S0-AGA-433

Untidy
ORIGINS

Untidy ORIGINS

A STORY OF WOMAN'S RIGHTS
IN ANTEBELLUM NEW YORK

⟿ Lori D. Ginzberg ⟿

The University of North Carolina Press

Chapel Hill and London

© 2005

The University of North Carolina Press

All rights reserved

Designed by Heidi Perov

Set in Adobe Garamond and Madrone

by Keystone Typesetting, Inc.

Manufactured in the United States of America

The paper in this book meets the guidelines for
permanence and durability of the Committee on Production
Guidelines for Book Longevity of the Council on Library Resources.

LIBRARY OF CONGRESS CATALOGING-IN-PUBLICATION DATA

Ginzberg, Lori D.

Untidy origins : a story of woman's rights in antebellum
New York / by Lori D. Ginzberg.

p. cm.

Includes bibliographical references and index.

ISBN 0-8078-2947-1 (cloth: alk. paper)

ISBN 0-8078-5608-8 (pbk.: alk. paper)

1. Women's rights—New York (State)—History—19th century.

2. Women in politics—New York (State)—History—19th century.

3. Women—New York (State)—Social conditions—19th century.

I. Title.

HQ1236.5.U6G56   2005

305.42'09747'109034—dc22

2004024837

cloth   09 08 07 06 05   5 4 3 2 1

paper   09 08 07 06 05   5 4 3 2 1

for Janet and Joel

Contents

Illustrations
and Maps

Acknowledgments

This book is the result of several projects that were not, I once thought, related, and I am delighted to thank the many people who helped guide it along its rather convoluted path. Several institutions provided funding without demanding that I produce exactly what I promised; I thank them for that flexibility, which may soon be extinct. Early on I benefited from a Mellon postdoctoral fellowship at the University of Pennsylvania to research a book about women and freethought. The Penn history department has generously granted me visiting scholar privileges ever since. A Fulbright senior teaching fellowship at Hebrew University in Jerusalem allowed me to read broadly in a setting that demanded global thinking. The Library Company of Philadelphia and the Historical Society of Pennsylvania afforded me a month-long residence as a visiting scholar in the finest of research facilities. Pennsylvania State University provided a year's sabbatical as well as a grant from the Research and Graduate Studies Office.

Librarians were unfailingly helpful. In addition to the incomparable Phil Lapsansky and Connie King at the Library Company, I am indebted to librarians and archivists at Penn State's Pattee and Paterno Libraries; the University of Pennsylvania's Van Pelt Library; the Flower Memorial Library (Watertown, N.Y.); the Jefferson County Historical Society (Watertown); the Hawn Memorial Library (Clayton, N.Y.); the Historical Society of Wisconsin; the National Archives and Records Administration (Washington, D.C., and Philadelphia); the Family History Center of the Church of Latter-Day Saints (Philadelphia); the New York Public Library; the Syracuse University Library; the Boston Public Library/Rare Books Department; the Southern Baptist Theological Seminary; and the State Library of New York. When I began this research, there was no Internet; I wish to thank those who design and maintain the websites that now make vast resources accessible from the historian's desk.

In Jefferson County, Laura Lynne Scharer, formerly the county historian, first located the petitioning women and offered essential advice on researching the area. Benjamin J. Cobb, records management coordinator in the County Clerk's Office, as well as the staff at the Jefferson County Surrogate's Court, offered generous assistance with deeds and legal records. Lisa Carr made available the *Watertown Daily Times* microfilm collection of nineteenth-century Jefferson County newspapers. The Thousand Island/Clayton Historical Society welcomed me to their meeting and suggested that I place an article in the *Thousand Island Sun*, which led to several valuable leads. Members of the Jefferson County, New York, Genealogical Society, which publishes the *Informer*, were also helpful. Descendants of the petitioners provided pieces of information and lively e-mail correspondence. I wish to acknowledge Richard Osborn, Stephen Ormsby, Thelma Moye, and Debbie Quick, who is also the director of the South Jefferson Historical Society. Among the residents of the North Country, none was more generous than Nan and Bill Dixon. Without their command of local genealogy and their management of Jefferson County's website, <rootsweb.com/~nyjeffer/>, this book would not have been feasible.

I have enjoyed numerous opportunities to speak about my work and have received helpful suggestions from one and all. I thank the Webb lecture series at the University of Texas, Arlington; the Berkshire Conference of Women's History; the University of Delaware History Colloquium; the Historical Society of Pennsylvania; the Center for the Study of Philanthropy at City University's Graduate Center; the 2003 Conference on Researching New York; and Penn State's Gender and History workshops.

The chance to work with Chuck Grench (again), Amanda McMillan, and Stephanie Wenzel at the University of North Carolina Press has been a privilege. I thank Chuck for his commitment to this book when it was at an early stage, and all for their support and efficiency at every stage that followed.

All historians are tourists among the people we study, but few have been as naive as I was when I began this trip. I am grateful to those who offered encouragement or who responded to my shameless appeals for guidance and translation, some so long ago that they may not recall what they did: Jeanie Attie, Gail Bederman, Howard Bodenhorn, Stephen Browne, John Caskey, Jonathan Earle, Shan Holt, Mary Kelley, Alan Kraut, Kathleen McCarthy, Katherine M. J. McKenna, Sally McMurry, Joanne Meyerowitz, Benedicte Monicat, Seth Rockman, Annie Rose, Mrinalini Sinha, Mike Smith, Olivia Smith Storey, Lisa Tetrault, Judith Wellman, Karen

Younger, and Susan Zaeske. Nancy Cott, Anne Boylan, and Nancy Hewitt have consistently offered valuable insights and generous support. Sarah Barringer Gordon helped me through the maze of nineteenth-century blasphemy law. Stephanie McCurry and the students in her University of Pennsylvania graduate seminar read the entire manuscript at a critical moment and offered excellent suggestions and warm support. Special thanks to Anne Boylan, Nancy Hewitt, and Charles McCurdy for contributing their exceptional skills as readers for the University of North Carolina Press; their enthusiasm for this book bolstered my own. My association with Jacob Katz Cogan in tracing the petition's signers launched this project, though neither of us knew it at the time. I thank him for his blessing as I continued to write the story of "our" women.

I have had the extraordinary good luck to be a member of Penn State's history department and its women's studies program. It is a real pleasure to thank Robin Becker, Bill Blair, Lorraine Dowler, Joan Landes, Dan Letwin, Sally McMurry, Jennifer Mittelstadt, Carolyn Sachs, Mrinalini Sinha, Melissa Wright, and most of all, Nan Woodruff. Numerous other friends, especially Rebecca Alpert, Christie Balka, Bob Eskind, Debora Kodish, Ann Listerud, Amy Neukrug, Kathy Schultz, and Beth Weitzman, may not realize how much they have helped this book along, but I thank them here. Jeanne Boydston has been this project's archaeologist, sifting through the rubble and finding whatever useful bits may lie below. The conversation she and I began more than a quarter of a century ago has left its mark on every page.

As always, my parents, Shirley and David Ginzberg, provided abundant love, humor, and encouragement. Robert and Steven Ginzberg and Francine Steiker, as well as the rest of the Ginzberg and Steiker clans, offered copious advice (occasionally solicited) and unending support.

My understanding of how change becomes possible has been deepened by my children, Kate and Eli Steiker-Ginzberg, who have given me the intense and wonderful experience of watching two young people become fine thinkers. I thank them for the sharpness of mind they've demanded of me at every stage of the process.

Finally, if I have been at all successful in understanding the six bold women whose story shapes this book, it is because of the two people to whom it is dedicated. It is a source of great and daily pleasure that my sister Janet Ginzberg shares my outrage at abuses of justice and of grammar and that she helps me find the right words. I often wonder if the Jefferson County women would identify with our conviction that we have the same brain. Joel Steiker has believed in me and this book with more confidence and far, far more patience than we deserved. I thank him for countless rereadings, for insisting that ideas matter, and for making sure that I take along a sense of adventure on my, and our, travels. I hope the final product satisfies Joel's hope that I will abandon my training to indulge in leaps of imagination—and that Janet is happy with all the endnotes.

Untidy ORIGINS

PETITION
FOR WOMAN'S RIGHTS (1846)

SATURDAY, (63d day,) August 15.
Prayer by the Rev. Mr. RAWSON.

Mr. GREENE presented the memorial of six ladies in Jefferson county, asking for the extension of the elective franchise to women. It was read and referred to standing committee No. 4.

The following is the Petition:

To the Constitutional Convention of the State of New-York:

Your Memorialists inhabitants of Jefferson county, believing that civil government has its foundation in the laws of our existence, as moral and social beings, that the specific object and end of civil government is to protect all in the exercise of all their natural rights, by combining the strength of society for the defence of the individual—believing that the province of civil government is not to create new rights, but to declare and enforce those which originally existed. Believing likewise that all governments must derive their just powers from the consent of the governed "from the great body of society, and not from a favored class, although that favored class may be even a majority of the inhabitants," therefore respectfully represent: That the present government of this state has widely departed from the true democratic principles upon which all just governments must be based by denying to the female portion of community the right of suffrage and any participation in forming the government and laws under which they live, and to which they are amenable, and by imposing upon them burdens of taxation, both directly and indirectly, without admitting them the right of representation, thereby striking down the only safeguards of their individual and personal liberties. Your Memorialists therefore ask your honorable body, to remove this just cause of complaint, by modifying the present Constitution of this State, so as to extend to women equal, and civil and political rights with men. In proposing this change, your petitioners ask you to confer upon them no new right but only to declare and enforce those which they originally inherited, but which have ungenerously been withheld from them, rights, which they as citizens of the state of New York may reasonably and rightfully claim. We, might adduce arguments both numerous and decisive in support of our position, but believing that a self evident truth is sufficiently plain without argument, and in view of our necessarily limited space, we forbear offering any and respectfully submit it for consideration.

ELEANOR VINCENT,	SUSAN ORMSBY,
LYDIA A. WILLIAMS,	AMY ORMSBY,
LYDIA OSBORN,	ANNA BISHOP.

Aug. 8th, 1846.

[William G. Bishop and William H. Attree, *Report of the Debates and Proceedings of the Convention for the Revision of the Constitution of the State of New-York, 1846* (Albany: Evening Atlas, 1846), 646]

chapter one
Puzzles
"the female portion of community"

Every event in history is a beginning, a middle, and an end; it just depends
on where you pick up the thread and what story you choose to tell. In
studying the history of an idea, we might ask how it changed from being
considered unthinkable to merely outrageous, from radical to common
sense, and thus how transformations in beliefs and ideologies occur. In
social history, too, changes that span lifetimes affect individuals at different points, and seemingly abstract events (the "industrial revolution"
or the "panic of 1837") bump into and alter a person, a family, a community, or a state in very different ways. We can understand the ideas and
identities that drive people's politics, religious beliefs, and actions as products of the individual mind, but also of the interactions that take place
daily among people living amidst wars, migrations, elections, newspapers,
sermons, and friends. I want here to underscore the histories of ideas as
they emerge from the experiences (personal, local, and national) of actual
people. And I want, further, to show how those ideas enter wider conversations—all of which contribute to the complex story of people's political
identities and of political and intellectual change. To put it another way,
this is a story that describes how people, shaped by their particular communities, time, and place, have an idea, chew it over, say it aloud, and prod
it onto the path of debate and action.

This book explores nineteenth-century women's political identities by
addressing two disparate but simple notions. First, it shows how, in myriad and often oblique ways, people argued that the idea of women as full
citizens was unthinkable, too dangerous even to contemplate. It does this,
in part, by offering a framework for rethinking how people's full membership in their state or nation is shaped not only by formal mechanisms,
the literal "rules" of legal status, but by rhetorics of religion, sexuality, and
respectability. Second, it shows that some women embraced the idea—and
insisted on the significance—of women's full citizenship notwithstanding

their formal exclusion, and it tries to explain why. Much of this is speculation, not to say fiction, and I offer few definite conclusions. But I hope that
this book suggests one model for rethinking how we put ideas back into
the context of people's lives where they originated. It argues vehemently
that in living that everyday life, and in the conviction of people that they
have the right to make claims on those in power, ideas matter. It demands
that we attend pointedly to the local, to the specificity of people's daily
intellectual lives, in order to make claims about the national and the
abstraction we call political identity. In a larger sense, it offers a few tiny
shards from the past that may shift our assumptions about women's sense
of themselves *as Americans*, as full members of the nation itself.

Some ideas are proclaimed too shocking to mention, too threatening to
entertain. Throughout much of American history, racial intermarriage,
open homosexuality, and women's sexual autonomy have been on that
short list. So has the idea of women's full equality as citizens. It was not so
long ago that the notion of a Catholic president held a spot on that
inventory; the idea of an openly atheist president still does, as does the
notion of granting children a vote. As Foucault has shown us in his work
on Victorian sexuality, we are convinced that these ideas were unspeakable because those who dominated public speech—ministers, writers, politicians, lawyers, social reformers, and others—kept insisting that they
were. Foucault's unspeakable opposite must be imagined, of course, in
order to be declared unimaginable. It constitutes the notions that define a
boundary around appropriate stances, acceptable behavior, and possible
change. To argue that women should be, simply and unapologetically, as
free and equal citizens as men was described as blasphemous and unrespectable; it was thus more easily dismissed than discussed.[1]

As Michel-Rolph Trouillot has so brilliantly shown in an entirely different context, this silencing of possibility, of reasonable thought, has
serious implications for historians' treatment of events. "The Haitian
Revolution," he writes, "thus entered history with the peculiar characteristic of being unthinkable even as it happened." The questions Trouillot raises about the historical and historiographical importance of this
silencing resound in the far smaller story that this book tells: "How," he
asks, "does one write a history of the impossible?" Brilliantly detailing
what he calls "failures of narration," Trouillot suggests that under some
circumstances, "worldview wins over the facts" and so the story is written
to reinforce historical silence.[2]

The virulence of those who insisted that women's political equality lay outside the boundaries of Americans' worldview indicates that consideration of woman's rights very much existed in public thought and private conversation. A great deal of noisy, self-righteous, and exaggerated defensiveness during the 1820s and increasingly through the 1840s over any mention of the subject suggests that some folks were worried. By the late 1830s nearly everyone in the reading or sermon-hearing public must have been aware of the attacks against outspoken or radical women. No doubt many women, disinclined to be labeled obnoxious, agreed that women should occupy a more limited citizenship based on a special moral duty. Although many women must have noticed their unequal status, few complained openly of its unfairness.

But some did. Tucked between the lines of ponderous debates among men are hints of what suffragist Inez Irwin called "little lights . . . small knots of men, circles of women, [who] dared to look the idea in the face."[3] On a Saturday morning in August 1846, Alpheus S. Greene, a Democrat from Watertown, New York, presented a petition to the state constitutional convention from "six ladies in Jefferson county." The petition asserted "that the present government of this state has widely departed from the true democratic principles upon which all just governments must be based by denying the female portion of community the right of suffrage and any participation in forming the government and laws under which they live." The women, Eleanor Vincent, Susan Ormsby, Amy Ormsby, Anna Bishop, Lydia A. Williams, and Lydia Osborn, firmly demanded "equal, and civil and political rights with men."[4]

There are several things that are odd about this petition, not least that the women wrote it at all. Women's public demand for suffrage, we have long assumed, burst upon the world two summers later, when several hundred people, under the leadership of Elizabeth Cady Stanton, Lucretia Mott, and other longtime antislavery activists, launched the woman's rights movement in Seneca Falls, New York. This 1846 document and other petitions that are being, and likely will be, discovered add another challenge to the legend of the origin of the nineteenth-century feminist movement by demonstrating that there were both private conversations and public appeals for women's political rights years earlier. Even the oft-repeated story that, faced with the "popular voice" against them, "most of the ladies who had attended the [Seneca Falls] convention and signed the declaration [of sentiments], one by one, withdrew their names and influence and joined our persecutors" seems increasingly far-fetched.[5] Indeed, there is no evidence, aside from Stanton's recollection, that this retreat occurred, that a group of seasoned antislavery activists recoiled in horror and amazement when the mainstream press belittled their demand for woman suffrage. I make no claim here that support for woman suffrage was ubiquitous; how widespread these women's views were remains an open question, although I suspect they were more commonly entertained than we have assumed. Nor do I mean to imply that the events at Seneca Falls were insignificant. And certainly Stanton was neither the first nor the last advocate of social change who helped, inadvertently or not, distort historical recollections of a movement she led.[6] Clearly, however, the celebration (by Stanton as well as by historians) of this watershed is complicated by the story of several ordinary women's brazen demand for their rights.

The petition and its creators offer additional mysteries as well. First, that it was printed in the constitutional convention debates was peculiar. Virtually every other petition to the convention was simply noted as having been presented and referred to the appropriate committee, with no mention made of the numbers who signed or the specifics of their demands. Indeed, that is how the Jefferson County petition appears in the *Albany Argus*'s version of the proceedings, and I have been unable to discover why William Bishop and William Attree, the editors of the competing *Albany Atlas*, published this and no other appeal.[7] Bishop and Attree's decision to describe the petition as one "for the extension of the elective franchise to women," rather than by the often derogatory term "woman's rights," may hint at their greater sympathy, but I cannot say for certain. As it happens, the likelihood that anyone would ever see these petitions was dramatically reduced in 1911 when a fire in the state capitol building in Albany destroyed the originals. It is pure good luck that we have the Jefferson County text and its attached names and its hint of what other petitions might have said.

Published is not, of course, the same as publicized, and the petition's virtual disappearance from the story of woman's rights offers further mysteries. Major newspapers in Albany and New York City duly mentioned the petition, but nothing more. Only the convention correspondent for the *New-York Daily Tribune* scoffed, at the end of his report, that "it would have been unpardonable had I forgotten to mention that Dr. Greene, a worthy bachelor Delegate from Jefferson County, took the opportunity . . . to present the memorial of six lovely ladies in Jefferson County." In what would become a familiar tone he added, "What a time for courting, love matches, etc., an election will be when that petition succeeds. It is said to be grounded on the fact that men have managed badly, and that women might do better but could not do worse."[8] Here he anticipated, albeit sarcastically, an argument to be made in the future by some suffragists, but not one made in the petition itself.

The petition has not fared much better with historians. Charles Z. Lincoln, in his five-volume *Constitutional History of New York*, first mentions woman suffrage with the comment that "in 1855 a petition was presented by [male?] citizens of Rochester for an amendment extending the elective franchise to women."[9] The 1846 petition and its signers do not appear in most accounts of the emergence of woman's rights in America, in part because of the extraordinary ability of Elizabeth Cady Stanton and Susan B. Anthony to shape the history of the movement they led. Although their six-volume *History of Woman Suffrage* fails to mention the petition, I cannot be convinced that Stanton, who followed that summer's convention proceedings closely, was unaware of it. Only Judith Wellman, in recognizing that "the ideas expressed at Seneca Falls did not burst full-grown upon the scene," quotes from the petition that the Jefferson County women wrote.[10] Also peculiar is the petition's absence from Franklin Hough's exhaustive *History of Jefferson County*, published in 1854, for which the author visited every town and gathered anecdotes from numerous inhabitants. Hough eagerly sought and wrote about indications of either scandalous or unusual behavior; apparently the women's petition was not noteworthy as either.[11]

But the petition itself is stunning. The "memorial of six ladies in Jefferson county" is not the deferential and tentative plea that is often associated with petitioning by the disfranchised. These women did not adopt the stance of supplicants or quasi-citizens or, for that matter, "ladies." (It was either Greene or, more likely, the convention's reporters who, intending respect, called them that.) Nor did they fortify their plea for full citizenship with the rhetorical arsenal of motherhood, as those familiar with the language of antebellum activism might expect. They did not use the honorifics "Mrs." or "Miss," as was customary for non-Quakers. On the contrary, they simply confronted their exclusion as full citizens and objected to it. Strangest of all, given that woman suffrage had not yet received serious consideration, the six women declared that they were forgoing the opportunity to offer arguments for their position, confident that "a self evident truth is sufficiently plain without argument."

There are so many ways we can read these words, so many stories of which they are part. The petition itself floats in time as a "source" that can teach students about rhetoric, about Madisonian concepts of political authority, and about woman's rights in these particular women's time and place. From the point of view of the rhetoric of petitioning, of rights talk, of constitution making, and of woman suffrage, the petition challenges what we thought we knew about women's political identities before 1848: six women in Jefferson County, New York, did not find the idea of women's full rights unthinkable and said so. There is no evidence that, as a result of their actions, they lost their husbands, abandoned their domestic duties, or went insane, as later opponents of woman's rights would predict (though Alpheus Greene did become "bereft of reason" and die several years later in the State Lunatic Asylum in Utica).[12]

Like a piece of a jigsaw puzzle, the petition can fit into several historiographical discussions. Seeing it as one, though doubtless not the only, beginning of the struggle for woman's rights, we might easily graft it onto the historiography of a feminist tradition. The history of women's political identities, and of their claims to full membership in the nation, thus turns out to be even messier than we have thought. Once, the story seemed both simple and dramatic: the 1848 woman's rights convention in Seneca Falls, New York, represented women's first public demand for suffrage, understood as the key marker of membership in the political community, and the movement for woman's rights took off from there. In that tale, the personal revelations of several extraordinary women— Lucretia Mott, Martha Coffin Wright, and Stanton herself—inspired a demand for women's political and legal rights, as well as their right to "a thorough education," "profitable employments," and self-respect.[13] The feminism that emerges from this particular story spoke of women's personal discontent and described their individual rights—the right to own property, to gain an education, and to vote—as group achievements. Though some historians—notably Elsa Barkley Brown in her provocative essay about freedwomen's political involvement in Reconstruction Era Richmond—have urged us to rethink the vote itself as a community, rather than merely as an individual, possession, the central story of feminism continues to be told largely in terms of individual dissatisfaction with prescribed roles and a battle for personal autonomy and fulfillment.[14] It is a triumphant, as well as a triumphalist, narrative.

The story I tell here is not the first to complicate that older tale. In recent years, historians of women have undertaken a critical revision of the traditional narrative of woman's rights, suggesting, among other things, that Elizabeth Cady Stanton's own unabashed self-promotion helps account for the gaps and biases in the *History of Woman Suffrage.*

With each rethinking, the story of women's political identities, their status as American-born or naturalized wives, and the relationship between their class standing and their access to political authority has grown more complex. Both the racism and class blindness that inhered in the old narrative and the gendered nature of citizens' rights and obligations have come under scrutiny, as scholars have increasingly revealed the complicated meanings of membership, rights, public activism, individualism, and gender itself. Nancy Isenberg underscores a "shared community of discourse" about woman's rights in a variety of settings that, taken together, offered a "coherent feminist critique" of American democracy.[15] Rosalyn Terborg-Penn, Bonnie Anderson, and Louise Michele Newman have taken the emergence of woman's rights as a starting point and recast the movement's significance from the perspective of black women's activism, European feminism, and a critical analysis of the racialized assumptions in the woman's rights movement itself. Still other historians have expanded our sense of what constitutes politics and have offered nuanced analyses of the many partisan and nonpartisan ways women participated. Most recently, Susan Zaeske has underscored the importance of petitioning in shaping the rhetoric of rights and citizenship that some activist women expressed.[16]

But there is another way to read the 1846 petition. We can view it not only as an early, dramatic demand for women's full rights but as a mystery story, a window into the women's own lives, into the details of their experiences, influences, and context. We might see it as part of an ongoing conversation coming about midpoint in six women's lives. Reading the petition this way, we could recast these rural women's relationship to "high" intellectual history, to political events, to religious teachings, to social and economic changes, and to one another—as well as to the stories of the movement for woman's rights that feminists would later tell. From abstract conceptions of natural rights to the more mundane question of how busy women found the time to head to a neighbor's farm to share their views with like-minded friends, this petition offers an unusual intervention in a larger inquiry into women's understanding of their own place in political culture. It demands that we rethink the boundaries of respectable behavior and legitimate claims in light of much political posturing over the sexual and domestic chaos that would result from discussion of woman's rights: How outrageous, how unusual, how brave, or how ordinary did these women think they were? What did other people think of them? And did they care?

[11]

The origins of this book were as untidy as the story it tells. When I first came across the 1846 petition of six women of Jefferson County for the full rights of citizenship, I was interested in abstractions. I was, and remain, fascinated by the ways people manipulate ideas about gender, sexuality, religion, and race to describe the fringes of respectability and thus shape the boundaries of full belonging in the nation. I was also, however, dissatisfied with historical writing that seemed to erase or ignore the intersections between intellectual life and lived experience. I became increasingly drawn to the story of these women as a key to understanding women's political identities, as well as the possibilities for dissent, in the real life of the nineteenth century. Their petition, I hoped, would allow me, in Alexander Keyssar's words, "to puzzle over the story, to avoid taking familiar things for granted, to interrogate the past with wonder."[17]

Ideas get expressed and shared in convention halls, pulpits, and newspapers, but they emerge and matter someplace else as well. The notion of kitchen-table conversation haunts me when I imagine Eleanor Vincent, Susan Ormsby, Amy Ormsby, Anna Bishop, Lydia Williams, and Lydia Osborn working on their petition. Who first mentioned it? Who put pen to paper? Which of their husbands and brothers—Abraham, Hiram, Luther, Nahum, Bailey, and Joseph—objected to or supported or laughed at or dismissed their effort? What did their fathers and mothers think, and what about the sisters and daughters who did not sign? Most of this I will never know, and so my efforts to locate the spark between identity and action, between ideas and experience, will inevitably fall short. I know that Susan Ormsby owned both a "Fall leaf table" that was "old & poor" and one that was "better," but not what happened around those or other farm tables.[18] Still, I can guess and try to reconstruct the conversations that took place by figuring out whom the women knew, with whom they interacted, and which events might have spoken to feelings of entitlement, resentment, exclusion, and belonging—things that, taken together, make up the identities and interests that can launch claims to equal citizenship itself. The petition offers a way to listen to a conversation about which rights and privileges were not on the table and which were too obvious to require "arguments both numerous and decisive" in their support.

Let us turn to this conversation that took place among six women during the summer of 1846 and that, astonishingly, resulted in a "memorial of six ladies in Jefferson county" whose words and signers' names survived. That

Bishop and Attree printed the memorial in their version of the 1846 constitutional convention proceedings may well be serendipity. But there it is, a bold and unabashed statement of the nature of government, of the rights accorded to citizens, of the fact that women had been denied those rights, and of the obviousness of their demands.

We have not been prepared for these words by what women's history has taught us. Yet perhaps we should have been, for we have long understood that some women, and especially women from Protestant, middle-class families, participated actively in political life. In addition to delineating the limits of women's formal citizenship, historians have noted for some time that women expressed their concerns to the men who ran state, local, and federal governments in myriad ways. These concerns did not reflect a universal womanhood but were closely (if imperfectly) related to women's own standing in their communities, to the political culture of their region, and to the differences between rural and urban life. Some women of the middle and upper classes, who enjoyed closer contact with politicians by virtue of their social standing, used that access on behalf of local charities, tract and Bible societies, and asylums intended to reform the poor and the "fallen." Others lobbied their legislatures for laws against seduction or alcohol sales or prostitution. Working-class women sometimes testified to legislative committees on behalf of specific goals designed to ameliorate the conditions of the laboring poor. Others participated in partisan parades, stood alongside politicians in dedications of public memorials, or simply sat in the visitors' sections of state legislative and congressional hearings, demonstrating their interest in the outcome of policy debates. From textile workers' calls for a ten-hour day to Dorothea Dix's demands for state-run asylums for the insane, the frequent pleas of women for political patronage, funds, authority, and legislation belie contemporaries' insistence that they were removed from and had no interest in the political world.[19]

By the 1830s, the written word had long constituted an essential means by which women assured their place in civic life. Many women who wanted their views heard in the realm of public discourse wrote tracts, articles, fictional short stories, and novels, as well as authoring and presenting political speeches. Written and read largely by middle-class women, magazines such as *Godey's Lady's Book*—packed with fashion plates and patterns, fiction, domestic advice, and reports by travelers throughout the world—circulated widely.[20] While female authors may have enhanced women's public authority, by no means did they all support what were known as woman's rights. Catharine Beecher, most famously, articulated a vision of American society that was both hierarchical and gendered—and that underscored women's dependence—through her domestic advice manuals as well as in publications opposing women's antislavery activism.[21]

Increasingly, those who wished to make their views heard and their numbers recognized by policymakers and the public turned to petitioning. Petitioning had long been the traditional means by which the unenfranchised were heard; it was their primary formal access to those in power. Early petitions by women had focused on personal matters, such as a plea for a divorce, for pensions due them as the widows of veterans, or for the settlement of a claim to land. Other women, acting on behalf of organizations, petitioned for corporate status or appealed to city and state legislatures for funds with which to build asylums or charitable institutions. Increasingly through the 1830s, petitions carried the words of ordinary women directly to politicians. The demands of women, which mirrored their class, their cause, and their outspokenness, ranged widely, as what had once been an individual act increasingly reflected a political culture characterized by democratic participation. Legislators at all levels of government heard from tens of thousands of female petitioners throughout these years; these petitions shaped both particular policy discussions and Americans' understanding of women's place in political life. It was women's antislavery petitions in the 1830s that "signalled the growth of an identity of national citizenship" and forced the first explicit "examination of women's political rights" in Congress.[22] Clearly, the efforts of women to transform public opinion reflected their own recognition that they were entitled to enter the larger political conversation and thus to make demands on those in power.

Once the woman's rights movement had begun, the gathering of seasoned abolitionists at Seneca Falls ensured that petitions would be a primary means both of transforming public opinion and of achieving their political goals. Statewide campaigns were held throughout the northern states. In 1854, for example, Susan B. Anthony enlisted sixty women throughout New York as "captains" and sent them off to collect signatures on a wide range of woman's rights petitions. Given the conditions of rural travel and the demoralizing effects of facing women who "rudely shut the door in her face," it is astonishing that in that year alone the women gathered some 6,000 names. A year later Anthony traveled to fifty-four of New York's sixty counties, lecturing, gaining signatures on petitions, and raising funds and support for a controversial cause.[23]

Petitions themselves and the attacks against them underscored connections that historians have long noted between the antislavery campaign and the later movement for woman's rights. Some women, schooled in the rhetoric and tactics of the movement against slavery, learned how to think and to act on behalf of their own rights and obligations as activist citizens. The story of Angelina and Sarah Grimké as antislavery lecturers who, under attack, asserted their rights as women is by now a classic in women's history, but there are others.[24] Certainly discussion about woman's rights—both for and against—arose frequently in the context of demands for the rights of African Americans, slave and free. In June 1834 a group of women from Harrisville, Harrison County, Ohio, submitted a petition "To the Senate & House of Representatives, of the United States, in Congress Assembled." Written in the early days of the movement for immediate abolition, the petition laid out much of the rhetoric that would inspire numerous northern white women to join the cause. Referring to themselves as Christians, wives, mothers, sisters, and daughters and as "good citizens," the authors intended to awaken "the females of our country" to the "degrading and unprecedented sufferings, to which our brethren of the African race are subjected," in the face of which "christianity can but mourn." They pleaded with other women to observe the "unmasked picture" of slavery and to act on their religious feelings to "bind up the broken heart, to loose the bands of wickedness, to open the prison doors, to suffer the gospel to be preached to the poor."[25]

In addition to calling for an end to slavery in the District of Columbia, the memorialists asked for "the immediate enfranchisement of every human being that shall tread this soil." Demanding voting rights for black men was a radical step in 1834. But did the women intend by the phrase "every human being" to reflect openly on their own political status? Did they intend to include children among the nation's voters? What was thinkable for the women who penned these words? In a context where "universal" was often taken and intended to mean "men" or even "white men," their use of the term "every human being," however suggestive, remains ambiguous.

It was also, in the 1830s, largely irrelevant as a matter of policy. For it was the states, not Congress, that pondered and determined the daily political rights of antebellum citizens. Thus, state constitutional conventions offered people unusual opportunities to participate in a discussion about citizens' rights and, indeed, to rethink the very underpinnings of the institutions that governed them. Rather than reflecting the ordinary workings of government, these conventions reenvisioned the political compact that bound citizens to one another and to the state and that made explicit their reciprocal rights and obligations. As such their proceedings elicited strong passions on behalf of tradition and equally intense hopes for change. Indeed, Jefferson County's petition for woman's rights was not the first to suggest that convention delegates consider why only men had full political rights. A group of Burlington County, New Jersey, men petitioned their state's 1844 constitutional convention "asking that the right of suffrage be extended to women." John C. Ten Eyck, the Whig delegate who presented the petition, said he did not favor its adoption "because it did not come from the females themselves—but he believed that they were generally as well fitted to exercise the elective franchise, as those who style themselves the 'Lords of the Creation.' "[26]

At least two other petitions for woman's rights made their way to the New York constitutional convention during the summer of 1846. One, from "females of Covington, Wyoming County, in favor of woman's rights," was evidently lost in the 1911 fire in the capitol. Another "somewhat important memorial, very numerously and respectably signed by some of the first citizens of Albany," was presented, "related to the disfranchisement of clergymen from holding office, and of women from voting in elections."[27] The language of this petition might have been lost as well had not both the *Albany Patriot* and the *National Anti-Slavery Standard* thought it worth reprinting.[28] The *Standard* also suggested that such talk may have been more widespread in upstate New York that summer than the record otherwise suggests.

The Albany memorialists (possibly all men, given the reference to "first citizens," though the petitioners referred to themselves as "inhabitants" of Albany) asserted that "the present Constitution of this State is blemished in two respects—by restrictions, unjust, injurious, and contrary to its otherwise equitable intent and provisions: these are the ineligibility of clergymen to office, and the disfranchisement of the female half of community."[29] Focusing mostly on the second issue, the petition filled three newspaper columns with the arguments the Jefferson County petitioners omitted. In its defense of woman's rights, it drew on the Declaration of Independence, the question of taxation without representation, the strength of women's intellect, and the writings of Democratic lawyer

Elisha Hurlbut, who had played an important role in arguing for a state convention. The petitioners insisted that great benefit would be conferred on society and on women themselves by the expansion of the rights of citizenship.

The Albany memorial differs dramatically from the Jefferson County appeal in more than its length, for the Albany petitioners moderated their demands in hopes of achieving a more limited goal. Although confident that politicians and voters, "as fathers, brothers, sons, husbands, guardians, Christians, and as MEN, . . . will vote to restore to the injured half of the human family those plain, natural, legal rights, which will enable them to elevate their sex to a state of much greater utility, independence and happiness, than their present one," they retreated to safer, if not higher, ground: "But if the [*sic*] allowing their simple civil rights to females be considered too sudden an advance for the spirit of the times, we would petition that the amendment of the Constitution secure to the married women of this State the interest, use and control of their own property." The Albany memorial is a rare and wonderful document, one that lets us in on a conversation about balancing a demand for women's political rights with a candid assessment of political reality. It also raises the possibility of the reverse: that others who called for limited rights for women, however anxiously they insisted that they would never ask for full legal equality, may have been consciously making concessions to that "spirit of the times" that declared woman suffrage unrespectable.

A passing remark in the *National Anti-Slavery Standard* suggests that Susan and Amy Ormsby, Lydia Osborn, Anna Bishop, Lydia Williams, and Eleanor Vincent may have known that they were not alone in talking about woman's rights that summer: "The following memorial, we understand, has had an extensive circulation through this State, though we have never heard of it in the Convention." If the Jefferson County women did see the Albany petition, however, they chose not to imitate it, in content or tone. There is no language in the women's own petition that precisely mirrors the Albany memorial, though copying a petition in whole or part was a standard practice. Only the odd phrase "female half of community" comes close to the Jefferson reference to the "female portion of community." But far more than words and phrases underscores their decision to adopt an entirely different tenor, especially in light of this memorial's "extensive circulation." For one thing, they did not defend their case, declaring argument superfluous. For another, they refused to compromise either rhetorically or in their demands. Whether they were politically foolish, unreasonably optimistic, or simply irritated beyond moderation, they did not equivocate in their demands or soften them for the tender nerves of politicians.

The Jefferson County petition was unconventional in other respects. The six women did not, like the Harrisville, Ohio, petitioners a decade earlier and thousands since, speak of moral rights, nor did they demand to be heard as Christians or as mothers. There is nothing oblique in their words, little that requires interpretation. Instead, they offer as purely an Enlightenment text as one might hope to find in the mid-1840s. The purpose of government, they began, was "not to create new rights" but to guarantee and protect the rights "which originally existed," "by combining the strength of society for the defence of the individual." Such governments, they affirmed, citing the Declaration of Independence, "derive their just powers from the consent of the governed." Then, in the petitioners' only other attempt at attribution (and their only use of quotation marks), they seem to paraphrase James Madison: those who govern, they wrote, come " 'from the great body of society, and not from a favored class, although that favored class may be even a majority of the inhabitants.' "

In "Federalist No. 39," Madison argued that only a republican form of government could reflect "the fundamental principles of the Revolution" by demonstrating "the capacity of mankind for self-government." A republican government was that which "derives all its powers directly or indirectly from the great body of people, and is administered by persons holding their offices during pleasure, for a limited period, or during good behavior." "It is *essential* to such a government," he continued, in words that the women would echo half a century later, "that it be derived from the great body of society, not from an inconsiderable proportion, or a favored class of it; otherwise a handful of tyrannical nobles, exercising their oppressions by a delegation of their powers, might aspire to the rank of republicans and claim for their government the honorable title of republic." He went on to defend the proposed constitution of the United States as "conformable" to this standard.[30]

As part of his effort to convince voters that the proposed federal constitution would best protect the people's liberties, Madison argued against the potentially oppressive dominance of a popular majority; the worst faction, he believed, was one composed of the majority itself. But in the words quoted here, he describes the dangers of dominance by a clique, or "an inconsiderable proportion" of the people. Why did the Jefferson County petitioners choose this phrase to point out New York State's inconsistencies? Did a copy of the Federalist papers sit in one of their house-holds? Or had the women only seen Madison's words quoted, perhaps incorrectly? It is impossible to say. But by echoing these words, the women placed their demands firmly in the tradition of their nation's founders. It was a tradition they shared with other groups seeking access and inclusion throughout American history. These foundational documents offered ideas that remained vital for citizens making particular claims and for marginalized groups asserting their own membership, indicating that wide-ranging versions of belonging were, in fact, available.

In spite of the Revolutionary context in which these words arose, these appeals were not directed only to the federal government. Indeed, the Jefferson County women found "just cause of complaint" precisely in their *state's* claim to be an honorable republic; that is, the source of their grievance was that the state of New York had not lived up to the promise set out by its founders. In the face of Madisonian principles, the "present government of this state has widely departed from the true democratic principles upon which all just governments must be based," they wrote, "by denying to the female portion of community the right of suffrage and any participation in forming the government and laws under which they live, and to which they are amenable, and by imposing upon them bur-dens of taxation . . . without admitting them the right of representation." They wanted nothing more than those "rights, which they as citizens of the state of New York may reasonably and rightfully claim." The denial of these rights, they argued, had the effect of "striking down the only safe-guards of their individual and personal liberties." Their demand was as simple as it was unlikely: that the new constitution of New York "extend to women equal, and civil and political rights with men."

These were radical words indeed in 1846, unpopular at best and, at worst, we have been told, outside the boundaries of polite discussion. Yet the women self-consciously drew upon a long-standing tradition in Amer-ican political thought: that people who were "amenable" to the "govern-ment and laws under which they live[d]" were entitled to be included in making them. There is no sense in the petition itself that the Jefferson County women worried much about provoking outrage or derision. They did nothing to temper its radicalism or to soften the bluntness of their appeal, nor did they employ the traditional rhetorical tools of prayer, modesty, or deference. They offer no hint that they viewed their demand for equal civil and political standing as competing with or undermining their domestic or farm roles, or even that their duties in one arena had anything to do with their rights in another. Rather, the women asserted that they sought "no new right but only . . . those which they originally inherited, but which have ungenerously been withheld from them." In closing, they noted (with perhaps a touch of impatience) that the points in favor of their demands were "numerous and decisive" but essentially consisted of a "self evident truth . . . sufficiently plain without argument," and so they chose not to waste their own or anyone else's time in offering them.

Who were these women who sat down in the summer of 1846 to make these demands? Eleanor Vincent, Lydia Williams, Lydia Osborn, Susan Ormsby, Amy Ormsby, and Anna Bishop have remained virtually invisible and impressively resistant to efforts to uncover their stories. Most of them were ordinary middle-aged farmwives; all were linked by family and friendship. Most lived on adjoining or nearby farms in the Depauville section of Clayton in Jefferson County, on remote and lately settled land near the St. Lawrence River and the edge of the nation. Theirs were not among their town's leading families, nor were they well connected politically, although I believe their families had known Alpheus Greene for some time. None of the women's fathers or husbands appears in the boastful entries of collective local biographies that counted men as "notable." The women themselves did not have the broad experience of associational life that would prepare some women for the struggle for woman's rights; none of them attended the Seneca Falls convention two years later; and none is mentioned in Stanton and Anthony's *History of Woman Suffrage*.

What we know about the six Jefferson County petitioners individually is minimal, the barest biographical data gleaned from census records, deeds, surrogate court documents, and genealogical information gathered by their descendants and local researchers. By nearly any standard of historical research, the evidence that has survived about these six women and their families is slim. This is especially the case considering that these were native-born Americans, longtime owners of land, and literate and established members of their communities. For a mystery reader like myself, finding clues about their lives has been a great pleasure, but these clues do not, finally, complete a puzzle with any precision. Except for that one act of writing and signing an extraordinary petition, these women were striking in their ordinariness. Embedded in the larger story of the

Eleanor [O'Connor] Vincent (1806–1886)
Married to Abraham Vincent (1796–1886)

Lydia A. Williams (1815–1882)
Married to Nahum D. Williams (ca. 1804–1863)

Lydia [Ormsby] Osborn (ca. 1803–1875)
Married to Joseph Osborn (ca. 1807–1876)
Sister of Susan, Hiram,
and Bailey Ormsby (1811–1848)
and others

Susan Ormsby (1815–1895)
Sister of Lydia Osborn
and Hiram and Bailey Ormsby (1811–1848)
and others

Amy [Eldridge] Ormsby (ca. 1786–1885)
Married to Hiram Ormsby (1799–1876)
Sister-in-law of Susan Ormsby and Lydia Osborn

Anna [Carter] Bishop (1790–1860)
Married to Luther Bishop (1783–1857)

North Country, their individual lives offer few clues as to why they saw themselves as fully entitled to the rights of citizens.

It was a custom of nineteenth-century petitioning that the most prominent or most central or most assertive petitioner sign her name first. But if Eleanor [O'Connor] Vincent, whose name heads the list, undertook its writing, there is no other evidence of it. She is remarkable in the record only for having lived in the least wealthy and most populated household; she would become pregnant with her tenth child soon after the petition was submitted to the constitutional convention. At thirty-nine years old, she fell in the middle range of the women in terms of age: Anna [Carter] Bishop and Amy [Eldridge] Ormsby were in their mid- to late fifties in

1846; Lydia [Ormsby] Osborn was forty-three; Lydia A. Williams and Susan Ormsby, born the same year as Elizabeth Cady Stanton, were only thirty-one.[31]

Five of the six women were married, four of them to farmers. None of their households was quiet, wealthy, or leisured; all were productive and well populated. The Vincents generated the most noise and the most laborers with their ten children. Amy and Hiram Ormsby had four, three of whom died before their mother. Anna and Luther Bishop had two children, but their son's children sometimes lived with them as well. Like other nineteenth-century households, some of these were complicated and—given the lack of marriage, birth, and death records—difficult to sort out.

Take the Williamses. Although I know that Lydia A. Williams was born in 1815 in Herkimer County, I have been unable to unearth her unmarried name. At some point she met and married Nahum D. Williams, a farmer about a decade her senior.[32] That Lydia was Nahum's second wife I know only because of a single deed and a worn-down gravestone. In 1830 Nahum and his wife Zerviah sold land to Bailey Ormsby, brother of Susan Ormsby and Lydia Osborn. In the absence of vital records, and given the barely legible carving on Zerviah's gravestone, I know only that Lydia and Nahum were married before 1846, when her name appears on the petition.[33] Of the five children in the Williams household in 1850, it is likely that Walter, born in 1833, and at least some of the next three children were Zerviah's. Only Susan, born in 1846 after a gap of seven years, was unquestionably Lydia's child. (Lydia Williams and Susan Ormsby were born the same year. Despite the lack of evidence, may we imagine that naming this child Susan indicated their particular friendship and respect?) There was at least one other baby, George, born in 1848, who apparently died soon after.

Lydia and Joseph Osborn had no children, but their household was hardly quiet and was likely the center of the storm. It was also something of a magnet for various female relatives. In 1850 it included Lydia's seventy-eight-year-old mother, Jane, and her younger sister Susan Ormsby. (That these two petitioners were, in fact, sisters was a thrilling research moment when I stumbled on Lydia's unmarried name.) In later years Ursula Whitney, the tailoress daughter of Abagail, Lydia and Susan's dead sister, would live with them as well. Susan Ormsby, the only one of the signers who never married, lived there for much of her adult life. But something other than economic dependence accounts for this arrangement, for Susan was a woman of property. In 1848, when her thirty-five-year-old brother Bailey died, Susan became the sole owner of his personal property and real estate; later she would buy other properties. By 1870 Susan Ormsby was, at least on paper, the wealthiest of the group.

The women in this group who did marry would eventually be widowed. Luther Bishop died in 1857, three years before Anna; Nahum Williams died in 1863; Joseph Osborn died seven years before Lydia in 1868; and Hiram Ormsby predeceased Amy, though she was about a decade older. Although most were widows for less than a decade, Lydia Williams had been a widow for nearly twenty years when she died in 1882 at age sixty-seven. Susan Ormsby, twelve years younger than her sister Lydia and sixteen years younger than brother Hiram, lived until 1895, the last of her siblings and of the petitioners to die. Eleanor Vincent and her husband Abraham both died around 1886 and are buried together in the Depauville cemetery. Their tombstone, unusual for that place, is topped with an open book; whether this statuary is meant to suggest intellect, piety, or their children's aesthetic sense, I have no idea.

Although their individual biographies are meager, the connections among these women and their families are rich indeed. The petition itself was a collective effort that mirrored much-longer-term patterns in their lives. Indeed, discovering the complex connections among them, as sisters, friends, and longtime neighbors, has been among the delights of writing this book. If we know little about them as individuals, we do know this: It is as a group that these women make sense historically, for it was as members of a community that they settled new farms, raised their families, nurtured their ideas, and expressed their political identities. Historian Eleanor Flexner remarks that, following the Seneca Falls convention, "it was possible for women who rebelled against the circumstances of their lives, to know that they were not alone."[34] Clearly, some women had known that for some time.

Buried in the historical sources, in the maps and the renamings of towns, and in the deeds and the wills is evidence that these women were more than acquaintances, more than a network drawn together to sign a petition. On the simplest level, they lived near one another. Reading the 1820 census as a trip along the road that joined Catfish Falls (then part of Brownville and later called Depauville) with what would become Clayton, one comes upon Osborns, Ormsbys, Vincents, O'Connors, and Williamses in quick succession. Timothy O'Connor's farm was near that of Benjamin and Polly [Frier] Vincent; the O'Connors' and Vincents' children, Eleanor and Abraham, would marry and establish their own household nearby. Abraham and Eleanor Vincent's nearest neighbor, Phineas A. Osborn, was one of Phineas Osborn's several sons; the others, Thomas, Schuyler, James, and Joseph (Lydia's husband), also lived nearby. Nahum and Lydia Williams's land was just around the corner. Elias and Jane Ormsby's farm was there, too, and their sons Hiram and Bailey settled on adjacent or nearby land. Even Anna and Luther Bishop, who lived for some time in the Henderson section of Ellisburgh, moved to Clayton after 1840, when Luther purchased ten acres near his brother Sylvester, another close neighbor.[35] The names of other neighbors—Frame, Haddock, Thomas, Rogers, and Halladay—are those of relatives or longtime friends as well.[36] Ironically, in an article we wrote some years ago, Jacob Katz Cogan and I wondered aloud what the women's "near neighbors, the Garlocks, the Thomases," thought of their petition.[37] Only much later did I discover that Cynthia Thomas, a minister's wife, was Anna Bishop's daughter; as to what she thought of the petition, I still have no clue.

Obviously more than proximity bound these petitioners. Susan Ormsby and Lydia Osborn were sisters, Amy Ormsby was their brother Hiram's wife and possibly had been Susan's teacher, and the evidence from wills suggests that they sustained close relationships with one another's children. But the relationships went back in time as well. An astonishing number of these families, as well as others among their neighbors, migrated to Depauville from Russia Township in Herkimer County. Elias and Jane [Lewis] Ormsby had been born in Vermont, and their son Hiram was born in Rhode Island; but they were residing in Russia when the census taker came around in 1810. Their near neighbors included Benjamin Vincent and Phineas Osborn. Even Amy Ormsby (then Eldridge) and her sister, Mrs. John Smith, who together left Hancock, Massachusetts, in 1818, stopped in Russia to visit relatives prior to moving on to Jefferson County. They may well have joined Ormsbys, Osborns, Vincents, and O'Connors for the final leg of their trip. (The 1820 census for Brownville in Jefferson County shows a John Smith, his young wife, and their two small children living next to Hiram and Amy Ormsby, having built one of the first houses on Francis Depau's land.) The numbers and the timing suggest that the families had known one another for some time and had undertaken this new move together.[38]

These women's fathers, husbands, and brothers were as closely connected as the women to their land, their families, and one another. That these families married one another with great consistency may not be surprising in a community where people's closest acquaintances were also their nearest neighbors.[39] But their lives remained tightly intermeshed. They frequently bought land from one another, cutting and pasting, as it were, to compose a coherent and profitable farm: Bailey Ormsby bought land from Nahum Williams in 1835, Nahum bought some from Bailey in 1837 and from Hiram Ormsby in 1838, Abraham Vincent purchased land from Joseph and Lydia Osborn in 1840, and so on. They witnessed one another's transactions, traveling to Watertown to swear out purchases, wills, or claims. As in other rural communities, they likely provided one another with mortgages, short-term loans, and other forms of financial assistance as well.[40] Women were clearly involved in these transactions. Indeed, in the list of debts that Lydia Williams paid from her husband's estate, the single largest amount was to S. Ormsby; Nahum also, interestingly, owed money to Lydia herself.[41] Although they were "pioneers" in the sense of having settled in Depauville in its early decades, they were neither isolated nor afflicted with wanderlust. Most of them, their siblings, and their children remained in Jefferson and nearby counties decades later, though close family members were also among emigrants to Wisconsin, Michigan, and Ohio. Having migrated and grown old together, they would help with the sad, final work of settling one another's estates after they died.

One more neighbor deserves mention. Alpheus S. Greene was born in Rhode Island about 1787. Like many of the Depauville families, he moved to Herkimer County before traveling to Jefferson, where he settled on Perch River in Brownville, possibly as early as 1812.[42] There he became a respected local doctor, a judge of the common pleas court, and a two-term member of the New York Assembly. According to the 1820 census, Greene lived two households away from Phineas Osborn. Only in 1829, when he accepted the appointment of postmaster in Watertown, did he move away from his Brownville neighbors. Seventeen years later he was one of three delegates from Jefferson County, all Democrats, who attended the constitutional convention in Albany. There, on August 15, 1846, the nearly sixty-year-old bachelor presented a petition by the daughters, sisters, and wives of his former neighbors to demand their rights.

There is no evidence that these women were spoken of widely as rabble-rousers. Quite the contrary: They were ordinary rural women who lived in dense and particular personal and economic and political networks. They had been involved in settling new communities, had witnessed those communities' growing isolation from both the prosperity and the intellectual bustle of their state, and had remained invisible outside those communities until, faced with the prospect of a new political compact for their state, they spoke up. There is little in the record that might have alerted us that they would do this.

But they did it, and so they force us to confront our assumptions about the intellectual possibilities of their time. Even if we cannot with great assurance generalize from these women's experience to that of other women of their class, region, religious affiliation, or age, their very ordinariness suggests that sympathy for their views was more widespread, at least within particular communities, than historians and contemporaries have assumed. Still, these women provided evidence of their opinions, and their neighbors did not. That women's legal standing differed from that of men was something that these women already knew and considered unfair. Members of a tightly knit, property-owning community of shared experiences and shared convictions, the women offer a window into what they felt entitled to as citizens of the state of New York. By speaking up they entered a conversation long under way, undermining its comfortable assumptions and shifting the ground on which men would defend their own exclusive claim to full membership in the nation.

chapter two
The Limits of Citizenship
"equal, and civil and political rights"

When six women from Jefferson County, New York, petitioned the 1846 constitutional convention for equal rights with men, they entered a conversation that was older than the nation itself. Yet at the time they composed their demand, it was one that political orthodoxy deemed unthinkable, outside the bounds of legitimate conversation. The idea of writing the petition would have begun with an individual, of course. Whoever first said it aloud must have known which of her sisters or friends would sympathize; maybe she already knew who among their neighbors or husbands or mothers and fathers would support them and who would be shocked. Perhaps they all knew better than to ask Eleanor Vincent's unmarried sisters, Sally and Susan, or Anna Bishop's daughter, Cynthia, to sign the petition, or perhaps they simply ran out of time. But however the women's action emerged from individual decisions, they all knew that they were joining a larger conversation, that ideas have lives that must be nurtured and nudged into public discussion. There is never simply one beginning of an idea. As George Geddes remarked in recalling the struggle for New York's act to protect married women's property rights in 1848, "Great measures often occupy the thoughts of men and women, long before they take substantial form and become things of life."[1] How the idea of women's political and legal equality with men became such a thing of life is a complex tale.

The words of Eleanor Vincent, Lydia Williams, Lydia Osborn, Susan Ormsby, Amy Ormsby, and Anna Bishop make perfect sense to us as a classic liberal statement of women's legal equality with men. In these words, the phrases and the logic of the nation's Revolutionary thinkers reverberate across time. Even more specifically, in their declaration that they demanded no new rights, we hear echoes of an 1802 "Plan for the Emancipation of the Fair Sex" that sought to "re-establish" women's lost standing.[2] Yet in their own time and place, in the context of other conversations then under way, the words seem shocking. To most of the men who had assumed the task of constructing political thought—politicians, convention delegates, lawyers, judges, and ministers—as well as many women authors and editors, the issues the women raised were best treated as either dangerous or absurd. Some thought women petitioners themselves intruders, while others believed them simply misguided. Only a very few agreed publicly that men had been "ungenerous" in withholding rights the women had "originally inherited." And yet we have only to listen closely to the denials and defenses that dominated public speech to recognize that, insulted and dismissed though they may have felt, the women were not talking to themselves.

Questions about the discursive shaping of citizenship and political identity pervade every aspect of this story: the settlement of Jefferson County, the conflicts between New York's political parties, the debates over voting and property rights at the constitutional convention in 1846, and the actions of six rural women that summer. Gender played an important role in debates over who belonged and who had what rights, and it helped shape the worldview of every player in this tale. But much had changed since the nation's early days, including the place of gender itself in political discourse, and with those changes came a new and decidedly unfriendly climate for advocating women's legal equality. At the same time, appeals for the rights of propertyless white men and African Americans had come to dominate public debate, and this broader discussion about the full rights of citizens likely deepened some women's sense of outrage and contradiction. Through the 1830s and into the 1840s, the right of women to participate in political debate, to declare themselves citizens with claims to being heard, and especially to advocate on behalf of African Americans was subject to intense scrutiny, long-winded theorizing, and congressional censorship.

" 'Citizen' is an equalizing word" of ancient origin, writes Linda Kerber, one that American Revolutionaries reinvented as "a new and reciprocal relationship between state and citizen."[3] Among the citizens of the new nation were free women and children who, by virtue of having been born in the United States, received passports and protection and were expected to pay taxes and obey the laws of the land.[4] Yet, dichotomous ideas about the sexes permeated republican assumptions about political rights and obligations, individual and communal interest, and group loyalty. As in other emerging nations, the laws of political rights and obligations in the early republic frequently conflicted with laws underpinning family status. Such contradictions were typically resolved by deferring to traditional and religious conventions of domestic life. Thus, for all their innovations, the various states and territories left largely intact common-law assumptions about women's—especially married women's—relationship to property, rights, and the government under which they lived.

From the earliest days of the American republic, women's citizenship was an ambiguous thing. If we understand citizenship to encompass various rights and obligations determined by legal forms, clearly free white women did not experience it in the same ways the men closest to them did. In most instances women could neither vote nor, if married, own, buy, or sell property or make contracts, and they were neither required nor permitted to perform military service, serve on juries, or work on the public roads. Often the inconsistencies of the nation's founding philosophies bubbled below the surface only to emerge in debates about the practical meanings of rights for propertyless men, immigrants, free African Americans, slaves, and non-Christians. Most often, republican thinkers insisted on the "natural" dependency of all women and smoothly, if illogically, conflated married women's status under coverture with unmarried women's awkward positioning between free men and wives. Over time, and more insistently with the entrance of propertyless white men into electoral politics, each proposal for new rights prompted vigorous denial and much redrawing of lines. Rather than viewing citizenship as a single "thing," a legal status that labels rights and duties unambiguously, we might attend to how the gender, race, religion, and marital status of citizens have modified people's sense of their own membership in the nation itself.[5]

There were women and men who lived and wrote at the time of the nation's founding who recognized the inconsistency in not counting women as full citizens, as cosigners, as it were, of the social contract. As Kerber has argued, that revolutionary men "explicitly denied married women entry into the new political regime" indicates that "it *was* possible to conceive of alternatives." Many more chose not to notice or simply declared women's status natural and immutable, the "outer limit of natural rights ideology . . . , the line that even the Jeffersonians would not cross."[6] When James Otis asked publicly whether "apple women and orange girls," with "as good a right to give their respectable suffrages" as men, had been consulted in forming the new nation, he knew the answer even as he raised the question. Sometimes courts and legislators felt compelled to articulate and justify the nature of women's citizenship and standing. Wives, the high court of Massachusetts declared in 1801, had "obligations to their husbands and families [that] overrode their obligation to the state."[7] Enough people raised the question to alarm some of the nation's founders. Students of American history will recall that when Abigail Adams pleaded with her husband to "remember the ladies" in the new nation's laws, he laughed. But if his laughter was dismissive, it was also shaky. Soon after, writing to lawyer and future Massachusetts judge James Sullivan, John Adams admitted that even to allow such talk in political conversation would set republicans atop a slippery slope. "It is dangerous to open So fruitfull a Source of Controversy and Altercation," he warned. "There will be no End of it. New Claims will arise. Women will demand a Vote." He pleaded with Sullivan, who had asked, "Whence arises the Right of the Men to govern Women, without their Consent?" to keep such thoughts to himself.[8]

Even before the nineteenth century had begun, ideas about women's political role—indeed, about the very nature of gender in public life—had undergone a major shift. Wealthy and educated women had long assumed their standing, what Jeanne Boydston calls their "confidence of membership," in the colonial elite. Given that economic rank among free white people was the most salient criterion for assuming that one belonged, women such as Judith Sargent Murray "asserted strong public, and even partisan, identities at the founding of the Republic." Some explicitly discussed the place of suffrage, seen as only one of several markers of that identity. Only after the 1790s, and increasingly with the achievement by propertyless white men of political rights, did "a discourse of public authority in which gender designated a distinct relation to the public for women" emerge, leaving women like Murray inhabiting a specifically female place in relation to the state.[9] In the age of "democratic revolutions," writes a historian of France, " 'women' came into being as political outsiders through the discourse of sexual difference," but this was not the uncontested or the inevitable product of Revolutionary Era debates.[10]

A "discourse of sexual difference" was not in itself new, of course, but it took on a special import in a time of republican experiments, both in the United States and elsewhere. Indeed, the very Enlightenment that drove a wedge into the absolute authority of religious institutions and the divine rule of kings in the name of liberty, equality, and human progress offered convenient and convincing categories with which to describe a citizenship distinguished by sex. Characterized in part by the creation of new forms of civic life, the French Revolution has been an especially fertile area for such theoretical insights. In her groundbreaking work on women and civic culture in the French Revolution, Joan Landes taught theorists and historians that "the bourgeois public is essentially, not just contingently, masculinist" in its structure and self-representation; the "exclusion of women from the bourgeois public," she writes, "was not incidental but central to its incarnation." Scholars have differed over specific aspects of women's exclusion and over whether political rights constitute the most salient category for assessing women's standing in civic life. But all have noted that the late eighteenth and very early nineteenth centuries offer a particularly important moment in which the exclusion of women, as women, from formal political life was made explicit.[11]

The author, leading character, and audience in the republican creation myth was the free, white, property-owning male citizen. Only he and his peers, rational, independent, and selfless, had been party to the social contract that defined civil society. Only he was capable of the reason and selfless devotion to the public good that virtuous republics demanded. He both embodied the citizen and controlled the representation of the outsider. Efforts to dissociate women from political life in a republic—not to be confused with women's actual experience of politics—emerged from the assumption that while the male citizen focused on the universal (state and nation), women were bound to the particular (family and home). Men in republics consented to a social contract, with the reciprocal rights and duties that that implied; women, at least most of them, consented to marriage. This concentration on (and duty toward) home and hearth precluded female involvement in that larger world, declaring women unsuited to take on the rights and responsibilities of property-owning men. Metaphors about gender difference were ubiquitous in describing and justifying various forms of exclusion. Their frequency and familiarity help account for the passion with which so many male thinkers defended their own assumptions about women and marriage as based in nature, truth, and reason.

In real life, the notion that some people act only out of "self-interest" and others for the "common good" is absurd, even aside from the thorny question of whose good counts as common. No male citizen is a free-floating, universal member of the nation, for men, too, are members of families, communities, classes, and regions. For men as for women, families offer support and labor, but also duty and distraction. But according to republican ideas, for men such personal ties were aids, not hindrances,

[31]

to fulfilling a political role. "Marriage gave men a familial stake in the community," writes Mark Kann in his work on the "grammar of manhood" in the early republic. "A married man had a family to provision and protect and, therefore, a family interest to join with neighbors in mutual aid projects that promoted family prosperity and in military ventures against enemies who threatened family welfare."[12] Whereas for women the intimate loyalties of marriage and family were distractions from the larger good, those loyalties provided men with an important stake in society; if marriage made women dependents, it made men adults. Rarely were the citizenship rights of white men explicitly tied to their marital status, though the idea was occasionally raised in terms of men's legal age. Working to define eligibility for office in the new state of Maine, Mr. Holmes proposed that rather than bar from office young men of twenty-one, Holmes "would infinitely prefer excluding *batchelors*," whom he thought "rather a useless animal." "Were we to exclude men from public employment, until they were *married*," he insisted, "the provisions would be *politic*, and the constitution would be *popular*."[13] His proposal failed.

In 1801 the "revolution" of the rise to power of Thomas Jefferson and the Republican Party came at the expense of elite women's claim to a political voice. Increasingly, even women's right to be heard in political conversation would be subject to debate. The disfranchisement of New Jersey's single, propertied women voters in 1807 simply marked a growing consensus about the limitations of women's citizenship.[14] Still, the Revolutionary Era, and especially Mary Wollstonecraft's 1792 *Vindication of the Rights of Woman*, which insisted on women's rational independence, had inserted a vocabulary of rights into the political discourse that would be impossible to ignore.[15] Even as the nature of political life became more overtly gendered, post-Revolutionary writers and political theorists assumed that "women along with men should be regarded as the bearers of rights." "Once women had attained the status of rights bearers," Rosemarie Zagarri concludes, "no formal theory . . . could contain the radical power of rights talk."[16]

If the first years of the nineteenth century witnessed a new and more explicitly gendered discourse about whose voice mattered in political conversations, the 1820s signaled yet another shift. White men without property demanded and gained a direct voice in the making of law. At the same time, the vote itself, organized through political parties, emerged as the primary tool for putting that voice into effect. In a pattern that would become more marked throughout the following decades, the right to vote was becoming the central, not to say the only, measure of citizenship. As the traditional relationship between property and suffrage was transformed, politicians engaged in hairsplitting debate, seeking to determine whether citizens and voters were one and the same. Through it all, the idea of women as full citizens provided a useful anchor in "natural" law, a rhetorical barricade against the full implications of democracy. Thus, when he advocated expanding the vote to all white men, Alexander Campbell, a delegate to the 1829 Virginia constitutional convention, explained that "a citizen is a freeman, who has a voice in the Government under which he lives. . . . No disfranchised man is a citizen. He may be an inhabitant, alien, or what you please, but without a vote he cannot be a citizen." This was ridiculous, retorted Benjamin Leigh: "It is not a necessary qualification of a citizen that he should be entitled to vote." If it were, "it would be most absurd to exclude from the privilege of citizenship, every female, and every minor in the community."[17] This inconsistency did not go unnoticed by those few who were interested in addressing women's status. "The truth is," editor John Neal admitted that same year, "that women are *not* citizens here; they have none of the rights of citizens; they pay taxes without being represented." He predicted that "the child is now born who will be a witness to the sweeping away forever of such mockery."[18] But such critical appraisal was extremely rare. Far more commonly, Leigh's suggestion either underscored the absurdity of universal suffrage or caused the advocates of greater democracy to protest and blush.

This debate would not end quickly, of course, as more groups clamored for the full rights of citizenship, and as those rights were increasingly embodied, or made effective, by the vote. Thus, recognizing that there remained some "diversity of opinion [about] what constitutes citizenship; or who are citizens," legal writers such as Samuel Jones urgently opposed the "loose and improper sense, [in which] the word citizen is sometimes used to denote any inhabitant of the country." On the contrary, citizens were those "who were parties to the original compact by which the government was formed, or their successors who are qualified and entitled to take a part in the affairs of government. . . . Women and children . . . are not properly citizens. They are members of the State, and fully entitled to the advantages of its laws and institutions for the protection of their rights." Satisfied with his spectacularly circular reasoning, Jones remained silent as to which rights of women and children warranted protection by the state of which they were "members." "It has been quite a common error, to confound the right of *citizenship*, with the right of *suffrage*," wrote Edward D. Mansfield. "The two are in reality distinct things."[19] In an intriguing twist, delegates to the 1846 Wisconsin constitutional convention reversed the usual equation and declared that one could have suffrage without being a citizen. As Moses Strong put it, "A man may be a citizen and not be a voter, and so he may be a voter and not be a citizen of the state or of the United States. The power to make foreigners citizens of the United States belongs to the United States; the power to prescribe the qualifications of electors has been lodged in the states, plainly showing that they are distinct powers."[20] If in the early days of the republic few had cared to distinguish clearly between citizens and voters, from the 1820s on the distinction remained highly contested and subject to constant renegotiation. Only in 1874, faced with a growing clamor for votes for women, did the Supreme Court settle the question in *Minor v. Happersett*, ruling unanimously that U.S. citizenship did not automatically confer upon its bearers the right to vote.[21]

Still, the men who decided who had rights and who did not had trouble defining their terms. From the 1889 Wyoming constitutional convention debates emerges the following pithy exchange:

MR. TESCHEMACHER. I would like to ask the gentleman a question. Mr. Fox, what is a state?

MR. FOX. I don't know.

MR. TESCHEMACHER. What is the use of trying to define what a citizen of a state is when we don't know the meaning of the word state.

MR. FOX. I don't claim to be a dictionary.[22]

We do not have to be a dictionary to ask with Teschemacher what men meant by the terms they threw about. In the United States, with its federal and state governments and competing sets of laws, people held multiple political memberships; the dance, or duel, between federal and state claims on their loyalties continues to the present. While the national government defined U.S. citizenship, it was states that delineated the most pertinent rights of individuals through much of the nineteenth century, determining (until the Reconstruction and woman suffrage amendments partially limited them) who could own property, who could marry whom, and who could vote.

The emergence of the vote as the focal point of political life, like the expansion of the suffrage itself, reflected changes in the nation's economic life as well as its political and intellectual culture. These changes, taken together, demand a more nuanced understanding of what constituted people's sense of belonging to the nation itself—and how those identities were, in turn, informed by the rhetoric of religious exclusiveness that came to permeate public life. By the late 1820s, motivated by the influx of refugees from Europe and by changes in an industrializing and highly fluctuating economy, a working-class movement of union organizers, mechanics, female laborers, and freethinkers had emerged, most visibly in New York City's Workingmen's Party. From that working-class milieu surfaced a vision of woman's rights that drew on and departed from Enlightenment thinkers' consideration of citizens' standing in law. Among freethinkers, Fanny Wright located the source of women's status in the sexual and legal constraints of marriage. Her support for women's freedom to marry, reproduce, and divorce as they chose instantly alerted her attackers to the danger she represented. But many of her views seem to have been shared or at least condoned by the greater body of freethinkers. Reporting on one of her lectures in Philadelphia, the *Mechanic's Free Press* observed that "in advocating the rights of women, she did not fail to insure the approbation of every body in the house."[23]

For all their support of woman's rights, freethinkers viewed women with some ambivalence and not a little condescension.[24] Many felt they had been daring enough in raising the question of women's equality but had little inclination to follow it to a logical conclusion. One freethinking writer mused, "In the next generation, when our females have from infancy been properly educated, we shall have a fair opportunity of ascertaining whether . . . to admit of their participation in the legislative proceedings of the country." Still, he accepted for the present that "when a woman married the man of her choice, her husband becomes her political representative."[25] Less complacent, some working-class women openly demanded their rights both as women and as workers. In 1831, New York tailoresses struck for better working conditions and wages, declaring it "a mighty work . . . namely, that of gaining our liberty." Sarah Monroe called on working-class women to organize both against bosses and against conventional notions of women's place. "My friends," she proclaimed, "if it is unfashionable for the men to bear oppression in silence, why should it not also become unfashionable with the women?" Louise Mitchell, the secretary of the United Tailoresses Society, urged women to "have more confidence in our own abilities, and less in the sincerity of man." "Are we not a species of the human race, and is not this a free country?" cried Mitchell. "Then why may not we enjoy that freedom? Because we have been taught to believe ourselves far less noble and far less wise than the other sex."[26] This tradition of working-class women speaking out on behalf of their sex did not produce an ongoing feminist movement, but neither did these views vanish entirely. Throughout the 1830s and 1840s, striking textile workers at the Lowell mills viewed the Revolutionary Era inheritance of equal rights as their own, describing themselves as "daughters of freemen" and on occasion making a "flaming Mary Woolstonecroft [sic] speech on the rights of women and the iniquities of the 'monied aristocracy.' "[27] When they organized petition drives to demand a ten-hour day or formed labor unions, these early female industrial workers insisted that "our voice be heard and our rights acknowledged."[28]

But if women's equal political rights were *not* more widely embraced in this climate, it was in part because a competing discourse about religion and respectability was establishing middle-class women's membership in the nation on new grounds. As many working-class and freethinking activists knew—and as historians have shown since—the 1820s were a religiously turbulent time. In that context, a revived and repoliticized Protestantism created a discourse counter to the one about political rights and Enlightenment reason. Having survived and, indeed, prospered from disestablishment, the clergy gained through revivals a strong cultural influence that often took a political form—and that played a dramatic role in reconceptualizing middle-class women's political identities. Leading members of the clergy organized to reinforce that influence both within churches and through national benevolent organizations. By the 1830s the nation would be awash with the campaigns of religious activists to transform Americans' habits of drinking, healing, dressing, and educating in light of their efforts to ensure the cultural ascendancy of Protestantism. By most measures, historians have agreed, the clergy, with women's help as congregants, authors, missionaries, and reformers, had won, and the intellectual landscape was transformed. So widespread was this cultural shift that by the 1840s one observer would note that the younger folks who attended an "Infidel Convention" universally believed in God; only "the old gray heads are Atheists."[29]

This transformation in the religious and intellectual climate of the 1820s was a battle for Americans' loyalties. It was a contest against both working-class activism and freethinking rationality that helped shape a middle-class identity with a language not of class division but of Protestant self-control and female morality. It is by now a truism that the antebellum United States witnessed and encouraged an intense association between middle-class women and religion. Although this association has come to seem inevitable, and religion the only possible framework for understanding women's place in civic life, neither was the case. As attacks against irreligion show, women had to be convinced of the utter evil—the absolute unthinkableness—of freethought and, by extension, of any ideas that could be attributed to Fanny Wright herself. These attacks took on an increasingly virulent tone throughout the 1830s, as allegations of infidelity worked alongside revivals to shore up evangelical dominance. As evidenced in the sermons of ministers, the writings on domesticity, and the newspaper debates between the religiously orthodox and the "infidel," the insistence on and the celebration of the evangelical victory hints at a vanquished enemy, an elusive yet profoundly threatening disbelief in the tenets of both "true religion" and "true womanhood." To the religiously and politically conservative, Wright, "the Red Harlot of Infidelity," provided an astonishingly resilient symbol of irreligion, sexual transgression, and urban working-class radicalism.

Throughout the 1820s and 1830s, writers employed the Fanny Wright epithet to evoke the dangerous threat of irreligion, ministers called on women to devote themselves to religious goals, and conservative activists sought to enforce the Christian Sabbath as a path to national salvation. But this rhetoric had a far wider impact than simply stifling freethinking radicals; there were far too few of them to have merited the scale and intensity of the attack. By the 1830s the power and pervasiveness of Protestantism had effectively shaped many aspects of American life. Some politicians were especially anxious about establishing a closer link between religion and politics to prevent the state their fathers had established from becoming entirely secular. In 1838 Henry Whiting Warner railed against the threat of "*political irreligion.*" Fuming over the "cant among us, that *as electors* we have nothing to do with men's religious sentiments," the author argued that tolerance could only lead to irreligion and worse. Several years earlier, New York's legislature had debated the merits of appointing chaplains to that body. Warner was appalled: "Nothing else could have . . . prepared us as a people to be tamely satisfied with, the corrupting and scandalous exhibition we have lately witnessed in New-York for the first time—may it be the last—*an unpraying legislature.*"[30]

Disbelief itself was impossible to outlaw, but its alleged dangers could be curtailed, and states went to some effort to do so. They sketched the boundaries of full citizenship not by outlawing one particular religion or establishing another, but by defining the edges of respectability that declared who had standing within the community and who did not. For example, agreeing that "the testimony of the atheist and the infidel, ought not to be placed upon an equality with others," most states required officeholders and witnesses in court to swear to a belief in God and eternal punishment. Some additionally mandated that officeholders and federal appointees swear to a belief in either Jesus Christ or the New Testament.[31] Far from viewing these limitations as relics of a less enlightened time, antebellum politicians devoted significant effort to upholding them. Delegates drawing up the first constitution for Maine in 1819 voted by a narrow margin not to require Christian oaths for officers of the state. Fearful of the implications of this decision, Judge Thacher "hoped none of the Convention wished to secure to themselves, or any body of people, *the right not to worship at all.*"[32] These requirements were widely understood as harmless, even liberal, guarantees of good government. The first Maryland constitution of 1776, for instance, had tolerantly asserted "that *no other* test or qualification ought to be required on admission to any office of trust or profit, *than* such oath of support and fidelity to this state . . . and a declaration of a belief in the christian religion." Only in 1818 did the Maryland legislature begin to consider revising this law so that Jews could become officers and lawyers in that state. Supporters of the so-called Jew bill (and of the religious tolerance it implied) went to some length to assure their constituents that they need not fear that a Jew might ever rule a Christian nation. Although the bill's main sponsor, Thomas Kennedy, had wanted to abolish all religious tests, the version that finally passed in 1825 merely substituted references to Jesus Christ with "a belief in a future state of rewards and punishments." Apparently the Jews of Maryland "were not and did not want to be linked with infidels and atheists," and the practice of drawing religious and moral boundaries around citizenship remained intact.[33]

In cases regarding legitimate witnesses in court and in blasphemy cases, questions about citizenship, religion, and sexual respectability were explicitly and forcefully debated. Each of these discussions implicitly linked political standing with conformity to the religious standards of the day. Antebellum judges, for example, considered whether Universalists (who believed that all persons were universally saved after death and that there was no divine punishment) could serve as witnesses in civil cases.

With an extreme sense of urgency about the safety of the nation and their courts, they decided that they could not. Judges in *Atwood v. Walton* (1830) declared that a person who denied heavenly accountability could not be trusted as a witness in a case where "life, liberty, property or reputation are to be affected by his testimony." The implications of this were vast, because without a sworn belief in eternal punishment, anarchy would reign. "Whatever strikes at the root of christianity," Justice James Kent had written in 1811 in *People v. Ruggles*, "tends manifestly to the dissolution of civil government,"[34] and many continued to hold that view implicitly. The separation of church and state, which Americans claimed to have perfected, meant that people could believe as they wished—could, even, deny a belief in eternal punishment. It did not mean that they could testify in court. As late as New York's constitutional convention in 1846 a significant minority of delegates expressed a similar concern. The men were preparing to take a new constitution to their constituents when Moses Taggart of Genesee County suggested that "no person shall be rendered incompetent to be a witness on account of his opinions in matters of religious belief." Whig George Simmons "considered this to be a most dangerous proposition." After all, "the only individuals now excluded from giving testimony, were those who denied the existence of a supreme being, and the moral power of the government to punish false swearing." Horatio Stow's fear ran even deeper, as he worried that "the laws [might] recognize that there might be even a doubt as to the existence of a Deity." "The making of such a question," he warned darkly, "implied such a doubt."[35] Taggart's amendment passed, 53 to 46, thus granting Universalists and freethinkers the right to testify in court. Still, that 46 delegates voted against the measure suggests that politicians remained alarmed by any hint of unbelief in the state's laws and were anxious to draw boundaries around those whose religious respectability was in doubt.

Opponents of religious tests should not be mistaken for freethinkers or atheists, for even liberals expressed confidence that religious tolerance would not shake the Protestant foundations of the state.[36] In the United States the dialectic between politics and religion had become so tightly woven as to be most visible to the irreligious or foreigners. "Religion in America," Tocqueville observed, "must be regarded as the first of their political institutions. . . . I do not know whether all Americans have a sincere faith in their religion—for who can search the human heart?—but I am certain that they hold it to be indispensable to the maintenance of republican institutions."[37] Nor did anyone doubt which religion most Americans intended to uphold or that, for instance, in Warner's words, "the chaplains of the army and navy are necessarily of the christian faith." "Jews," he stated firmly, "are out of the question."[38] Indeed, the nation's very air was saturated with the understanding that Christianity lay at the foundation of Americans' (and especially American women's) freedom and liberty. Politicians rarely hesitated to note that the United States was a Protestant nation. On those occasions when their assumptions were challenged, they expressed surprise that anyone had ever imagined otherwise.

By the 1830s, Protestantism in the United States had proved to be an especially effective and largely uncontested means by which to describe and limit the boundaries of civic belonging. Very few antebellum activists, with the notable exception of Polish-born Jew and freethinker Ernestine Rose, suggested that Christianity ought to be wholly irrelevant to women's, or anyone's, full membership in political life.[39] Ideas about women were central and essential to this consensus. In countless arenas of public discourse, the concept of female sexual purity provided the most salient rhetoric for advancing a view of the republic as Christian, for marginalizing particular groups through warnings of sexual chaos, and for justifying limitations on suffrage as natural and just. Avowals of this consensus pop up frequently, as when the Democratic Party of Wisconsin, deep in debate about a proposed constitution in 1847, *"resolved, . . . that . . . the integrity of our people, to say nothing of the chastity of our women, may safely be trusted to Him who made man in His own image and the religious constitution of the Christian revelation."*[40] Furthermore, the "gendering" of religion had important implications for the ways many women would enter the conversation about their rights. Certainly the 1830s were not the first time that an association with religion helped to sustain a sexual hierarchy in the political world, for an emphasis on the spiritual duties of women had long undermined sustained discussion of their political rights.[41] Yet the antebellum North offers a fascinating time and place to study that association. It was a time when religious language pervaded political life to a great extent and when women's purportedly moral role in civic life took on a noticeably political cast. Indeed, by the 1830s, many middle-class women, in their work for reform, charitable, and benevolent societies and describing themselves as Christians, as Americans, and as mothers, had declared their intention to act in the larger world. Religious rhetoric provided a mandate for their political activities even as it narrowed the grounds on which women, at least in theory, could speak openly about their rights.

Language that associated religion, female respectability, and political belonging provided a shorthand that helped conflate what was un-Christian and un-American—"not us"—in the antebellum years.[42] Antebellum Protestants were adept at imagining, describing, and expressing enormous anxiety about those whose full membership in the nation they declared unthinkable. Ideas that no one wished to debate were dismissed as infidelity, just as the proponents of almost any reform in women's status were labeled Fanny Wrighters. Phrases that branded outsiders as "Jews, Turks, and Infidels" or "Turks and Mohomedans" provided the rhetorical boundary encircling "Christian" nations and peoples and had little to do with the presence of actual Jews, Muslims, and nonbelievers within the nation itself.[43] (It did, however, have a great deal to do with justifying missionary expeditions among those peoples, both at home and abroad.) But it remained a useful grouping, not least because everyone seemed to agree. In no sense was Christianity an *established* religion in the United States, Rufus King assured his fellow delegates to the 1821 New York constitutional convention, "yet the religious professions of the Pagan, the Mahommedan and the Christian, are not, in the eye of the law, of equal truth and excellence."[44]

Depictions of non-Christians as un-American "others," in turn, had special salience in defining women's political identities. This was, after all, the nineteenth century; few questioned openly whether white women had rights to be protected. But on many levels of public discourse, those rights had taken on a decidedly spiritual cast. Just as they had drawn boundaries around (middle-class) female virtue by thwarting the threat posed by (largely working-class) freethought, so writers, ministers, politicians, and many women themselves considered women's civic standing in light of Christianity. American women, they insisted, gained their greatest rights from having been born in a Christian nation; religious, not political, rights were at the heart of women's standing in their communities and their nation. Women themselves, in this framework, came to be understood not as "fully accountable citizens" but as "the best of all possible moral subjects."[45] Thus American writers employed a "pervasive characterization of Islamic societies as backward and particularly degrading to women."[46] "The sad story of woman's wrongs, where the true God is not worshiped, is, or should be, familiar to my fair readers," remarked a writer in the *Ladies' Repository* who went on to praise missionaries' "redemption of their sisters from the servility and degradation of paganism."[47] Supporters of woman's rights often appealed to this kind of reasoning as well. John Neal, for one, insisted that as an ostensibly Christian country, the United States had to be "better" than the non-Christian. "Are the Egyptians, the Hindoos, the Chinese, and the rudest barbarians of all the earth, *right* in their doctrines and practices, with regard to women?" he asked. He delineated the wrongs supposedly done to women in those countries only to condemn his own, where "women are under a perpetual guardianship" and where "it is their *privilege* to be taxed without their own consent."[48] Underscoring these assertions of religious superiority was a defense of Americans' own moral standards, civil inequalities, and economic disparities that made common rhetorical use of the boundaries of national belonging.

Religion thus served as a justification for marginalizing some Americans, for proselytizing around the world, and for limiting women's standing and authority in political debate. Those who bore responsibilities of a religious nature, according to this logic, should not be granted or did not desire or would be diminished by full political rights. Thus were clergymen prohibited in most states from "holding any civil or military office or place." The language used to defend one form of exclusion, to limit one group's claims on the state, was remarkably like the other. New Yorker George Crooker "believed it was wisdom to keep [clergymen] free and unspotted from the defilements of political ambition. . . . Was it wise to invite a holy and highminded ministry to mingle in the corrupting conflicts of our political elections? Would it not hazard the sacredness of their piety and soil their robes of office?"[49] Sometimes the analogy between ministers and women was made explicit, as in Virginia's 1829 constitutional convention debate. Although women had not yet been mentioned in the debate over allowing clergymen to run for office, Mr. Randolph opined that "there is not greater indecency and incompatibility in a woman's thrusting herself into a political assembly and all its cabals, than in a clergyman's undertaking the same thing." "If women will unsex themselves," he warned, "and if priests . . . will degrade themselves, . . . they must take the consequences. . . . If ladies will plunge into the affairs of men, . . . they will be treated roughly—like men. Just so it is with priests. They lose all the deference which belongs, and which is paid to their office."[50]

The obligation of Americans to be virtuous citizens was both fundamentally Protestant and profoundly gendered, a conflation that helped define the boundaries of female belonging throughout the nineteenth century. To challenge religion was to threaten domestic and sexual purity as well. Thus it was without irony or humor that a Pennsylvania court agreed that permitting blasphemous speech "would provide a nursery of vice, a school of preparation to qualify young men for the gallows, and young women for the brothel." If blasphemy were allowed, "every debating club might dedicate the club-room to the worship of the Goddess of Reason, and adore the deity in the person of a naked prostitute."[51] The fear of religious and sexual infidelity was especially effective in attacking feminism. In a political culture suffused with the assumption that men acquired their rights through a political compact and that women gained theirs by virtue of Christianity, women's full citizenship could seem respectable only if it was gendered, if it seemed to uphold rather than undermine sexual differences. Thus the threat of female deviance, both sexual and religious, was ubiquitous in those political and legal settings that set the terms for women's citizenship.

These views were powerful and long standing. At many levels of political conversation, as well as in movements for temperance, charitable work, and antislavery, the pervasiveness of Protestant thought, the association of women with religion, and the rhetoric that linked irreligion with sexual chaos sustained the view that women's political equality was beyond the boundaries of legitimate debate. Rather, the most important "right" of women, that of being protected, which was itself utterly mired in assumptions about class standing and privilege, was said to be guaranteed by their religious loyalty. It was this view that the Jefferson County petitioners implicitly addressed—and rejected—when they insisted that their disfranchisement denied them "the only safeguards of their individual and personal liberties."

The conflation of respectable womanhood with restricted religious and sexual practices pervaded antebellum claims to the rights of citizens—and to the denial of those rights. To the extent that political thinkers associated rights with independence, the idea of the female citizen was fraught with dangers. The phrase "independent woman" connoted prostitution, and so the notion of women as citizens slid easily into some predictable sexual slurs. In turn, woman's rights were evoked in numerous contexts to measure the limits of legitimate debate, to disparage *other* claims to rights. So common was this rhetoric that, reading constitutional convention proceedings, I could predict its approach. Opponents of universal white male suffrage frequently mentioned woman suffrage as the horrible result at the bottom of the suffrage-granting slope. Women's exclusion from voting, these delegates frequently proclaimed, was proof that the suffrage was an arbitrary and *not* a natural right. In contrast, supporters of expanding the suffrage to other men, trapped by the habits of boundary making and unwilling to rethink the meaning of gender in political life, declared themselves unable to imagine such a thing. The notion of women as independent citizens was too ridiculous to merit discussion but conveniently served to warn of the dangers or highlight the necessity of political innovation. In deciding the limits of white men's voting rights or of Jewish men's officeholding or of free black men's right to petition, politicians made explicit assumptions that both reaffirmed and helped establish women's equality as absurd. Merely to consider the woman as voter was not only to challenge gender conventions but to shatter the connection between republicanism and morality itself. As late as 1872, Pennsylvania's W. H. Smith claimed to be "as much astonished as pained, to find that this startling innovation, this pernicious heresy of woman suffrage" had wormed its way into political life.[52] As abolitionists painfully discovered, the insistence on their own piety did not protect radical women. To propose that women be granted their rights as American citizens was to open oneself to charges of both sexual and religious transgression. To overcome that association—to make woman's rights palatable —required significant reworking of those assumptions but not, I argue, a complete break with them.

Yet the rhetoric that declared the world black and white, Christian and infidel, or respectable and radical never wholly matched the experiences of women within the political culture of their own town, state, or region. The rules of citizenship, that is to say, as well as the rhetoric of respectability fit imperfectly alongside the experience of membership. When Boston lawyer George Blake argued in 1801 that a married woman "is not a member; has no *political relation* to the *state* any more than an *alien*," his was an extreme view.[53] For if free white women were denied the rights and freed of the duties of white male citizens, few imagined that they were actually aliens or slaves. Nor did all free women share an identical status. Sharp and very real differences between married and unmarried women complicated women's legal standing, just as wives of men who owned property, whether southern yeomen, midwestern farmers, or urban elites, likely understood their own relationship to the state or nation in ways that were shaped by landownership. White American women did not consider themselves noncitizens or strangers; much evidence suggests that they believed they were entitled to make claims on those in power. Through petitions, lobbying, and speeches, whether individually, in organizations, or in small groups, women made demands on the governments under which they lived. They acted, against so many assumptions to the contrary, as if the nation and its political traditions were theirs. If we are to judge by their anxiety in the face of any whisper of woman's rights, politicians, too, understood that free women had rights that could not be entirely ignored. Their full and equal citizenship may have been "unthinkable," but women themselves constructed political identities that reflected a more nuanced sense of belonging than one shaped entirely by legal rights. Something more tenuous than legal privileges, a more complex understanding of *membership* in civic life, may be central to understanding those identities.

I do not mean to suggest that full legal and political rights, or the struggles of those who sought them, were irrelevant; clearly, the Jefferson County women did not think so. I believe, however, that political identities are malleable and complex and are created at the junctions among people's legal rights, access to politicians, standing in their communities, and attitudes toward those who make the "rules" of political engagement. The puzzle I offer here—pieces of which include six ordinary women, the specific intellectual and economic history of their part of New York, the women's particular standing in their communities, and the petition itself —demands that we incorporate into the story of female political identity some women's sense of entitlement, their assumption that they should participate in shaping political life. The long and dreary years of suffrage activism, as well as its triumphant retelling, may have made women's demand for political rights seem more dangerous to wish for than it really was. We need to examine more closely what ideas were available in the language of the day and attend more carefully to what the silences of ordinary women may have meant. And we must look at the center—at moments when women said directly, without blinking or blushing, that they deserved and wanted the full rights of citizens.

Writing as "the female portion of community," six Jefferson County women declared their membership in the larger world. They wrote not as isolated individuals but as partners in making the social contract for their county and their state, as people who felt entitled to enter the conversation that was reframing its rules. Their language may have reflected a national rhetoric, but their concerns were more local. For while the Ormsby and Osborn women and their Vincent, Bishop, and Williams

friends were U.S. citizens, it was the state of New York (as they so pointedly put it) that "ungenerously withheld" their "equal, and civil and
political rights." For them, belonging and rights were inextricably linked.

Disparate and conflicting definitions of belonging, of place, race or
ethnicity, language, religion, governmental policies, and relationships
with whoever is "not us," infuse debates over the rights and obligations of
citizenship. It is here that I find much of the significance and the poi-
gnancy of the Jefferson County story—not in the fact that the women's
petition succeeded in transforming the legal forms of women's citizenship
or that it provides a new "start date" for the movement for woman's rights.
Rather, it is in the women's insistence, implicit in their petition and
underscored by the circumstances of their lives, that they were "us": full
members of their community, "amenable" to the government "under
which they live[d]," legitimate heirs to the American political tradition,
and active in expanding the egalitarian aspects of that tradition to all the
adult citizens of New York.

In noisy discussions about who could claim the full rights of citizenship, politicians insisted that women's equal rights were dangerous, im-
moral, and unthinkable. This conversation among men does not suggest
an ever-implicit and thus invisible sexual contract in republican thought.
It was, on the contrary, a source of much open pleasure and satisfaction to
the men who formed and ran state governments to note, again and again,
that on the issue of woman's rights, they and nature and God were in
agreement. It was also a topic of great anxiety, for in the state capitals that
politicians inhabited, discussion of woman's rights threatened to lay bare
basic assumptions about who belonged fully to the nation. This conversation among men obviously affected women's political identities; how
could it not? But to six women, this exclusion, this insistence that they
were not, in fact, parties to the political compact of their state, rankled in
a way that would push them to act.

The threat against women who dared to demand equal rights was
pervasive in antebellum political rhetoric. They forswore the protection of
a Christian nation; they would suffer lost deference and rough treatment.
Given all the noise about the danger of woman's rights, we would expect
thunder from Jefferson County pulpits, politicians, or newspapers in the
fall of 1846, when people caught wind of the petition of these six women.
We would expect outrage, backlash, and renewed warnings of the decline
of Christianity. We might expect to find evidence that they sought sympathetic companionship at the Seneca Falls convention two years later. We

might even hear from their descendants the echo of a distant memory of outrageous or mysterious female relatives. There is nothing. Quiet outrage, snubbing, small acts of hostility—all are possible and unlikely to have survived in a historical record that includes no memoirs. But the silence can as easily suggest something else: mild support, shrugged shoulders, and an easygoing tolerance of their action. Perhaps these six women differed from their neighbors not so much in *believing* that the laws of their state were unfair, but in *caring* so much. What is clear is this: if we want to know why this small community of women viewed woman's rights as eminently thinkable and why they felt entitled to say so in public, we are going to have to stop listening to the conversation politicians were holding on the subject and go to where the women lived.

MAP 1. *State of New York, ca. 1840s*

chapter three

Property and Place

"Your Memorialists inhabitants of Jefferson county"

Just as the study of ideas must encompass various levels of discourse—from politicians' debates to the writings of women authors to a petition by six ordinary women—so we can examine questions of property and place from the air, so to speak, or on the ground. From a distance, Jefferson County exhibited both vast emptiness and striking change. Although " 'gazeteers' still referred to the northern tier of counties as the 'remote counties' " in the decades after the Revolution, others considered this "a period of remarkable expansion and growth" when "settlers . . . spread into every nook and corner suitable for habitation." By 1825, "every district had been entered, no large blocks of farmland remained unsold, and . . . the basic patterns of farms and villages had been set."[1] Still, when a writer described nineteenth-century Watertown, Jefferson County's largest city, as "off the main tourist route," he greatly understated its isolation.[2] Remote, slow to settle, and quirky in its history, Jefferson County offers stories about land, property, and place that are central to our understanding of the lives of these women, their political identities, and their words.

Even its most exuberant boosters considered Jefferson County remote. It sits literally on the nation's edge, with Lake Ontario its western border and the St. Lawrence River and Canada on the north; to the east, the Adirondack Mountains, protected in 1882 as a 6-million-acre park, heighten its geographic isolation. Lately and sparsely settled, the county is barely mentioned in accounts of New York's population and mobility, lists of churches, records of roads, or surveys of agricultural production, although the placement of roads and fields signaled that native peoples had previously inhabited the land. Travelers rarely refer to Jefferson County except to note its fine harbors. Things that one might expect to find in New York by the second decade of the nineteenth century are simply not there. More than a decade after the Revolution, the North Country did indeed seem "an unexplored wilderness."[3]

The Ormsby, Vincent, Osborn, and O'Connor families all arrived in Jefferson County between 1817 and 1820 and so experienced its time of great (if short-lived) expansion and hope. Although their immediate neighborhood was well populated by their friends and relatives, all of them could recall when it was filled mostly with trees, for the land itself was just being surveyed, cleared, claimed, farmed, named, and settled when they arrived.[4] Dramatic claims were made about the region's expansion, but it took some imagination to describe its population growth as a flood. "In the spring of 1800," declared early settler Noadiah Hubbard, "people began to flock into the country by [the] hundreds." Indeed, when Hubbard boasted, "I was *the first white settler in the county*," only one or two others could compete for the claim.[5] By the time the families of the future petitioners arrived (in what was then part of Brownville), towns had been roughly laid out, but they consisted primarily of a few houses, sawmills and gristmills, and many immodest predictions about the area's still unmet expectations.[6] Certainly Jacob Brown had big plans for his town, and although it lost the contest for county seat to Watertown, by 1810 Brownville, with some 1,660 residents, could be considered "the most progressive and prosperous settlement in the county." Its population would more than double in the next decade, to 3,990.[7] So rapid did the settlement of Jefferson County seem that local leaders began to worry that "the county might be infested with criminals to the great danger and injury of its inhabitants," and so in 1808 they built a jail.[8]

We can get a sense of the newness and flux of the place simply by following the changes in town names and boundaries. When first glimpsed in Jefferson County in 1820, Hiram Ormsby, for example, lived in Brownville. In 1825 he was in Lyme; in 1832, buying land in Orleans; and in 1840, residing in Clayton, in the section that was known as Depauville. It is tempting to be fooled into believing that his family had packed up yet again. But he and Amy and their children, who, if asked, would probably call their neighborhood Catfish Falls, had not budged.[9] However "set" the geographic patterns by 1825, the region's settlement was extraordinarily raw and new for a northeastern state. By the time the women wrote their petition in 1846, the county was barely forty years old, and their immediate community of Depauville was much newer. Their families had introduced farms, markets, churches, legal stability, and political communities into their section of upstate New York. Further, at a time when cheaper western land was a constant temptation, Osborns, Ormsbys, Vincents, and Williamses remained in Jefferson County for the rest of their lives, very much

MAP 2. *Jefferson County, New York*

rooted in the place that they had helped establish and that made the women's political and legal inequality particularly salient. On the fringe of their state and nation but at the center of their own communities, they expressed a strong conviction that they were participants in the wider conversation about their own and others' political rights.

Even with the jail, a courthouse, and a board of supervisors in place, only after the War of 1812, when the fear of invasion from Canada or attacks by Indians no longer caused "constant agitation and an intense excitement of the public mind," did landowners promote the North Country to settlers. As one gazetteer recalled, "New roads were opened in every direction, and for a short time, the country advanced rapidly in population and improvements, which continued till the completion of the Erie Canal" in 1825.[10] There seemed little reason to question the most optimistic of hopes. The land was fertile and promised vast quantities of timber and ash, copious amounts of wheat, and excellent pastures for cattle and sheep. The market for selling agricultural products was superb, in large part because of the St. Lawrence River and its offshoots, as "farm and timber products were floated with small cost down to Montreal, which was then one of the best markets on the continent."[11] Still, although individual farms would become productive and comfortable, Jefferson County as a whole never achieved its hoped-for prosperity. The very markets for agricultural products that drew settlers would soon suffer from the timing and nature of the region's settlement.

As historian Jeanne Boydston has pointed out, "Most free Americans lived in middling households that already were deeply, deliberately, and contentedly immersed in commercial relations." In moving to new farms or expanding older ones, they sought "not splendid isolation, but successful negotiation of the market." This was precisely the North Country's appeal. "You were not preferably attracted to it merely by the goodness and fertility of the soil," James Le Ray de Chaumont, founder of Jefferson County's first agricultural society, admitted to an audience of farmers, "neither by the abundance of wild game and fish. . . . No; your marked preference was given to this county, more particularly by its superiority over all other new countries [sic] in the advantages of market." Given those ambitions, Le Ray commiserated with farmers over "the most extraordinary events and unexpected difficulties . . . which it was not in the reach of the human mind to foresee, when the majority of you came to settle in this county."[12]

The source of these difficulties was not hard to find. The Erie Canal transformed access to markets and the development of towns throughout New York State, but its effects were uneven. While the canal proved a great boon to some parts of the state, "cheap and better lands in western New York and on into Ohio soon drove farming operations in northern New York to the wall." Despite once high hopes, these residents of the "fastest growing, wealthiest, and most populous of the states" observed New York's progress literally from the margins. They had experienced the effects of political decisions made and economic changes occurring beyond their control, and this, in Le Ray's poignant phrase, had resulted in "almost the annihilation of their former and reasonable calculations."[13]

Like virtually everyone else in Jefferson County, the Vincents, Ormsbys, Osborns, Williamses, and Bishops came from someplace else. Many of the older generation, including most of the petitioners' parents, had already moved to New York State from New England, and their decision to uproot again suggests that they hoped to own their own farms. Theirs was a fairly typical migration pattern, one that expanded upstate New York even as it drained Vermont of its population, as ads for fine land elsewhere appeared in all fourteen of that state's weekly newspapers.[14] Some New Englanders, including Anna Bishop's family, crisscrossed the national boundary, and still others traversed the Adirondack wilderness, moving west along the Canadian line to get to Jefferson County. Far more stopped first, for a year or a decade, along a more southern route. Most of those who lived in the Depauville neighborhood had come north with their parents and siblings from Russia, in Herkimer County, New York, where their families may have rented land on the 37,000-acre Royal Grant patents.[15] The move must have seemed well timed; what with insects and the financial competition of the West, "between 1820 and 1830 the prospects of the Herkimer county agriculturist were not encouraging."[16] In any case, that so many of the people in this story migrated from the same place suggests that the families were acquaintances of long standing and that they made their decisions as part of a group. They would have found the area cluttered with former neighbors, including the father and son Doctors Frame, Elkanah and Lucy Corbin, and Nathaniel Norton Jr., a land agent, who had moved there only a year or two before the rest.

The Depauville families were the earliest rural community to settle this particular land while the county, "with its rich farming lands, its water power and its rapidly growing villages," was at its period of greatest expansion. Their decision to move north was made possible, quite literally, by the construction of the State, or Line, Road, authorized by the legislature in 1803 and paid for with $41,500 in public money.[17] Once finished, it ran right through the town of Russia and up to the St. Lawrence River. "The route is very direct and generally straight," reported George L. Johnson, "especially through Herkimer County; all the villages . . . are very nearly in a straight line." The state road quickly became a busy thoroughfare that "thronged with teams. . . . The carriage of grain, pork, potash, flax, wool, fish from Lake Ontario, venison, furs and other products from the field, forest and waters, made an animated scene along the whole road." Conveniently, "taverns stood at short intervals." While canals and transcontinental turnpikes would become the measure of a transportation and market revolution, men like Benjamin Vincent, Timothy O'Connor, and Elias Ormsby knew that it was the small road, dirt or plank, that would make or break individual farms and communities.[18] To them, the state road must have seemed a perfect way out and up, following an old Indian trail across the Chaumont River near Depauville, bordering Penet's Square, and dividing tracts 40, 41, and 60 on the east side and lots 261, 262, and 270 on the west. Ormsbys, Osborns, O'Connors, and Vincents built their homes and settled their farms on either side of it.

Regardless of what they had been told, acquiring the land was no simple matter. Indeed, whether out of optimism, gullibility, or simple disregard for the law, some of them established their farms before they had any legal claim to them. Though the practice of planting a crop in the ground before holding a deed to it was common throughout the United States, the politics of land is rarely seen so starkly as in New York State, with its deals and patents and ongoing feudal relationships. In the far north, major disputes—with Indians, the French, the British, Massachusetts, New Hampshire, and land patent holders—were still ongoing long after the rest of the state had been surveyed, rented, sold, and farmed.[19] Huge parcels of land were bought and sold by men who had never even seen it, much less shouldered an ax. All this tumult and speculation, many believed, resulted in "slow development . . . , squatterism, tax delinquency, title disputes, and tension between original owners and subsequent purchasers."[20] New York's "ways were different from those across the New England border," as one historian puts it, "partly because land here from the first was an active commercial commodity for private sale to any purchaser rather than the possession of town communities assignable for public good. New York, then, was the first paradise of speculation."[21]

Historians have written ruefully about the fervor with which wealthy New Yorkers undertook speculation in "vast tracts of wild lands." It was, one recalled, "an amazing fever . . . to which statesmen, army officers, ministers, and merchants of highest standing, in common with financiers and out-and-out adventurers, succumbed." As early as 1829, James Macauley fumed that "the peopling of the state since the revolution, although unexampled in the annals of colonization, has nevertheless been slower than it otherwise would have been, had not the state government thrown obstacles in the way." The main impediment to settlement, Macauley and others believed, was the "large land-jobbers" who "frittered away" the land.[22] Others were more sanguine. As one owner of vast lands, Gouverneur Morris, mused, "Speculators, as such, are not respectable, but they are necessary. . . . It is absurd to suppose a person with scarce a second shirt on his back can go two or three hundred miles to look out a farm, have it surveyed, travel back again to the office for a patent, etc., clear the land, cut a road, make a settlement, and build house and barn, and then an owner under a prior grant may come forward and take possession. . . . As things now stand, the conflict of title is generally between men able to stand the shock."[23]

Alexander Macomb exemplified this grand and sordid pattern and brings the larger story of speculation and investment literally into the Vincents', Ormsbys', and Osborns' backyards. Between 1791 and 1798, Macomb, a wealthy fur trader and an associate of John Jacob Astor, purchased from the state almost 4 million acres (for a price so low that some considered it a "gift"), making him the largest landowner in northern New York. Except for a tantalizing ten-mile square tract of land known as Penet's Square (to which we will return), he owned virtually all of what would become Jefferson County and more.[24] William Cooper, no small potato himself among owners of vast lands, "could not conceal his envy." "McComb and R. Morris has Skipped over Us all," Cooper wrote wistfully to Henry Drinker, "and in fact Done too much for any one American family. . . . This is Doing Buisiness at such [a] Monstrous rate that the Very thoughts of it flashes Over the mind Like Extravigant ideas." Some large landowners would reside splendidly on their Jefferson County holdings, symbols of gentility in the northern wilderness. Macomb planned to watch the value of his property rise from a distance and sell to small farmers at a great profit. But Macomb proved less able to "stand the shock" than other wealthy men. Bankrupt, he "lost his property, and was lodged in jail, and his name does not subsequently appear in the transfers of land" except to designate its location on deeds of sale.[25]

One contentious bit of real estate remained elusive even to Macomb, its ownership ambiguous for years after some of it was being farmed by Vincents, Osborns, and Ormsbys. The intriguing story of Penet's Square shows the complicated process of establishing both economic claims and political stability on the land. In a 1788 treaty, in which the Oneida Indians did "cede and grant, all their lands to the people of the State of New York, forever," they reserved a ten-mile square for their friend Pierre

Penet, a French gunrunner, treaty negotiator, and aide to George Washington. Penet chose his acres well, for they included the mouth of French
Creek, part of the Chaumont River, and fine access to the St. Lawrence
River from Lake Ontario. The state of New York, unable to gain title to
the land, agreed to recognize Penet's claim only after he had received U.S.
citizenship, for noncitizens were not then permitted to own property in
the state.[26] Penet applied for naturalization and left for the Caribbean; he
evidently died soon after. His 100 square miles of choice land, predictably,
became entangled in legal disputes that were convoluted even for New
York and that delayed its formal settlement and sale for decades. As Solon
Massey recalled, it was a "tract long owned by nobody but claimed by
everybody" and largely considered "as 'free booty,' where every man 'cut
and carved' for himself."[27] Indeed, no records tell how Eleanor O'Connor,
Abraham Vincent, the Ormsbys, the Osborns, and the Williamses first
came to live on this land.

An odd assortment of speculators and dreamers, many of whom were
French, bought the bankrupt Macomb's land, and their settlements soon
surrounded Penet's Square. Unswayed by the economic ramifications of
the embargo against Britain and comfortable in the pro-French climate,
the most influential of them, James Le Ray de Chaumont, moved there
with his wife and three children in 1808 and undertook to establish a
French aristocratic culture in the northern woods.[28] Le Ray "opened a
land office and proceeded to sell land to actual settlers," oversaw the
building of sawmills and roads, urged new agricultural industries, and
raised merino sheep and elaborate orchards.[29] He also owned three slaves,
which made him one of the largest slaveholders in the area.[30] His center
hall mansion was the headquarters for both wild visions and actual settlement of French refugees (including, notably, Napoleon's brother, Joseph
Bonaparte) in Jefferson County; his family names still dot the land.

But it was a "Frenchman of an entirely different type" who finally
sorted through the jumble of claims to Penet's Square. John La Farge,
Penet's "former fellow gun-runner," had heard Penet talk about this fine
and abundant land and began an arduous legal process in 1817 to stake a
claim to the square. By 1825 he owned large chunks of it. Yet as La Farge
discovered to his dismay, "a rough lot" of "Catfish people" or "Penayers"
already squatted on the land, cutting timber and living apart from the
formal restraints of the state, the surveys, and the landowners. Local lore
but very little written evidence surrounds these squatters, some of whom
were present as early as 1816; there were many more by 1820. A nearby

camp in Ellisburgh was first named No God, and slurs persisted in the area about "Catfish girls"; some early settlers apparently believed that a "free love" colony had been established in Depauville.[31] In any case, "the belief became general, that there was no legal owner of the tract, which . . . led great numbers . . . to come and select land and make locations." "Clearings began to crop out here and there," reports one local chronicler, and "dry land, hay-stacks and corn-cribs appeared; and log cabins took on a more homelike look. . . . Justice was administered and disputes settled mostly by what was called 'the Catfish Code.' "[32] Deeds to this land, as in so many areas newly claimed by the United States, would reflect its complicated past, recording both the surveyors' system of links and chains and the settlers' practice of marking a farm's borders with a neighbor's initials.[33]

Not surprisingly, one's opinion of the squatters closely paralleled one's interest in the land's legal title. For decades land speculators and their agents complained that squatters proved as prickly as the legal disputes themselves. Some, wrote Nathan Ford self-righteously, were wantonly cutting down trees; they "pretended to settle; their motive was only stealing off the timber." The ownership of lumber was in the eye of the beholder, of course, and opinions differed. The Catholic bishop of Ogdensburg, for instance, would later insist that these lumbermen were not "thieves" but "forerunners of colonization," which may amount to the same thing. But to Ford the issue was clear enough: "If something is not done about this business, great destruction will arise. An example ought to be made, and this can not be done without sending an officer from Fort Stanwix. They have got the timber so boldly that they say there is no law that can be executed upon them here."[34]

Yet there was not total chaos. To some, squatters were merely those, "chiefly of the poorer classes," who took advantage of ambiguous titles. Although many squatters made potash or farmed "in the most slovenly and careless manner," some observers admitted that the "squatters had adopted a kind of regulation among themselves, in relation to lands." Indeed, prior to the appearance of any legal authority, squatters commonly measured and bounded their land, often by "step[ping] out 250 double paces, or 440 yards, toward the sun at noon, stick[ing] in a marker, then march[ing] 250 double paces toward the point where the sun set . . . and put[ting] in another marker. That was it: 440 yards by 440 yards made a 40-acre lot." Although the situation invited "crowds of adventurers from various quarters, . . . rough, hardy, and enterprising, with

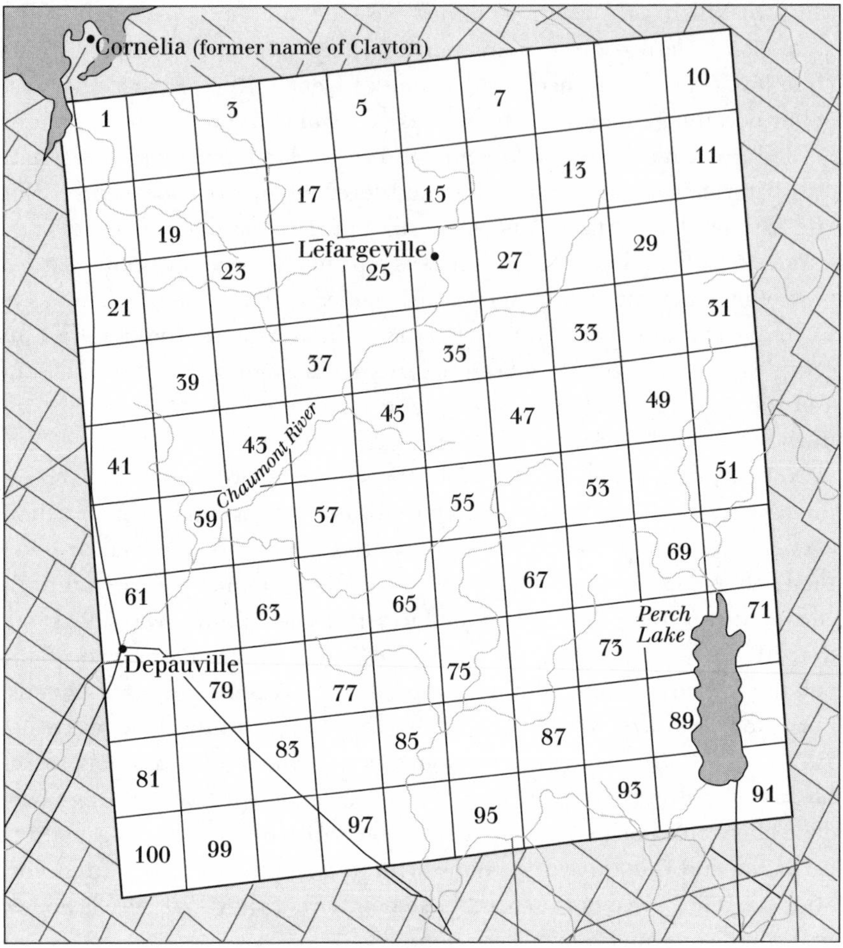

MAP 3. *Penet's Square (based on David H. Burr,*
An Atlas of the State of New York *[1829])*

nothing to lose and every thing to gain," they were "just the class to subdue a wilderness."[35]

Deeds reflected the legacy of shady land deals and greedy speculators that had literally shaped the landscape. Even for northern New York, few places experienced more speculation, squatting, and squabbling than the acres the newly arrived Depauville farmers chose as their own. Their very deeds identified parcels known decades later as "Lot 4 of Macomb's Purchase" or "Penet's Square" and recalled mysterious claims to the land. Only after these families had occupied their tracts for several years would deeds refer to "A. Vincent's farm" or to land "bordering Phineas Osborn."[36] The land they claimed was what a local historian calls "one of the few 'parcels of land' in Uncle Sams' [sic] domains which was never acquired by force or fraud from its aboriginal owners," and that in itself is a fascinating tale of political intrigue and negotiation, of Frenchmen and Indians, of lawyers and speculators, and of boom and bankruptcy.[37]

The connection between asserting one's ownership of land and developing a strong sense of place was probably inescapable in this setting. Whether the Ormsbys, Osborns, Vincents, and their friends thought of themselves as "squatters" or "settlers" or were an especially "rough lot" is impossible to know, but evidently they were among the several hundred families who had established homes and farms on Penet's Square by the time La Farge and the legal system he represented showed up. They can hardly have missed or been unaffected by the dissatisfaction with large landowners that grew after 1818 and may well have contributed to the discord rumbling through the neighborhood. Perhaps the men were among the Penet's Square settlers who petitioned the state in 1821 asking that the land they farmed be granted to them outright; surely they knew of it. As Solon Massey recalled, "Peneters had a nice sense of honor among themselves, but woe to . . . any man or set of men, claiming to hold a better title than a *peaceful squatter*."[38] John La Farge's appearance to stake his claim can only have heightened tension and deepened the sense of community identity and interest among the settlers. People "turned out in a body" to defend their hold on their land, and it took some years and much writing of contracts to pay all the taxes and stabilize the land claims.[39] A leading citizen of Watertown, William Smith, charged by the court of chancery to mediate a dispute concerning this land, understandably recalled this duty "as among the most onerous and delicate of his active and eventful life."[40] All these negotiations help explain why it was not until 1834 that the county clerk recorded the sale by John La Farge of 52.65 acres on Penet's Square to Abraham Vincent. But long before Abraham Vincent returned home from Watertown with this deed in hand, a "lime stone" marked the boundary between his and Phineas A. Osborn's farm with the initials "A.V.P.A.O." Thus, while it may well be true that by 1820 "the frontier stage in New York history had passed, for all of the territory in New York had come into the private or public possession of the white man," for the Vincents and Ormsbys and their friends, gaining firm title to the land was a matter of some struggle, and its accomplishment no doubt a great relief.[41]

What did the settlers expect when they headed north? If the state road made the North Country a place folks could reach, somehow the Herkimer County families must have gotten the impression that they would be able to purchase their new farms. The Vincents, O'Connors, and Ormsbys and their neighbors the Corbins and Frames probably heard about the North Country from Nathaniel Norton Jr., a former merchant from the town of Russia, who built a log house on land owned by Francis Depau and looked to sell the rest. Land agents were northern New York's earliest settlers and its most enthusiastic boosters; some, such as William Cooper of Cooperstown, had already become wealthy members of upstate New York gentry. Advertisements for "New-York Canal Lands on Sale" sought to balance the land's wild qualities with its access to the amenities of settled life. Thus Hezekiah B. Pierrepont described in glowing detail the "unsold part of that extensive tract bounded on the *East end of Lake Ontario*, . . . every part of the tract being within one day's easy drive of the *Erie Canal*" in 1823. Pierrepont bragged that this partially cleared land, "having been from 10 to 15 years regularly advancing in settlement, has a numerous population, and possesses most of the advantages of old countries, as to schools, public worship, mills, distilleries, mechanics, manufactories, &c." Priced between $2.50 and $5.00 per acre, plots could be selected by settlers "on arrival" with the assistance of "local agents and others." Perhaps Norton sent broadsides to Herkimer County boasting that "no country can possess a more *healthy climate*, or a greater abundance of living springs, and streams of *the purest water*," but word of mouth likely worked as well.[42]

The amenities associated with well-settled communities were scarce. The village of Brownville boasted a cotton and wool factory, but Clayton was barely established (and still unnamed) when the Depauville families settled on farms several miles away. William Angel opened the first store there in 1819 or 1820 and several others followed; the first store in the village of Depauville itself was not opened until several years later.[43] Soon Clayton had a tavern and, by 1825, a stone school building; after 1821, mail could be received and sent. By 1835 the town boasted some half-dozen stores and three taverns, a shipbuilding business, several machine, blacksmith, shoe, and tailor shops, and a plan to build a church. Only then did it give "the appearance of a thriving and business [sic] little village" with more than ninety buildings and a population of 426 people.[44]

The scarcity of retail trade would not have presented much of a hardship, since early settlers brought to Jefferson County what they would need to start their farms. "An inventory of the entire effects of each settler . . . would have been a short and easy matter," for several hundred dollars could equip a farm; $70 bought a yoke of oxen; $15, a cow; and $20, a man's farming tools.[45] Land itself was fairly cheap, but contrary to expectations, its value did not rise much. True, the price of property worth only a few cents per acre after the Revolution had risen to $2.50 in Henderson by 1805 and as much as $10 in Champion, but Abraham Vincent paid John La Farge only about $4 per acre for his farm in 1834.[46] Although prices fluctuated, these men were farmers, not realtors, and they would not become rich buying and selling Jefferson County land. James Le Ray de Chaumont sold land to such farmers starting at $3 per acre under contracts that would be paid off in seven years. As William Cooper had done decades earlier, he also widened roads, established taverns, donated lands for public streets, and built gristmills and sawmills in strategic locations. Other landowners and agents did the same.[47]

The Herkimer families' first view of Jefferson County probably met their expectations of abundance and of hard work. As promised, water power was plentiful, access to Canadian markets was excellent, and the land's first crop was abundant, even lush. Trees were everywhere, and timber was an essential component of commerce as well as a source of building material and cash. Plank roads, for instance, made from boards sawed at the side of the road and held in place by the wagons that trod on them, reflected the seemingly endless supply of wood and settlers' apparent unconcern that the roads would rot. Ash from fallen trees, boiled and sold as potash, provided settlers with their first commodity. Potash was an element in every transaction—in the complex relations over renting and buying land, in the politics of national embargoes, and in women's production of soap long after many other household products were being purchased. Sawmills emerged along the rivers before towns, and the sound of buzzing broke the silence regularly.[48]

An 1882 memoir described such settlers' first windowless, one-room cabins, built from twenty-four-foot logs and without a hearth or oven or cistern. But these conditions lasted only briefly. An oven "was built the second year out-of-doors," and almost immediately "three window sash [*sic*] were brought and glass was set"; "a fire-place was built . . . and on this a chimney was constructed," and "a floor was laid of white ash planks." By the second winter in Jefferson County both work and leisure time could be well spent around a "blazing fire": "Reading, sewing, spinning, knitting, or conversation could all go on around such a blaze, and the occupants of the cabin cared not whether or not it was cold outside." Not everyone, of course, was so fortunate. For families whose fathers were afflicted with wanderlust or who were unable to make their farms pay or who never did manage to own their land, mobility could be a severe trial. Their children, one settler recalled, were "half naked and sometimes hungry and cold and [we had] no place to lay our heads that we could call our own, free from all encumbrances."[49] But over time, each of the Depauville petitioners' families would build a frame house, yet another sign of increasing prosperity and comfort. What evidence there is suggests strongly that Eleanor and Abraham Vincent and their friends intended to remain on this land they and their parents worked so hard to call their own.

The Vincents, Ormsbys, Osborns, O'Connors, and Williamses did achieve a measure of "free[dom] from all encumbrances," but not without a struggle that tells its own story about property, place, and political identity. The ownership of land, described so often by political theorists as representing one's stake in society, was to them more than a metaphor, for they had participated collectively in building farms, families, and new communities all at once. Their story is not so much about class conflict, but it is no less about class. It points to the sense of entitlement, of standing, and of belonging that can emerge from people's material interest in the place and political community they call their own. Buying, selling, and farming the land—indeed, achieving membership in a class of property owners—were central to these women's and men's relationships not only to their work but to their communities, the state, and one another. Deeds and wills, the paperwork that formalized their transactions, tell a story of settlement and stability but also of contentiousness and greed. Few of these stories are straightforward, and many are impossibly convoluted.

Physical proximity of individuals to one another defined their migration and daily lives. Eleanor Vincent was only about seventeen years old in 1823 when she and Abraham moved to their own farm and had their first child, Leonard. During sixty years of marriage they would add nine or ten children to Jefferson County, far more than any of the other petitioning women. But even in the early years, when the work was hard and the children were small, Eleanor and Abraham Vincent would not have been isolated from adults and kin. Neighbors were family members, as the children of early settlers married one another and established adjoining farms of more or less comparable size. In 1825 Eleanor's father, Timothy O'Connor, farmed forty-five improved acres; Benjamin and Polly Vincent's farm next door was about the same size and wealth. Next to Abraham and Eleanor Vincent lived Phineas A. Osborn, with thirty improved acres. One of his brothers, Joseph Osborn, not yet twenty-one, likely still lived with his parents, but two other brothers, Schuyler and Thomas, lived on neighboring farms, on sixty and fifteen improved acres, respectively. Elias and Jane Ormsby and their children, including Hiram, Bailey, Susan, and Lydia, lived three addresses down from the Vincents on forty acres. Although Jefferson County land was cheap and plentiful, these farmers began small and never purchased more than they could farm or graze.[50] Still, by 1835, Hiram Ormsby, Joseph Osborn, and Abraham Vincent had cleared a lot more land, and no doubt they shared much of the labor. But their responsibilities toward one another and the property that reinforced those ties went deeper. Elias Ormsby died in 1828 when his youngest son, Bailey, was just fifteen years old. Surely Hiram and his brother-in-law Joseph Osborn helped keep the farm functioning over the next several years. When the state census taker came around in 1835, he recorded that twenty-two-year-old Bailey Ormsby headed a household that farmed and produced domestic goods on fifteen acres; most likely the two females living and working with him were his mother, Jane, and his sister Susan, then twenty.[51]

The men bought and sold land frequently. Their wives and sisters would do so when the law allowed, that is, when they were single, widowed, or after the passage of New York's Married Women's Property Act in 1848. But far from indicating movement and upheaval or, certainly, independence from familiar ties, these transactions bound them even more tightly to one another and to other neighbors and friends. In the absence of vital records, the deeds and tax assessments that record all this buying and selling of land provide much of the data about its inhabitants' lives. The documents suggest, for instance, that Abraham and Eleanor Vincent went through a complicated process before they owned outright the forty acres of land, fifteen of which were cultivated, on which they paid taxes in 1824. Not until a full decade later does a deed record the sale of those acres to Abraham Vincent, and it referred, in turn, to an 1830 contract between Vincent and John La Farge.[52] Information of a more intimate nature emerges from deeds as well, such as the fact that Lydia Williams was not Nahum's first wife or the mother of all of their children.[53] Similarly, in 1851 Abraham and Eleanor Vincent sold some land to their oldest son, Leonard; only because he resold that land one month later (a process that required a wife's formal consent) do I know that he had by then married Mary Johnson, a woman four years his junior.[54]

Deeds also suggest that if land and labor were at the center of these relationships, they were reinforced by friendship and trust. In 1838 twenty-five-year-old Bailey Ormsby bought an additional 22 acres of land for $220 from longtime neighbors Elkanah and Lucy Corbin and Ira H. and Elvira Corbin on lot 60 of Penet's Square.[55] Hiram Ormsby purchased 30 acres for $123 from Emer Woodin in 1832; his brother-in-law Joseph Osborn witnessed the sale.[56] Much swapping took place: Hiram Ormsby added to his holdings with numerous purchases, sold another 18 acres to Nahum Williams in 1838, and sold 50 acres back to Emer Woodin in 1835 (again with Joseph Osborn as witness). Joseph Osborn himself paid John La Farge $126.67 in 1833 for 52.78 acres adjacent to Abraham Vincent, part of lot 41 of Penet's Square; Abraham Vincent and Nahum Williams soon followed suit.[57] All these families added to their holdings during the first decades of settlement, showing every intention of remaining in what the deeds referred to hopefully as "quiet and peacable possession" of their land.[58]

But such peacefulness and stability took some time to achieve, for Penet's Square remained a somewhat raucous place. Town meetings could be heated affairs. Surely some of the recently arrived settlers from Herkimer County attended Brownville's 1820 meeting, held at Perch River, and so were party to the split between residents of different sections of the town. Whatever the cause of the dissension, some settlers in Penet's Square objected to "being thus robbed of their town meeting" and petitioned the legislature for one of their own. An early round of the dividing of towns soon followed. In Hough's sardonic account, this was called " 'stealing a town meeting,' which gave rise to much talk at the time, and about which many fabulous stories have been related. It is said that this heinous crime of robbery was made the subject of a painting, that formed a part of a traveling exhibition."[59]

As landlords went, La Farge was difficult, and Eleanor and Abraham Vincent and the various Ormsbys and Osborns were no doubt relieved when they finalized the purchase of their farms. According to some, the problem was the squatters: "Though apparently perfectly just in all his demands, La Farge was thoroughly hated by most of his squatter neighbors. His property was mutilated, and he himself was fired upon by the enraged people who wished to live on his land but were unwilling to be his tenants." But many thought the problem was La Farge himself: "He dispossessed squatters, insisted upon rigid adherence to terms of mortgages and leases and made himself as cordially hated as any man in all Northern New York." Still others reported that although he "was at first considered a hard and exacting landlord, [he] was afterwards acknowledged to have been just to individuals and liberal to the town."[60] Surely the Depauville folks might have resented a man who persisted in buying land even as "enraged tenants were continually shooting out the windows of [his] Perch Lake house." And then there was the time that La Farge and a lumberman became embroiled in a dispute over the profits of a sawmill on La Farge's land. Local sympathies went against La Farge, and people blamed "spiritual manifestations" when the boards of the sawmill were found floating in the bay.[61] Finally, in 1837, La Farge's young wife, Louisa, herself a member of the Binsse family of refugees from France, convinced him to sell their property in northern New York. An advertisement for its sale gives some idea of what he had, and what he lost, in the process: a 460-acre holding, 250 acres of which were improved land, a 4-acre vegetable garden, a mansion, many personal goods, and, poignantly, some 4,000 books.[62] Eleanor and Abraham Vincent, Hiram and Amy Ormsby, Nahum Williams, and the several Osborn brothers, deeds firmly in hand, remained.

A legal deed thus held far more meaning than simply outlining the boundaries of a farm or even declaring its owner's unassailable and individual title to it. For both women and men in rural communities, buying and selling land constituted their major contact with the legal authorities and their clerks. Trips to the clerk's office in Watertown to formalize landholdings were, at least during times of peace, the settlers' most immediate connection to the workings of the larger political community. The assumption that property ownership and collective rootedness were a basis for political identification was no abstraction but reflected the place of both women and men on their farms as well as in their towns, their county, and their state.

Owning and working the land represented a particular relationship to

[65]

the larger community, one that encompassed—and made tangible—identities of both gender and class. For men it meant earning an income, paying taxes, contributing to the public roads, and, as long as voting in New York was still tied to property, political rights. As historians have noted, the association between property and the right to vote was broken only erratically and incompletely. That it *was* unraveling, and that the very notion of a stake in society was undergoing dramatic change, cast the citizenship of women, of African American men, of tenant farmers, and of city dwellers in an increasingly bright light.[63] Just as owning land was a particular mark of manhood in the antebellum rural North, so married women's lack of access to property emerged early on as a sign of all women's exclusion from full membership in the rural community.

The relationship between property and full membership in the community was not a mere abstraction to these women. Every sale of land reminded the wives among them of their ambiguous status. Under the laws of the state of New York, a married woman could not own, buy, or sell property. She was, however, entitled to her dower right, or widow's third, and so had to agree to the sale of any property she stood to inherit upon the death of her husband. Every Jefferson County deed of sale by a married man named his wife and noted formulaically that she was "examined privately" to ensure that she "had executed the same freely and without any fears of or compulsion by her said husband." While intended to protect the wife's dower right, this ritual also reminded women (in Elisha Hurlbut's cutting phrase) that the husband had a "legal right to inspire fear in the wife."[64]

Eleanor Vincent, Amy Ormsby, Lydia Osborn, Anna Bishop, and Lydia Williams, as well as most of their mothers, participated in this legal ceremony, no doubt with varying degrees of acquiescence, irritation, or contempt. Whether they discussed the contracts with their husbands, or even read them; whether they merely signed over their claims; or whether they actually opposed some sales, we will never know. It is tempting, however, to imagine these particular women at a ritual that Hurlbut describes so vividly: Deed in hand, a "little officer," "the only legal remnant of the days of chivalry," "sendeth the husband sneakingly out of the room—he goeth up to the wife—he looketh in any direction but that of her face—he seemeth ashamed of his errand—he muttereth something about 'fear and compulsion of her husband'—attempts to laugh at the idea of *her* fearing her husband, but saith something about the law's requiring him to certify as to her bravery—he getteth out of the house as quick as possible, and feels that he hath done a foolish thing."[65] To Hurlbut this was more than foolish; it was humiliating and wrong. It might have seemed so as well to women who would later declare woman's rights too obvious to require debate.

Always present in the relationship of married women to the land were two facets that helped shape their daily lives and adult identities: their legal dependence and their labor. Although much of New York's vast land was, for some, a commodity and an object of speculation, for the families that populate this story it was the products of their labor on the land that signaled prosperity or failure. If the legal and political dependence of married women remained largely intact in the early antebellum years, their relationship to the farms they helped build and the products they manufactured was more complex, for in a rapidly expanding economy, that work, too, was undergoing dramatic change. Eventually those changes would force legislators, in New York as elsewhere, to adapt the legal rules of marriage to the realities of a commercial society in which wives' work took place. Historians have long argued that in these contradictions lay the roots of the ideology of woman's sphere, a framework that obscured the economic nature of women's work even as it reified the moral and spiritual value of the middle-class home.[66]

The notion of women's separate sphere was central to the ideological reworkings of the relationship between the middle-class household and the market. This notion, in turn, was crucial to the emergence of the northern middle class, which identified with the "moral" qualities of gender, religion, and individual character rather than the harsh material standards of industrial capitalism and market domination. This "renegotiation of gender systems," historians have noted, took place in the context of changes in rural capitalism that were closely tied to changes in women's labor. By the 1840s, Catherine Kelly has argued, provincial women who were becoming ever more distant from traditional household economies reframed the differences between household and market, and between women and men, as distinctions between town and country. The contradictions thus raised aided in the creation of a middle-class culture that was deeply tied to the market values rural women deplored.[67] Describing married women's standing in domestic and moral terms also helped shape women's political understanding of their place in the larger communities in particular ways.

The Depauville women came late to this process, however, and may have initially escaped the ideological implications of these changes. Still busy settling farms and communities through the 1830s, they may not have experienced the reworkings of gender, household, and market that were so important to the identities of many middle-class women.[68] Situated on their nation's border, they could not have imagined themselves "exempt from the influence of the growing world market," nor were they unaware of the relationship between their own work and the rumblings of change outside their community.[69] Nothing in the evidence suggests that they embraced an ideology of woman's sphere that would remove them, even in theory, from the economic and political labors of building new homes and communities, a project that was itself inseparable from their particular time and place. Even if these women had aspired to rural or domestic isolation, the economic depression of 1837, which so quickly followed their becoming well and truly settled on their land, would have cured them of that. Unlike women in longer-settled regions, they would not have felt by the 1840s that the notion of "women as producers and associates in the farm enterprise" was irrelevant to their own experience.[70] Instead, as they worked alongside men and one another in founding a new community, participating, it may have seemed, in establishing a new social contract, the very salience of ideas about gender in more settled areas may have made them feel as marginalized intellectually as they were geographically.

Amy Ormsby, Lydia Osborn, and Eleanor Vincent, married women whose husbands owned their land, lived alongside one another by the 1830s, and no doubt they labored together as well. Perhaps their awareness of their legal dependence was muted by an atmosphere of shared purpose and hard work, of membership in a larger social and economic community. But on the most personal level, these women would have known that women's citizenship was complex. Their small community and, by 1850, the Osborn household included Lydia's younger sister, Susan Ormsby, as well as their widowed mother, Jane, and their presence underscored the asymmetry of the relationship between women, the land, and the products of their labor. As an unmarried woman, Susan was legally independent, and her property and her earnings were her own. Indeed if, as I assume, she came to live with Lydia and Joseph Osborn after her brother Bailey died, she did so as the owner of a significant amount of land. Still, on a practical level her labor contributed to the Osborn household's property, on which every piece of cloth and each farm animal was the legal possession of her brother-in-law Joseph. Certainly the fifty-acre farm she inherited in 1848 was her separate property, as was its produce, but if the families farmed that land collectively, the crops and cash it produced could have blended imperceptibly into their overall earnings.

Yet however much the labors of Joseph Osborn's wife and sister-in-law added to his overall wealth, Susan Ormsby maintained the legal integrity of her property without, so far as I know, disrupting the harmonious functioning of the household. Susan's daily work—her care of chickens or making of butter and soap or cooking, cleaning, and weaving—probably became swallowed up in supporting the Osborn household, but the evidence suggests that she kept an eye on her own account. Whether through the receipt of rent on her farm or because she worked as a tailoress for cash (an occupation she reported to the census taker in 1860), Susan accumulated property. By 1870, still living with her widowed sister Lydia, she was the wealthiest of the petitioners.

As these women worked alongside each other in kitchen, yard, and barn, their tasks resembled those of countless other rural women. But the Jefferson County women were producing cloth, butter, soap, and perhaps cheese after dramatic changes in technology and the organization of work—not to mention ideological constructions of women's labor—had already begun elsewhere. By the 1820s, rural women on longer-settled farms, such as those in the Brandywine Valley of Pennsylvania, were already turning from the home production of cloth to the production and sale of massive quantities of butter.[71] In Depauville this was the decade of the hardest labor, as the families cleared land, made and sold potash, built houses and barns, and produced goods for their own use. Neither account books nor physical structures remain to offer evidence of their particular talents in making wool or butter. We can glimpse their specific labors only by observing that as early as 1825, with eight cattle, ten sheep, and five hogs, Eleanor Vincent probably made butter and sheared and prepared wool, and that she and Abraham were far from wealthy but also quite far from poor.[72]

Work and weather likely dominated the daily conversations of women and men in the North Country, as did their forays into new crops and manufactures. New York's farmers raised a wide variety of crops, and experiments were made, abandoned, or incorporated into both women's and men's work. The decline in their region's prospects reflected the ordinary farm family's despair. From 1843 until 1845, rot and pestilence effected "the partial or complete failure of the potato crop." The climate, observers claimed, was notable only for getting worse. On January 28, 1844, Saratoga experienced temperatures of thirty-four degrees below zero. But even under less extreme conditions, living in the far North was bracing. "Spring," one traveler reported, ". . . does not exist here." Occasionally a farmer advertised the sale of his profitable and well-managed farm *"cheap,"* "a milder climate being desirable."[73] For the hardy, winter had its advantages, since it was "the season allotted by the agriculturalist, for business and pleasure." Visiting friends and neighbors was simpler then, when "the highways have an even and firm bed, and the streams and lakes are bridged with ice" and "a sleigh could make twice the distance over snow that a wagon could on earth roads."[74]

Surely some writers have romanticized this period of rural life.[75] Fortunately, those few farmers who did well enough to brag about it offer a rare glimpse into the difficulties of farm labor. Asa Carter, the owner of a 150-acre Jefferson County farm, hoped to set an example for farmers who "occupy land and farm by guess." He noted proudly that he had earned $1,639.09, not including what his own family consumed.[76] Carter was also among those upstate New Yorkers who shared in the silkworm craze of the 1830s, a project that, agricultural journals maintained, would allow women and children to produce a cash crop in their "spare time." Writing to the *Cultivator*, Asa Carter "enclosed us a specimen of silk manufactured by his daughter, who never saw a silk worm nor a silk reel, till last summer." According to the journal, "This is a pretty good evidence that there is no great art or mystery in managing silk worms." Actually it was evidence of no such thing, for Carter's enthusiasm for silkworms soon ended.[77] Whether or not the families of the Jefferson County petitioners invested in the project (something the state census fails to record), the women must have known farm wives and children who plucked countless mulberry leaves to feed the squirmy little crunchers. Some had risked and lost a great deal after speculating wildly in mulberry trees, the price of which crashed in 1839.[78] By the mid-1840s the silkworm craze had died down, defeated by the northern climate, both meteorological and financial.

Every experiment in farm production and every change in taste held implications for farm women's labors. Probably only as adults, for example, did Anna Bishop or Eleanor Vincent taste tomatoes, which even the *Cultivator*, usually so amenable to agricultural experiment, thought merely evidence of "the mandates of imperious fashion." "Few like the tomato at first," the writer conceded, "but the taste soon becomes not only reconciled to it, but is much pleased with it." Ebenezer Emmons considered the tomato sufficiently novel in 1849 to mention its many uses in his official history of New York State agriculture, certainly no recipe book. By 1850 the *Working Farmer* could report that "this vegetable has, in a few years, not only got into general use, but to be one of the delicacies of the vegetable kingdom."[79]

Orchards, too, shaped women's work. Encouraged by the agricultural press, planting fruit trees signaled both people's intention to invest many years in the land and new chores for women in picking, preparing, and preserving fruit. Only in 1851 did one agriculturalist feel confident that "it is now well established that money can be made in raising good apples and pears; and there is probably no readier way by which a farmer can raise one hundred dollars, than by resorting to the avails of his orchard." Evidently this writer had to combat prejudices against peaches and other fruit. "The idea that effeminacy is somehow or other connected with such luxuries should not be entertained," he insisted. "The cultivation of these fruits belongs to a species of refined civilization. . . . The savage may plant his corn and dry his roots, but it only consists in acts but little higher than those performed by the rodents of the forest." Whatever the significance of fruit trees to masculinity or higher civilization, by 1860 Jefferson County's households were producing 215,431 bushels of apples, nearly 3,500 barrels of cider, and smaller quantities of plums. Viewing this output not as aggregate numbers but as the products of labor reminds us that it was women who added the work of canning, pickling, and drying tomatoes and other fruit to their usual chores.[80]

Although fungus, weather, and new crops could raise or dash farmers' hopes, dairy products were women's particular burden. When they sold butter and cheese, women in northern New York interacted most directly with distant markets and so experienced personally the changes under way in the commercial economy. Although the New York State censuses do not list dairy cattle or their products, surely Lydia Osborn and Eleanor Vincent churned, molded, and possibly sold butter and, somewhat less likely, cheese. In 1835 Abraham Vincent reported to the census taker that he had eight cattle. Joseph Osborn had nine, Hiram Ormsby had four, Bailey Ormsby owned seven, and Nahum Williams, wealthier than the others, had twenty.[81] The women in each of these households milked cows and produced enough butter for their families and, in some cases, for sale. It is difficult to know how to compare their productivity to that of farm women in Nanticoke Valley, New York, who churned more than 430,000 pounds of butter in 1879, only a small fraction of which could be consumed by their families. There, with an average of eight cows per household, "two-thirds of all farm families made enough butter to sell, and one-third made at least a thousand pounds a year." Butter could play an enormous role in a family's access to cash. "A family that milked seven cows," Nancy Osterud writes, "might receive $250 from the sale of butter in a year; this amounted to . . . as much as 70 percent of their annual cash income."[82] I have no idea if the Jefferson County families, who were acutely aware of their growing isolation from distant markets, could earn this much, but butter making was surely a significant part of the labor of these women. At the time of her death in 1875, Lydia Osborn, widowed for seven years, still owned some ten cows, each individually described by color, age, or breed in the inventory of her estate.[83]

The "dreaded churning day" was some women's undoing. "Mary," who enjoyed the "various pursuits and engagements connected with a small farm" on Long Island, begged the *Cultivator* to help with the "one employment that has of late given me 'a world of trouble,'—that of churning. . . . I have availed myself of the experience of my neighbors, but all to no purpose." In 1838 the *Cultivator* published a letter addressed to women by "the undersigned, dealers in butter and cheese," who "would call the attention of the manufacturers of these articles in the middle and western part of this state, to the existence of general and just complaints in regard to the quality and condition of both butter and cheese made in such section, together with the packages."[84] Indeed, the quality of dairy products varied widely, with Herkimer County gaining a particular reputation for the sweetest butter.[85] The connections between dairying and cash were not hard to find. "A thermometer . . . costs but one dollar," wrote the *Working Farmer* in 1850, "and such an investment every farmer ought to make, who has churning to do, and thus save labor and time, which is money—and make this much dreaded part of the duties of farmers' wives and daughters much pleasanter and easier."[86]

Whatever the Jefferson County women earned by selling butter, families in rural communities like theirs displayed a growing need for cash, a trend that reflected both individual decisions to purchase goods and the greater variety of items that came from distant markets. Writing in 1850, Solon Massey was amused by a Jefferson County merchant's account book for 1805–6. Purchases of rum figured high, with some $8.50 spent over a three-month period, though Massey, reflecting his own era's aversion to alcohol, assured his readers that "the family were well and favorably known, as an orderly, industrious, pious, and sober family." Molasses cost $1.00 per gallon; pepper and spice, 50 cents per pound. This early settler family spent only $68.91 over the course of the year at the local store.[87] But as we in our own time know well, the availability of new goods encourages new consumer needs, with the attendant mix of pleasure and dismay. In 1840 Henry Conklin's father purchased "a barrel of wheat flour raised out west somewhere and ground in the new style." "How they did talk about that barrel of flour that night," recalled Conklin, "and they decided to go over early in the morning and carry it home across lots so some of it could be baked for breakfast. . . . All of us children that could walk had to go along to see the curiosity." Soon, "we had some splendid white biscuit almost as white as snow. How we did live then and how the neighbors came to visit and have a taste."[88] A child's fascination reflected larger changes in the household economy, vividly illustrating how even the most rural households faced a growing demand for cash with which to purchase such exotic goods. Jefferson County's farmers, whether resigned to their region's failure to achieve great prosperity or distressed by it, often found that income in the dairying labor of their wives, sisters, and daughters.

Of the nearly seventy dollars spent by the family in Solon Massey's account, almost none went toward clothing or other necessities. Two decades later, like northern rural women elsewhere, Eleanor Vincent, Lydia Osborn, and their friends still produced a huge array and quantity of household goods. Timothy O'Connor's household, with five females at home in 1825, produced some 140 yards of linen and cotton cloth. Ten years later, Nahum Williams owned ten sheep, and his household (presumably with his first wife, Zerviah) produced 23 yards of woolen cloth "manufactured in the domestic way" as well as nearly 30 yards of other kinds of cloth. Eleanor Vincent, with twelve sheep, produced 16 yards of woolen cloth, as did Lydia Osborn, though she and Joseph owned twenty-five sheep. Both wives and daughters made much of the household's thread, cloth, wool, and clothing, but Eleanor's eldest daughter Cordelia, then only five, was too young to have contributed her own labor.[89]

Jefferson County women continued to produce considerable cloth even as domestic production began its decline. In 1810, when the county itself was five years old and the inland settlements barely begun, a population of 15,140 produced a total of 160,877 yards of cloth. Ten years later the census showed that Jefferson County had produced a total yardage of 276,310.[90] Some steps in the manufacturing of woolen cloth, such as fulling, were centralized early even in small towns. But to a large extent, the women who helped settle northern New York continued to make cloth for household use for some years.[91]

The more rural and inaccessible a particular farming community was, the slower and later its residents were to turn away from home production of essential items. But aggregate numbers about domestically produced cloth describe only part of a process that, in real life, was erratic and inconsistent and evoked ambivalent feelings. Mary Conklin "never did much weaving after [her last baby] was born" and may have welcomed the change, but her son evoked each piece of the machinery lovingly in its decline. "The old loom and its kindred parts were disposed of," he recalled. "Some of the reeds, shuttles, warping bars and little wheels were sold or traded or given away to others . . . , but the old loom was finally stowed away in the hog pen chamber and years after was used up piece by piece for kindling wood."[92] Women may have felt less sentimental about the tools of their labor. Many farm women, for instance, embraced the mechanization of cheese making as a worthwhile trade-off and felt that "life was wonderfully improved." The process of turning cream into butter and cheese, wool and flax into cloth, and cloth into clothing, blankets, linens, and carpets was arduous and neverending.[93] Whether middling farm women such as Eleanor Vincent, Lydia Osborn, and Lydia Williams still produced cloth in the mid-1840s or whether they turned, reluctantly or enthusiastically, to store-bought fabric is impossible to know. In any case, they were not sentimental enough to keep the tools of those labors, for none of their estates (we have inventories for Nahum D. Williams [1863], Lydia Osborn [1875], and Susan Ormsby [1895]) included looms or unfinished cloth.

What numbers do show is that with the rise of factory textile production throughout the North, home manufacture of cloth declined sharply after the mid-1840s. From a high of 307,175 yards in 1825, Jefferson County's textile production declined to 269,536 yards in 1835, 263,543 in 1845, and a mere 45,956 in 1855 even as the population increased. The total value of other household manufactures declined as well, from an 1840 high of $123,528 to $34,072 in 1860.[94] As early as 1836 the *Cultivator* reported that "THE CULTURE OF FLAX, Has very much diminished, with the decrease of household manufactures, since the establishment of cotton mills, until very little is now used in the domestic way," and gazetteers and censuses agreed. By 1850 the New York State Fair's committee on domestic manufactures, all men, would remark that "the exhibition in this class was much more limited than they had expected," and they urged "the wives and daughters of farmers to give more attention to this important branch of household industry."[95]

As in so much else in rural life, if the work was hard, it was likely shared. Cheese making, for instance, was often done collectively, with families sharing female help or even pooling their milk.[96] While the absence of account books and diaries makes it impossible to know whether the Jefferson County women hired one another's daughters or engaged in monetary exchanges among themselves, surely Lydia Osborn and her sister Susan Ormsby labored side by side. Given their proximity, the other women of this group may well have shared the daily duties of their lives and work. The distances between the Vincent, Ormsby, Williams, and Osborn farms could be covered in minutes, and the women probably moved among their houses easily, mixing visiting with shared labor. There is no evidence to suggest that they stood out from their neighbors in the kind of labor they performed, the wealth they accumulated, or how their particular households structured the work. Instead, they may have differed only in the conversations they had while they churned butter or stitched cloth and in the issues about which they felt passionately.

For these people, particular locations on a map represented a farm, a livelihood, and a life. Landownership reinforced men's political independence just as it underscored their wives' legal dependence. But for both women and men it signaled their ties to family, community, and the state, relationships that together constituted a sense of place and belonging. For Susan Ormsby, landownership may well have highlighted the incongruities of unmarried women's legal status. For all of them, I imagine, land, its sales, the labor it demanded, and the place in a community it confirmed helped shape their sense of themselves as members of that community and of its political culture.

Changes in that political culture—most notably in married women's legal standing—were inextricably tied to property as well. The authority of men had long been established and reinforced by their control over land. But throughout the antebellum years, as legislatures gradually permitted wives to inherit, buy, sell, and lease land, women who had married under an older set of rules entered a new relationship to the land itself. Four years after New York State passed its Married Women's Property Act in 1848, Eleanor's widowed father, Timothy O'Connor, died. In a will he had written only weeks before the new law was enacted, he left his land to

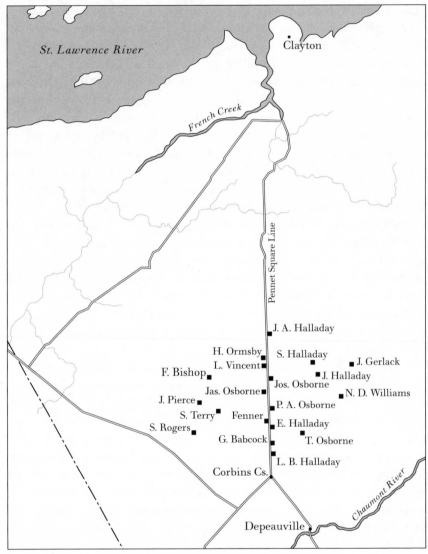

St. Lawrence River

Clayton

French Creek

Pennet Square Line

J. A. Halladay

H. Ormsby
S. Halladay
J. Gerlack
L. Vincent
J. Halladay
F. Bishop
Jos. Osborne
Jas. Osborne
N. D. Williams
J. Pierce
P. A. Osborne
S. Terry
Fenner
E. Halladay
S. Rogers
G. Babcock
T. Osborne
L. B. Halladay
Corbins Cs.

Chaumont River

Depeauville

MAP 4. *Clayton, 1855, with Landowners' Names*

three of his sons and his two unmarried daughters, Susan and Sally; his three married daughters, including Eleanor, inherited fifty dollars each.[97] Whether this was perceived as a slight or as reflecting real need, or whether O'Connor had previously transferred other land to his children, is unknown. Certainly Eleanor and Abraham were less wealthy than her father; their $1,000 farm was worth less than half of his and somewhat less than the farms of the other petitioners' families.[98] But even though Eleanor did not receive a sizable inheritance from her father, somehow her own wealth increased. In 1856 she paid a great deal of money, $2,500, to Robert and Esther Fenner for ninety acres of land in lots 269 and 262 of Macomb's purchase, across the road from Joseph and Lydia Osborn's place. Four years later she paid another $1,480 to Lucretia Flanders for a parcel of land in lots 322 and 321 in the adjacent town of Lyme.[99]

After all those years of men buying and selling land, Eleanor Vincent's transactions present an enigma. The 1860 and 1870 censuses do not mention that she owned her own property, but obviously she did. I do not know where Eleanor got this money or why she spent it in her own name or how she felt when she was able to do so. If the acquisition was a maneuver to protect land from Abraham's debts, the record does not say. All I know is that she used her money to buy land in the community where she and her family had settled decades earlier and where she and Abraham would live for the rest of their lives.

Other women also bought and sold land. When Bailey Ormsby, brother of Susan Ormsby and Lydia Osborn, died in 1848, Susan became the owner of a fifty-acre farm (most likely their father's original homestead) near her siblings' land. But this was not the only property Susan would own. In 1869 Lydia Osborn, recently widowed, sold Susan fifty acres of land adjoining her own farm on Penet's Square for $550. By 1870, Susan Ormsby, with $4,300 in real estate and $300 in personal property, and her sister Lydia each had more wealth than their brother Hiram. In 1886, the year that the last other surviving petitioner, Eleanor Vincent, died, Susan Ormsby made one final purchase, a house on three-quarters of an acre in the village of Depauville that cost her $350. Susan was seventy that year, and the decision to lease out her farm and move to town was probably a practical one. Susan and her sister-in-law Betsy Ormsby shared that home in town until Susan died in 1895. It was left to her nephew, Burton Whitney, to inventory her belongings, pay her taxes and other debts (the greatest claim, $1,000, was by her niece Ursula Whitney, who received only $52 of it), and sell her house and farm.[100]

Even in the face of meager evidence, I am certain that these women and men discussed their changing relationship to land, to the larger society, and to one another. Several of the men in this story left their estates outright to a wife or sister. Others showed more ambivalence but also signs of negotiation. Take Nahum D. Williams, whose second wife, Lydia, has remained the most elusive of the petition's signers. The will he wrote in late April 1863 is unusually convoluted, making his "beloved wife" Lydia his executrix, granting her "the use possession and controul of all my real estate for and during the term of five years from my decease," and then setting rather strict terms under which she should dispose of their farm. If Lydia were unable to sell the land for fifty dollars per acre, he wrote, she should continue to live on it for another few years and try again for "the best price [she] is able to realize for the same." He left other sums to his four remaining children and a grandchild; two sons, Edward and Walter, had died.[101]

That spring must have been an especially difficult time for the Williamses, though here, too, the evidence is scant. Edward Williams had evidently died in the still-ongoing Civil War, for Nahum poignantly bequeathed to his daughter Susan "the certificate and all moneys that may hereafter be received by me or my executor as Back pay and bounty for services rendered by Edward C. Williams deceased for services in the United States service and which I may be or am entitled to as his father." Nahum himself would die less than three months later, so he may have been ill as well as grieving. In any case, Nahum and Lydia Williams must have talked, for he apparently realized that the strings he had attached to his land and his wife were a bit taut. In June, Nahum Williams returned to the clerk's office to revise his will. He removed the controls he had set over Lydia's use of their estate, requiring only that "immediately after my decease only sufficient of my said Personal estate shall be sold by my Executrix to pay my debts and funeral expenses, and that the balance . . . shall be and remain in the possession and controul of said executrix for her use free of charge." When Nahum died the following month, this codicil gave his wife full control of their land. Even after Lydia had paid for the administration of her husband's estate and his funeral (including $33 for an impressive tombstone) and covered the next year's county, school, and road taxes, she was left with a considerable estate. Most intriguing among Nahum's debts were one to S. Ormsby (for $345.50) and one to Lydia herself (for $185).[102] I can guess how Susan Ormsby came to possess her own funds, but how Lydia acquired enough independently to lend money to her husband must remain a mystery.

With each new map of Clayton and each new census, the names changed as people married, died, moved, or watched their children settle far from home. Yet throughout the nineteenth century, the names Osborn, Ormsby, Vincent, and Bishop, as well as other relatives, such as Halladays, Rogerses, and Frames, dot the map on either side of the old Penet's Square boundary. Their stability of residence suggests a modest prosperity that was somewhat at odds with their region's overall decline and that resembles descriptions of "those who stayed behind" in rural Vermont.[103] By the 1840s, Jefferson County itself exuded a rather forlorn insularity and a sense of abandonment by the outside world. Petitioning for canal aid in 1841, a convention of towns complained that Jefferson County should have shared "in that State patronage, which has done so much for others, but nothing for us." Newspapers reveal a place both raw and established, with advertisements for "Wild Lands" appearing alongside cures for baldness, ads for *Godey's Lady's Book*, and articles about the "Wonders of Magnetism."[104] The growing number of reminiscences about the Revolution and of obituaries further marks Jefferson County as an aging community, and it was not an entirely happy one.

Inevitably, some Jefferson County residents looked west, took advantage of the cheap government-owned land, and sold their farms. The California gold rush made matters more unstable, as newspapers both described and fretted about the itch. Advertisements in the *Albany Atlas* cried "Ho! For California" and "For California Gold" and offered for sale a "New Map of California." Still others offered land, stores, and personal goods for sale so that the sellers could join the rush.[105] Surely no one was surprised when one of Henry Conklin's brothers, Abiah, heir to their father's wanderlust, was "smitten down with [gold fever] quite badly and all summer long it was nothing but going to California as soon as they could save enough money to go with." Agricultural and political writers expressed dismay at the trend and urged northern New Yorkers to figure out how to keep their sons and daughters close to home. "How are we to compete with the great west?" moaned one writer. "Railroads and canals are multiplying. . . . They can raise everything cheaper than we can. . . . [We must] stay where we are, and work head-work." Of course, the inclination of those who stay home is to disparage other choices, and so newspapers soon reported smugly, "if we do not yet get much gold from California, we at least are begining [*sic*] to get back some of our emigrants. Every paper we take up gives some account of the return of disappointed adventurers."[106]

There were good reasons to move on, and the Jefferson County petition families were not immune to the westward pull; each had siblings, children, or nieces and nephews who settled in the West. Two of Eleanor Vincent's sisters, Mary Perine and Louisa Wilson, had moved with their husbands to Wisconsin by 1852. When Nahum Williams died in 1863, his

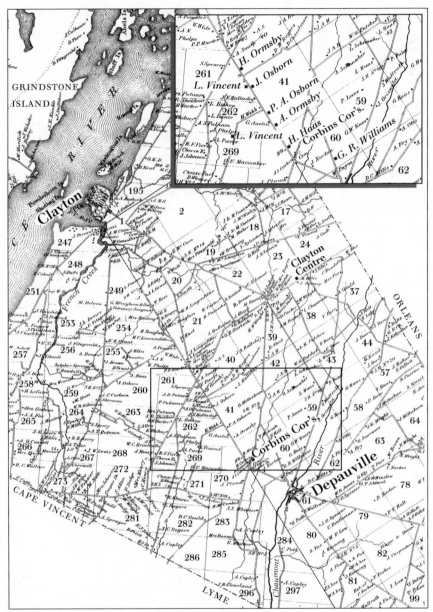

MAP 5. *Detail of Depauville Area of Clayton, 1864 (based on C. K. Stone,*
New Topographical Atlas of Jefferson Co., New York *[1864], 18)*

brother and sister had to be contacted in Fulton County, Ohio. Alpheus Greene's sister Nancy Moore had moved with her husband, a Baptist minister and missionary, to Ohio. Several of Joseph Osborn's relatives were living in Michigan when his will was read in 1868.[107]

But just as the decision to move north was a conscious and collective one, so must have been the decision to stay. The women who wrote the petition to their state's constitutional convention in 1846 remained firmly rooted in their land, their community, and their homes. Their sense of content, as well as their discontents, emerged from their experience of establishing, working on, and belonging to a particular place. In contrast to Elizabeth Cady Stanton, whose famous "intellectual repression, a woman's rights convulsion!" exploded against the constraints of the life of a provincial housewife, the evidence from Jefferson County suggests that these women developed their views from a less individualistic and perhaps less personally rebellious experience.[108] Their demand for equal rights reflected both their pride in what they had built and their indignation that it was nevertheless not fully theirs. By the time they expressed those ideas on paper and in public, there were more material comforts in their households and fewer dramatic decisions to be made. There was also more time to think.

chapter four
_____

Intellectual
Influences

"arguments both numerous and decisive"

Nothing in the story of land and labor could have predicted the turn these particular women's thoughts would take. After all, so far as we know, their neighbors (the Garlocks and the Halladays, for example) did not petition for woman's rights. There is little in the historical record to suggest that Jefferson County was a hotbed of radical ideas or that its populace was unusually well educated or well read—though one observer considered "the New York farmer . . . the most inquisitive mortal on earth . . . [who] sought news from every passer-by and remembered what he was told."[1] Yet clearly the mid-1840s were a contentious time, when New Yorkers focused intensely on men's economic and political relationships and talk about rights was ubiquitous—in religious discourse, Native American politics, international events, antislavery activism, and debates about expanding the political rights of men. In that setting, six middling farm women in Jefferson County found the idea of asserting their own rights far from unthinkable. Exploring the ideas that were "out there" in their households, their community, their churches, and their state helps us understand how people come to embrace a radical demand. It also helps us locate the source of their conviction that they had a right to express that demand. The evidence of a backlash against female outspokenness (as abolitionists, most notably, but also as preachers) signals that all this talk could be frightening. For rights, as conservatives have long warned, do not enter discussion singly, nor is talk about them easily contained; the myth of Pandora's box remains a metaphor of great power. Once an idea is raised, even in a negative sense, someone is going to mull it over.

If property and place offered these women standing in their households and communities, what were the sources for their particular ideas about their rights? What in their religious and intellectual experiences—in the reading, the arguments, the meetings, the political campaigns, and the

[83]

newspapers that entered their homes—made them think as they did? What sermon, what article caused them to storm over to a neighbor's or a sister's farm to share their reaction with friends? Whatever the degree of local support for their views, they evidently believed more ardently in woman's rights than other neighbors and friends did, or perhaps they simply felt more compelled to speak out. Perhaps they were just more annoyed. For whatever reasons, these women took time from the routines of a busy summer season to assert their claim to be recognized as full citizens under the new constitution being adopted by their state.

However she arrived at her decision to sign the 1846 petition for woman's rights, Anna [Carter] Bishop traveled a different route, both geographically and intellectually, from that of her five cosigners. She had not come to Jefferson County from a more southern county, nor had she been among those who established the first farms in Depauville. Born in 1790, she was nine when her family moved from Wallingford, Connecticut, to Canada. Some years later the Carters moved again, recrossing the border, to Jefferson County, New York. There, in 1807, she married Luther Bishop, born in Chesterfield, New Hampshire, in 1783, whose family was among the earliest settlers of Henderson.[2] Although Anna and Luther first lived alongside Luther's brothers in that town, in 1840 Luther purchased ten acres of land in Clayton, and soon he and Anna and two of their grandsons had become neighbors of the other petition signers.[3] They may not have known their Osborn and Ormsby neighbors before, but they already had strong connections in the community. Only two households away was the Bishops' daughter Cynthia and her husband, John Thomas. Also nearby were Luther's brother Sylvester and sister-in-law Almeda Bishop and their children.

Among the petitioning women, only Anna Bishop's husband did not identify himself as a farmer. One record reports that Luther was a Methodist minister; another describes him as a Baptist.[4] But in 1850, when asked for his occupation by the census taker, Luther Bishop called himself a New Jerusalem, or Swedenborgian, clergyman. Neither Luther nor Anna was among the thirteen members, most of whom were from Henderson and five of whom were women, who founded a society of Swedenborgians in nearby Ellisburgh on Christmas Day in 1825. But if the sources of Luther's religious inclinations are murky, a religious calling was common among the Bishops. Luther's brother Calvin was a trustee of Henderson's Methodist society, which organized in 1830 and erected a building on Bishop Street. Sylvester was a "widely known and highly

esteemed local minister of the Methodist Episcopal Church" in Depauville. Luther and Anna's son, John Fletcher Bishop, and their son-in-law,
John Thomas, were ministers as well.[5]

Like other historians of U.S. women and of antebellum politics and
reform, I look to religion for insights into Protestant women's sense of
their place in civic and political life. After all, these women lived in an era
drenched in religious rhetoric. The 1820s and 1830s, the very period of
Depauville's settlement, was a time of particular religious intensity, and
churches were often "the cohesive and sustaining force in an otherwise
scattered, fearful community." Perhaps Anna Bishop's experience in a
family of ministers and her marriage to a Swedenborgian offer a key to
her boldness, or perhaps religion simply offered Bishop, as it did so many
nineteenth-century women, a framework for expanding her ideas about
women's duties and woman's rights. Certainly historians have assumed
that Protestantism constituted the scaffolding for her generation's understanding of the world, that "the first generation of United States citizens
may have lived in the shadow of Christ's second coming more intensely
than any generation since." American society by the 1830s was deeply
Protestant; religious assumptions pervaded the nation's political culture
and movements for social reform, set boundaries between groups, and
provided the vocabulary for many people's vision of an orderly or just
society. As we have seen, religion and morality were evoked regularly in
the political conversations about citizenship and belonging that the advocates of woman's rights would enter. Christianity served, to a large degree,
as "part of the axiomatic bundle of truths on which the nation rested—
those assumptions that made everything possible and were not themselves disputable."[6]

A conversation about the status and role of women was ongoing in this
religious discourse, as both those who endorsed religious faith and those
who worried about ministers' cultural dominance asked, "What has Religion done for Women?"[7] Both sides recognized that women were essential
both to describing and to deploying Protestant virtues. Anticlerical thinkers considered women peculiarly and dangerously susceptible to religion
itself: "Error," wrote an acerbic William Andrews, "seeks access to the
female mind first." Freethinkers and religious liberals pointed to the
constraints that orthodox theology placed on women's willingness to
speak publicly against injustice, to expand their educations, and to open
what some called their "weak minds."[8] Ministers and religious writers
protested such insults. Reflecting the intersection of religion and na-

tionalism, many Protestants argued that Christianity had accorded American women their highest status on earth and that women themselves should respond with loyalty and gratitude. And many did. Women filled church pews, did much of the work of charity, and seemed to exemplify the Protestant virtues of piety, purity, and humility. Some women also preached, especially within the dissenting churches that were prevalent in upstate New York, though the 1830s and 1840s witnessed growing restrictions on, and thus debate about, their outspokenness.[9] Historians have long recognized as well that Protestant revivals motivated thousands of women to join antebellum movements for temperance, moral reform, Sunday schools, missionary activity, and antislavery; these, in turn, helped shape a version of female citizenship based on women's standing as moral actors. Protestant thought undoubtedly helped define the intellectual terms in which many women would express their political identities and assert their rights.

Yet for all the burning it did in the western regions of the state, religion seems not to have been the main passion of these early settlers. While observers agree that most northern New Yorkers sprang from "Puritan" roots, they also note the diminishing intensity of religious observance, the tolerance for previously dissenting faiths, and New Yorkers' greater passion for partisan, rather than religious, considerations. Indeed, one observer believed that the "tumult of infidelity" itself was widespread in New York, and that "Tom Paine's *Age of Reason* was one of the commonest books in every town and farming community, and was read and studied zealously by many."[10] Although the signers of the 1846 petition were undoubtedly Protestants, they do not seem to have been members of a single congregation. Nor were they members of Jefferson County's small community of Quakers, although they chose not to list themselves as Miss or Mrs. on their petition. Perhaps their decades- or generation-long sojourn in central New York had tempered their religious intensity; perhaps Elias and Jane Ormsby or Benjamin and Polly Vincent had moved to put some distance between themselves and the orthodox faith of their parents in the first place. Perhaps they carried with them a tradition of dissent nurtured in northern New England, which witnessed the "most militant religious radicals" of the Revolutionary Era.[11] Or maybe Jefferson County's early residents were just too far away, too recently settled, and too busy to have been caught up in the decade's religious fervor.

I am not suggesting that religious influences were absent. From the earliest days of white settlement, missionaries roamed the North Country.

Early religious activity began with the arrival of the Reverend Mr. Bascomb, sent on a missionary tour by a Ladies Charitable Society in Connecticut in 1801. The Reverend John Taylor, whose travel journal offers some of the best descriptions of the North Country's early years, soon followed. Noadiah Hubbard, Champion's founder, stressed his town's rapid settlement by pointing to the arrival in about 1805 of the Reverend Nathaniel Dutton, sent by a missionary society "at the east" and invited to remain. But to the outside world, Jefferson County was a sparse field for religious labors, a situation described succinctly by Taylor, who found in one town of seventy-five families "2 or 3 baptists, 3 or 4 Deists."[12]

Religious excitement did pick up with the growing population. In 1817 Dutton led a revival that drew 168 new members to his Congregational church.[13] In 1823 the General Assembly of the Presbyterian Church reported a long list of New York congregations that had been "graciously visited" and mentioned "the continuation of former revivals, in Brownville, Adams and Watertown."[14] The revival in Adams was of unusual significance, for among those converted was the young Charles Finney, who had returned to Jefferson County to practice law. Two years after he joined the Presbyterian Church of Adams, Finney himself led one of the revivals in Brownville, which split the Presbyterian church.[15] Well into the century, such revivals provided religious and communal fellowship. Henry Conklin, whose mother had been raised in a very religious household, welcomed the revival meetings that came to their Herkimer County town in 1850. "We had been deprived of having meetings or going to church so long that we had almost become like the heathen," he recalled years later, "and needed a good shaking by something."[16]

The churches that early settlers in Depauville established reflected a broad diversity of Protestant sects and little effective orthodoxy. Largely local and self-governing, they seem to have had few ties to national missionary and benevolent societies that mattered. A few Sunday schools appeared in the 1820s when six missionary agents were sent to establish auxiliaries in some ten New York counties. But as late as 1835, although New York State generously funded its work, the American Baptist Home Missionary Society could list no life members (contributors who had sent thirty dollars) in Jefferson County and supported only one agent, John Peck, in all of New York.[17] By 1843 the New York Convention reported that John N. Webb in Carthage, Jefferson County, had in two years supplied four stations, baptized thirteen individuals, and welcomed seventy children to the Sunday school.[18] D. D. Reed had performed similar labors in Pillar Point, Jefferson County, and both the Black River Association in Lefargeville, with thirty churches, and the Jefferson Union, with six, were flourishing.[19] But in the North Country, as in Cooperstown a generation earlier, "churches were slow to organize," and church building lagged behind other, arguably more essential, construction such as sawmills, gristmills, jails, schools, taverns, and stores.[20]

What is striking about the religious character of Jefferson County is not so much the number of churches as their diversity and mutual tolerance. Baptists, Methodists, Presbyterians, and Catholics formed congregations almost simultaneously, sharing buildings in a spirit of cooperation that did not characterize more settled or wealthier areas. Universalists were present in a number of Jefferson County towns as early as 1823.[21] Even if, as seems likely, the Depauville petitioners attended the same stone church, built in 1837, they did not necessarily share a service, a minister, or a religious community, for the building housed Universalists, Freewill Baptists, Congregationalists, and Baptists. We should not assume that Quakerism was the sole critical source for dissenting ideas, for what little evidence we have about these folks' religious proclivities suggests that a diversity of Protestant faiths and, especially, a strong presence of sects with a tradition of flexibility on gender issues made for fertile ground for talk about rights.[22] Indeed, the county's churches welcomed discussion of the most controversial issues; as abolitionist Gerrit Smith noted admiringly, "Meeting Houses in every part of [Jefferson] county are open to the advocates of our cause." Nor was religious observance itself universal, for even in the 1850s an impressive array of individuals apparently remained unchurched. As John Fletcher Bishop boasted in the prospectus for his magazine, *The Revivalist*, recent converts in the area included "formalists, moralists, spiritualists, skeptics, downright infidels, mockers and scoffers, swearers, liars, fist-pugilists, Sabbath desecraters, drunkards, gamblers, and otherwise vile and abandoned" people.[23]

In matters religious Jefferson County's experience resembled that of less settled areas decades earlier. The growth of the Baptist Church was rapid in the nation's first decades and surpassed that of other Protestant groups. From a position as a tiny dissenting church "made up largely of the underprivileged classes, economically and educationally," Baptists, with their deep distrust of centralized authority, had become a leading force among migrating communities. Not surprisingly, then, although a Presbyterian church had formed in Brownville in 1818, the first congregation in the immediate vicinity of Depauville was a Free Communion

Baptist congregation, formed in 1820.[24] Others soon followed, including, in 1841, a Baptist society, which had both Nahum Williams and Joseph Osborn's brother, Phineas A., as trustees. Among Brownville's devout Baptists were Alpheus Greene and various members of his family, including his brother-in-law John L. Moore, a missionary. Greene's church affiliation suggests another link to the petitioning families; according to Amy Ormsby's obituary, "in early life she sought and found Christ as her Savior," and it was the Baptist church's minister, Amasa Dodge of Lowville, who baptized her.[25]

Methodist meetings, too, were ubiquitous in newly settled regions such as Jefferson County. "When the new homesteader drove his stakes into the ground," remarks Edwin Gaustad, "the echo was heard somewhere by a Methodist preacher." Indeed, however the first Methodist minister arrived in northern New York, by 1850 there were more Methodist churches than any other denomination in New York and more Methodists than any other sect in Depauville itself. In 1834 a Methodist society formed in Depauville, of which Timothy O'Connor, Eleanor Vincent's father, was a trustee; the congregation would build its own church in that village in 1852, the year O'Connor died.[26] With the founding of Methodist churches came, in the North, a commitment to social issues, to antislavery, and to the "affairs of world-wide Protestantism."[27]

The malleability of religious allegiance and the sense that orthodoxy held little sway emerges from even the most conventional of stories, that of Luther Bishop, an early preacher in Jefferson County. Luther and Anna's son, evangelist John Fletcher Bishop, paid sober tribute to his "venerable father" as one of "Several Pioneer or Prominent Ministers" in upstate New York. He entered the "Gospel ministry" at eighteen, John Bishop reported, and was an early circuit preacher, responsible for "many powerful revivals" and working "free of charge." John Bishop's reminiscence was an entirely typical one of a "young itinerant Methodist minister [who], aided by the Divine Spirit, wrought wonders in promoting Christian revivals." Only at the end of his brief recollection did he hint at religious turmoil within the Bishop household. "Though his religious sentiments, in some respects, were changed for many years prior to his recent decease," John Bishop admitted, "yet his living and experimental piety remained essentially unchanged."[28]

"Experimental" indeed. Even if we accept that progressive elements existed among a range of denominations and that the struggles of dissenting sects over women's authority highlight an important conversation,

Luther Bishop's affiliation with the Swedenborgians is striking, suggesting the kind of religious quirkiness that historians associate with unconventional political ideas. Combining "many of the liberal religious doctrines with the new sociological ideas of the time," the ideas of Emanuel Swedenborg enjoyed a widespread influence among intellectuals and progressive thinkers. The church itself grew slowly, claiming some 360 members in nine states in 1817 and never more than 10,000. Still, "by 1848 these concepts had deeply penetrated the thinking of the Universalists and some of the Quakers" and influenced "more diverse types of dissenters" than any of the "unconventional currents streaming through the many levels of American religion."[29] Although Swedenborg's ideas were interpreted in various ways, his notion that "marriage was a process of mutual regeneration" and his followers' association with Fourierism encouraged some of his adherents in radical ideas about divorce and property.[30] To some, the Swedenborgians helped define the very fringes of religious thought. When Henry and William James asked their father what was their "church home," Henry Sr. asserted that "there was no communion, even that of the Catholics, even that of the Jews, even that of the Swedenborgians, from which we find ourselves excluded."[31] That Luther Bishop labeled himself a New Jerusalem, or Swedenborgian, minister suggests that he took a progressive view on many social matters and considered himself something of an intellectual, though not necessarily that he was among the church's "innumerable frontier quacks."[32] That such a community emerged in the tiny and obscure town of Ellisburgh in 1825 is nothing short of astonishing.

Membership in Protestant churches and a wide-ranging conversation among various sects may have offered women in upstate New York opportunities to consider themselves full members of their community. But religion was only one stream of the complex intellectual currents that contributed to their views of the world and of their rights. Among those influences must be counted the Iroquois peoples of northern New York who, though few in number by the 1820s, were far from invisible in the region's culture. Women and men who were alert to the history of their state would have known that family lineage among the Iroquois nations was matrilineal, that land belonged collectively to women, and that a council of women selected tribal leaders.[33] The Jefferson County women could not have missed the point, expressed in a wide range of contexts, that Iroquois women enjoyed significant leadership roles in their community. Lydia Osborn's household, for one, received the *Albany Patriot*, which in 1844 noted approvingly that among the Cherokee "the property of the wife cannot be sold without her consent."[34] One New York historian writing in the 1950s fancifully attributed his own (male) contemporaries' attitudes to the state's former residents: "Iroquois women had once ruled their tribes and spoken to be listened to in council," he remarked, suggesting that "perhaps something of this clung to our earth and infected our air." New York's men, he bragged, "have come to fancy this breed of women with their blunt truths and their speaking out in meeting; confident men are not abashed by confident women."[35]

However oddly phrased, the example of Iroquois women's standing may well have clung to the very land these women inhabited. For if claims to owning Penet's Square left a whiff of outlaw life and distrust of authority, they also left a legacy of competing ideas about women's economic and political standing. In the fall of 1788 Penet and a group of Oneida Indians set about doing what other Americans were doing: they wrote a constitution. In striking contrast to the one being ratified by the United States, the Oneida constitution declared that land was to be divided among every person in the Oneida nation, "equal with the daughter as with the son, without any distinction." In addition, every person over eighteen could speak at the General Assembly. The constitution was passed and signed by twenty-three men and four women. Even those who rejected Penet's treaty (some Oneida considered him "a great liar and graceless rascal") did not dissent from this view of women's authority. In 1789 twenty representatives wrote Governor George Clinton to say that only the chiefs followed Penet, "and we the chief warriors and the majority of our nation, even women, follow the State of New York."[36] Perhaps Jefferson County women and men felt pride that the "honest freeholders of old 'Penet Square,' enjoy[ed] as unblemished a title to their soil as can be found upon the planet."[37] But they may also have found special meaning, tinged perhaps with irony, in men's and women's previous shared ownership of that land.

The example set by the Iroquois may have had a more significant impact on American rights talk than historians have assumed. Elizabeth Cady Stanton, Lucretia Mott, and Matilda Joslyn Gage were "at most, one person away from direct familiarity with Iroquois people," and "suffragists regularly read newspaper accounts of everyday Iroquois activities." Indeed, during her visit to upstate New York in the summer of 1848 that was made famous by the Seneca Falls convention, Lucretia Mott also visited the Cattaraugus community, where women were helping to design the Seneca nation's new constitution. Surely the Jefferson County women, farther north and in newer communities, appreciated from the Iroquois experience that "human harmony, respect for women's lives, and equal rights for women" were possible.[38] Local evidence of Native American women's control over property, rights to their children, access to political and religious authority, and relative freedom from male violence may well have helped shape other women's understanding of and opposition to their own status.[39] That the Jefferson County women claimed "no new right," but only those they had "originally inherited," suggests as much.

In addition to whatever oral traditions their community shared, the Jefferson County petitioners were informed by what they read. Though the women's only remaining words—the petition itself—establish that at least one of them was unusually articulate, their formal education was probably no more than typical. Given the ages of Eleanor Vincent and Lydia Osborn, their education was surely interrupted by migration to a place where only the roughest school facilities had been established. But all of the women petitioners had likely attended common schools for several years, and at least some were more literate than their parents.[40] Back home in Massachusetts, Amy Eldridge Ormsby had received "as good a common school education as the place afforded," and after she moved to Jefferson County in 1819, she taught at a district school.[41] Bailey Ormsby was apparently also a schoolteacher, indicating his parents' willingness to give up a son's labor for his education. His sister Susan, two years younger than he, probably received as much. In any case, when she died in 1895, Susan Ormsby's estate included "1 Lot of old books" valued at three dollars.[42]

Lydia Williams and Susan Ormsby may have attended Amy Eldridge Ormsby's classroom; there were not many choices. The area they settled was simply too new and too remote, and their parents' financial standing too tenuous, to support such extravagances as girls' seminaries. A female school "of the first character" was established in a brick building in Watertown as early as 1815, but only in 1836, with the founding of the coeducational Black River Religious and Literary Institution, did private academies begin to appear in the county seat. In 1849 a Brownville Female Seminary offered both day and boarding school for girls.[43] What records I have found of early academies offer no evidence that any of these women or their close relatives attended. Although a very few young women from Jefferson County attended Emma Willard's Troy Female Seminary, they were (like Elizabeth Cady and her sisters Margaret and Catharine) far more likely to be the daughters of judges and merchants than of middling farmers.[44] Still, some women in Jefferson County had clearly absorbed the language of civic belonging and republican ideals that increasingly characterized girls' education. If they did not directly benefit from the dramatic rise in girls' seminary education, by 1833, when Susan Ormsby and Lydia Williams turned eighteen, news of these opportunities had likely reached the North Country. Possibly they heard about Zeruviah Porter from nearby Whitestown, who entered Oberlin College's Ladies Department in 1836 and became the first woman graduate of a coeducational college two years later.[45] Surely they had picked up stories of other young women who had used such educational opportunities to become missionaries to the West, to Indians, and to foreign lands.

For talk was everywhere about the effects of exposing rural daughters to the higher branches of learning. Newspapers reported a rise in female seminary attendance among farmers' daughters and, in turn, helped shape literate New Yorkers' attitudes toward the education of girls. "Nothing but a newspaper," as Tocqueville famously put it, "can drop the same thought into a thousand minds at the same moment," and newspapers were clearly spreading the notion that girls' education was worth discussing.[46] The agricultural press, in particular, offered a forum for a vigorous debate about what constituted an appropriate education for farmers' daughters, emphasizing, as it did for farming men, the value of "practical" learning.

Correspondents to these papers confirmed the sense that "provincial parents and daughters agreed on the value of an education" even though "they were uncertain as to how the particulars of that education might be turned to the service of kin and community."[47] For some, the tension between the "fashionable education of the present day" and the mundane demands of farm life were irreconcilable. Annette believed that seminaries ruined farmers' daughters; they "return home, refined and accomplished it is true, but totally unfitted for their situation in life, and soon become discontented and miserable."[48] A "Farmer's Daughter" from Seneca County disagreed, arguing that it was girls' "affectation of effeminate gentility" that caused their discontent. Fanny, a seminary graduate, insisted that schools were not to blame for rural girls' purported vanity: "It is no matter whether they are Merchants', Lawyers', or Farmers' daughters," she wrote, "if they go to improve, they will improve; and just what they aim to be, they will be. If . . . Annette wishes a reformation in the present system of education, she . . . [should] *reform the mothers at home*."[49]

Men, predictably, had something to say about women's education. D.C. was made nervous by all this learning and lamented that it made girls ill suited to marry farmers' sons: "The daughters . . . having equally active minds, . . . study to better advantage and make greater acquisitions," he wrote. He viewed this situation as tragic for "the sons of farmers [who] are thus thrown into back ground, mortified, repelled" and who "wonder at a state of things over which they have no control." "However much the sister may have," warned D.C., "let the brother have far more means of education." A very few, unfazed by the specter of female superiority, tied women's education explicitly to their membership in the civic community. "It is true, our women do not vote at our elections, or hold political office, or manage the out door concerns of the farm," one Columbia County farmer admitted, but "they exercise their full share of influence in all our concerns" and so should be given "an equal chance with our sons."[50]

The more than 400 agricultural newspapers in circulation in the antebellum years offer an important, if perhaps unexpected, source for exploring rural women's and men's civic identities. It was often in these pages that farmers made claims on state and federal governments and entered debates about farm life, new crops, and new methods, taking sides for and against what had been known, disparagingly, as "book-farming."[51] ("It is one of the shallowest prejudices which ever crept into the mind of man," grumbled R. G. Pardee before the Wayne County Agricultural Society, "that a fact loses its power and value because printed in a book.")[52] In one woman's view, the papers' focus on "manures, crops, short-horned cattle, sheep, swine, &c." benefited everyone, for the men "seem to talk less of politics, and other everlasting subjects about which they never could come to any satisfactory conclusion."[53] Yet politics was never entirely absent. While farm journals declared themselves staunchly against government intrusion, they were vocal in demanding public assistance in building roads and canals and in supporting tariffs, agricultural education, patents, and subsidies of crops—for farmers "rarely permitted limitations to concern them when they sought favors."[54] The New York state legislature acknowledged this relationship when it gave financial aid to county societies, fairs, and the state's agricultural journal, the *Cultivator*, founded in 1834.

Civic concerns were also expressed and enacted in agricultural societies. Much like state and national governments themselves, early agricultural societies such as Jefferson County's, founded in 1817 by James Le Ray de Chaumont, were peopled by "gentlemen-farmers," men who continued to garner most of the prizes at agricultural fairs. By the 1840s, as ordinary farmers began to subject these organizations to greater scrutiny, agricultural reformers responded by becoming more self-consciously democratic.[55] Like politicians, agricultural editors were ambivalent about their newly expanded constituency, and many farmers, in turn, resented the conceit their attitude conveyed. Criticism and disrespect went both ways in the declining years of rural deference. "That our fathers subsisted without agricultural papers, is no satisfactory answer," one writer scoffed. "They even lived without rail-roads, steam-engines, and not a few without hats, boots or breeches." When it folded, the *American Farmer* took a last jab at the "dirt farmer," who remained trapped, as one historian characterizes its editorial view, by "prejudice of ignorance, and the obstinate and blind perseverance in bad habits."[56]

But where agriculture was losing its competitive edge or communities felt threatened by migration to the West, some farmers were quietly open to new ideas. In far northern New York, worried or curious or restless farmers began to take note of their neighbors' experiments; the silkworm enthusiasm of the 1830s was only the most manic example of this experimentation.[57] While it is impossible to know how many, and which, farm households received agricultural papers or even if any of the 6,950 subscribers to the *Cultivator* in New York State in 1837 lived in Jefferson County, it is clear that times were changing. We know that by 1839 copies of the state's leading agricultural newspaper had made their way to the county because the paper suddenly lists an agent in Watertown, A. S. Greene, postmaster.

Agricultural historian Paul Wallace Gates thought the journals themselves offered "surprisingly little of interest, and less of use, to farm women." Yet women read the agricultural press, attended local farmers' clubs, and viewed agricultural curiosities. Sometimes men noticed: speaking about homespun, part of the labor of the "*fairer* portion of the human race," Vincent Le Ray de Chaumont reminded his audience "that our assembly is graced as usual by their presence, in a number which is a reward and an encouragement for our labors."[58] An occasional editor fretted that "farmers' wives and daughters ought not to be neglected" and sought articles of particular interest to women readers.[59] But even without a "ladies' department," many rural women read the *Cultivator* and the *Genesee Farmer*. Prudence Reynolds of Stamford, Connecticut, had "had your Cultivator so long in our family, that it scarcely entered my mind while writing, that *personally* we are strangers." Reynolds evidently felt entitled to call on the larger farming community's resources, having written for information on making cream cheese, which Arabella Sheldrick of Hereford Hall promptly supplied.[60] These papers, insisted Annette, a frequent correspondent to the *New Genesee Farmer*, were "read as much by the female members of families as by the other portion." "I can assure you that your paper is not thrown aside or destroyed like common political trash," she insisted, but "is carefully read by the whole family and preserved for future reference." Reflecting the interests of those readers, by the 1850s agricultural papers "furnished a battleground for conflicting views on woman's rights." While the *Ohio Cultivator*, whose Ladies' Department had long been dominated by reformers, openly endorsed woman's rights, others simply, and increasingly, welcomed a range of views.[61]

Farm journals offer historians possible sources both for the ideas available to literate women and for some women's grievances about farm life itself. Among the most vociferous contributors was Susan, who complained that men ignored the advice in the Philadelphia *Farmer's Cabinet* regarding the needs of women, who "constitute . . . no unimportant part of the agricultural community." Susan's concerns were specific:

> A year or two ago you published a very good essay about a "wood-house," for the comfort and convenience of females; it was much talked of, and every man in our neighborhood, except an old bachelor, approved of it . . . ; one even went so far as to get the stuff for it, but afterwards used it for an other purpose, and to this day there has not been built a wood-house in our township; so we have to burn wet wood, and go out in the rain and snow to get it; sometimes the breakfast or dinner is delayed . . . , and whenever this happens, we are sure to hear of it in the way of complaint, although the fault lays precisely where the complaint comes from.

She pleaded with the editors to "write another essay about keeping wood in the dry, and having it cut and split to proper sizes for current family use." The editors of the *New Genesee Farmer* were amused to hear "such warlike threatenings from the descendants of the peaceful WM. PENN." Nevertheless, they reprinted Susan's complaint in its entirety.[62]

As in so much else, there is hardly a whisper from Jefferson County before the mid-1840s, although the county's elite had been at the forefront of founding agricultural societies. In 1845 the *Cultivator* acknowledged as much by declaring itself "glad to receive any agricultural facts from the county of Jefferson, which we know can boast of some as good farmers [sic] as any other section."[63] But each of the rare glimpses into Jefferson County's farming life supports Annette's contention that women were active in community discussion. Solon Robinson visited several Jefferson County dairy farms in 1850 and noted approvingly, "The women and children here take more interest in agricultural improvement and know more about it, than a majority of the men in some places." "Would you know the reason?" he continued. "They read."[64] Another male correspondent, H. H. T., writing from East Rodman, argued that the women of Jefferson County rejected the "false notion . . . that women's appropriate labor is strictly confined to the inside of the farm house." "In this section," he bragged, "where nearly every farmer keeps from ten to sixty cows, the women folks (to their honor be it said) generally help milk, without being *asked*, and consider it a *shame* to those women who refuse to maintain their right to share in the labors and toil, the joys and sorrows, of their husbands, brothers and lovers."[65]

From within the organized agricultural community came hints of changes in women's expectations and roles. In 1844 "a Farmer's Wife" from Onondaga challenged a long-standing policy: in judging domestic manufactures at agricultural fairs "would it not be judicious to consult the opinion of ladies who have been in the habit of manufacturing more or less of the same kind of goods; they certainly understand better than gentlemen can, the difficulty in performing different kinds of work, and the time and expense requisite for the completion of the articles." "No one can understand the difference in the labor required to make a yard of woolen or linen cloth," she declared mildly but firmly, "unless they have actually made both." The editors did not comment on the suggestion, and all of the officers and judges for that year's fair were male, due appreciation given for women's fine work. The following year as well, only men served as judges.[66]

The August 1846 issue of the *Cultivator*, published as the constitutional convention met to discuss its own weighty matters, covered such topics as "Nitrogenous Matter in Oats" and "The Potato." As usual, the paper announced the list of prizes to be awarded at the annual state fair, including a new category, "Ornamental, shell, Needle, and Wax Work." Also presented, without comment, was the list of judges, among whom were five women: Mrs. B. D. Coe (Buffalo), Mrs. Hanson Cox (Auburn), Mrs. Alvah Worden (Canandaigua), Mrs. Wetmore (Utica), and Mrs. W. W. Watson (Geneva).[67] (Alvah Worden, as we will see, was a delegate at the convention, where he was embroiled in a raucous discussion about married women's property rights.) The following year, the agricultural fair included several mixed-sex committees of judges, including the four men and six "ladies" who were to offer prizes for flowers.[68] Having women judge domestic products alongside men became common practice without evoking public controversy, and the *Cultivator* itself published no further discussion of the matter.

Perhaps such tiny changes stirred up so little debate simply because talk of woman's rights *was* in the air. However much politicians, ministers, and others declared women's political and legal equality with men unthinkable, talk about the inconsistencies in women's status was ubiquitous. John Neal, the editor of *Brother Jonathan*, forecast nearly a century's worth of arguments in favor of woman's rights when he spoke at the Tabernacle in New York City in 1843. "Where people do *not* govern themselves, either directly or indirectly by representation, they are slaves," he asserted. "Qualify it as we may, disguise the unpalatable truth as we may, they have not *rights* and all their *privileges* are at the mercy of the governing power." "In any given case," he remarked, "we have only to ask ourselves how we should bear such laws from women as they are called upon to bear from us—and not only to bear, but to be thankful for?"[69]

Let us return to Lazette Worden, tasked with judging domestic manufactures while her husband, Alvah, grappled with whether the new constitution should grant elite women such as herself other rights. Perhaps she was not paying attention to the debate over married women's property rights, or perhaps she resisted its implications. But talk of woman's rights was within her intellectual universe and would be increasingly impossible to ignore. The daughters of a judge, Lazette Miller and her sister Frances had attended the Troy Female Seminary. Lazette married lawyer Alvah Worden, and Frances married William Seward, New York's Whig governor. Both women moved in reform and political circles throughout their lives. Seward, although not a supporter of woman suffrage, would later relish telling the story of his then-widowed sister-in-law's hiring of her farm laborers. Having "examined them as to their capacity to perform the required labor," she would inquire into their partisan loyalties, since as "a woman and a widow, and having no one to represent her, she must have Republicans to do her voting." Worden, claimed Seward, considered that she had a "right to [vote] by proxy, hence I hire men to vote my principles."[70] Seward's own wife was apparently less bold. After a vigorous debate with William Seward and other men about woman's rights, Elizabeth Cady Stanton learned, in the privacy of the parlor, that Frances Seward agreed with her views but expressed herself "a born coward" who dreaded "Mr. Seward's ridicule."[71] The story has gone through several retellings; it is Elizabeth Cady Stanton's rendition, intended to show both upper-class wives' trepidation and their quiet support of her campaign, that provides our source. But what did Seward mean by telling this story about his sister-in-law? Was he making fun of the hired men or of Worden's insistence that she had standing in political life? Did he aim to support the logic of woman suffrage, or was he reminding Stanton that well-connected women exercised political influence without voting? I do not know. But all of the characters in this story recognized that woman's rights talk was in the air, in the press, and in their parlors.

Local newspapers, most of which were partisan, helped shape these conversations in people's kitchens as well as in convention halls. In the North Country, newspapers, beginning with the *Black River Gazette*, founded in 1807, arose and flourished briefly, only to fold and be replaced almost at once. Among the more enduring papers were the *Black River* (later *Northern State*) *Journal*, a Whig paper, and the *Watertown Jeffersonian* and *Jefferson County Democrat*, representing the other party's views. Thurlow Weed's *Albany Evening Journal* likely found its way into a few far north Whig households by the 1840s. Liberty Party newspapers were widely read; some seventy papers were subscribed to following a Watertown meeting in 1844, and the party's leader Gerrit Smith had no doubt that dozens more would follow.[72] Several bigger-city newspapers appealed to North Country readers as well. Most important was Horace Greeley's *New York Tribune*, which "came nearest to being a truly national paper." The editor's wide-ranging interests and practical concerns and his support of the movement for free soil and public support of agriculture made the semiweekly paper, available for three dollars per year, a popular choice.[73] That women read these papers was understood. "American women read newspapers as much as their liege lords," pronounced Henry Raymond of the *New York Times* in 1852. "The paper must accommodate itself to this fact, and hence the American sheet involves a variety of topics and a diversity of contents." "Our dailies," Raymond admitted, "have domestic habits. They possess the requirements of the family journal."[74]

If newspapers carried ideas from the rest of the nation to Jefferson County farms, nearby events in 1837 and 1838 "became the absorbing theme of discussion" that helped shape the political consciousness of women and men in far northern New York.[75] At the same time, these events show the porousness of national loyalties, and ideas about national rights, on the nation's borders. In the fall of 1837 an ongoing political revolt in Lower Canada was joined by a rebellion for Upper Canadian independence, bringing Canada "as close to revolution" as it ever came.[76] Full of parliamentary intrigue, republican and anticlerical rhetoric, and disputes over women's political status, what became known as the Patriot War, or, to the victors, the Rebellion, is a fascinating story. Although like many defeats it has been largely ignored or dismissed, it stirred great passion on the Canadian border. Hundreds of Jefferson County men participated, providing the small revolutionary forces with arms, joining insurrectionists, and hiding refugees from the law. William Lyon MacKenzie and his followers seized the steamer *Caroline* in the Niagara River; someone, reported variously as "a band of men from Canada"[77] or as British troops,[78] burned the ship. Congress appropriated some $625,000 to defend the "frontier," but defiant New Yorkers and Vermonters formed secret clubs (some 200,000 people strong) to help invade Canada.[79]

These actions could not easily have escaped the notice of the Depauville families, as crowds of men gathered in Clayton to undertake the invasion, federal troops arrived, and the Canadian militia demonstrated its loyalty to the British by squelching the uprising. "This was called the Patriot War," sniffed Enos Martin at Jefferson County's centennial celebration in 1905, "and a more absurd and quixotic filibustering expedition probably never went forth from any country. The Canadians did not want to be liberated." It was, one Jefferson County resident fumed a half-century after the event, "one of the most curious, and what would now be classed as inexcusable and insane episodes that Jefferson county and the whole northern frontier had ever witnessed—nothing more nor less than a popular effort on the part of American citizens to overthrow the government of Canada by an unwarranted invasion of the frontier towns."[80] Some residents experienced the events more intensely than others, of course. The young assemblyman Preston King of St. Lawrence County suffered an emotional breakdown after participating in the revolt, and his family confined him to an asylum in Hartford. (Several years later he became a congressman and a leading free-soil Democrat.)[81] Others were less lucky. Nineteen "patriots" were killed in the effort, 35 were wounded, and 190 prisoners were taken. Ten or 11 prisoners were hanged, and more than 140 were sent to the notorious Van Diemen's Land, where most remained for several years.[82] "What a comic affair it all was," wrote Harry Landon, "if one can forget the grim scaffold at Kingston and the bullet-torn bodies of North Country boys lying in the snow."[83]

Why did so many Jefferson County residents support a futile war in a bordering country even in the face of President Martin Van Buren's warning "that they forfeited all claims to the protection of their country if they engaged in armed invasions"? For some, the "hatred of all things British," the living memory of their own Revolution, and "the belief that it was the duty of Americans to propagate republican institutions" entered the decision.[84] But even after the conflict was over, residents in Depauville and elsewhere raised money for prisoners' defense. Others tried to mollify their neighbors' enthusiasm for a lost and dangerous cause, as statements of loyalty to the U.S. government were anxiously signed. These statements, which expressed "a deep commiseration for our misguided citizens . . . now in confinement at Fort Henry" and a hope "to see justice tempered with mercy, and . . . magnanimous treatment towards these unfortunate men, worthy of a brave and generous people," signaled how widespread was northern New Yorkers' sympathy for the revolt.[85] In any case, the rebellion was thoroughly crushed, with the Catholic church a "major winner" and "the forces of democratic secularism . . . badly weakened."[86]

But if they were listening closely, women in Jefferson County would have heard a different message in these events. The Patriot Party was at the forefront of a "wider shift in the politico-sexual order," one reminiscent of the American and French revolutionaries' own masculinist republicanism. "It was within its ranks that the democratic conception of a 'public sphere' open to every citizen without privilege or distinction was enunciated most clearly and forcefully," Allan Greer writes. "Since the patriots' definition of citizenship excluded women, their discourse of liberation was as much about sex as it was about politics."[87] Indeed, throughout much of this discourse, none of which worked to advance women's full citizenship, the patriots emulated the American Revolutionary experience. Did Jefferson County women hear an echo of their own national past in the appeals to women to boycott British goods, resist luxury, and advocate the national cause? Did *La Minerve*, the *Montreal Gazette*, and the *Vindicator*, all of which debated woman suffrage in the middle and late 1830s, travel the St. Lawrence River along with goods intended for Jefferson County? If so, women there might have learned, if they did not already know, that some propertied women had long voted in Lower Canada—and that efforts were afoot in the years before the Rebellion to restrict the practice. In 1834, *La Minerve* reported, legislators in Montreal argued that because "the right of women to vote . . . is still undecided," a law must be passed to prevent such improprieties. One, a future Patriot leader, harangued his fellow legislators on the evils of seeing women "dragged to the hustings by their husbands, daughters by their fathers, often even against their will"—thus signaling that even some married women could claim the right to vote. Did any of the six Jefferson County petitioners know and talk about it when, first in 1834 and (to make sure the act stuck) again in 1849, Canadian governments, with vocal support from Patriot leaders, explicitly prohibited women from voting?[88]

In important respects, Jefferson County residents' experience of political possibilities—as well as their notion of what counted as "local"—was shaped by their relationship to Canada and their place on the nation's border. Indeed, as late as the War of 1812, people in northern New York described those in New York City or Philadelphia as living in "the states."[89] Unlike settlers in western New York and those who moved to Illinois, Ohio, and Indiana, the Vincents, the O'Connors, and their friends had established their community on the very edge of the United States. They would have been aware of French people and Canadians joining them in New York as well as Loyalists, fugitive slaves, and French Canadian migrants moving to Canada. Goods sailed back and forth, so tariffs and embargoes were an immediate concern. During the very decades that forged what historians call an American identity, Jefferson County residents faced north. Only much later, with the rise of inland transportation systems, would a historian note that "the arrow has turned half way round and now points to the south and the west."[90] Even then, northern New Yorkers' points of reference could differ from those of residents in more central regions, as they participated in conversations across national lines that were, nevertheless, very close to home.

Perhaps these various discussions about woman's rights did not so much shape the Jefferson County women's beliefs as reinforce them; maybe the women were keeping an ear open all along for opportunities to discuss their own status as citizens. Certainly some nineteenth-century activists would later describe woman's rights as an idea whose time had simply come. Emily Collins of Ontario County recalled that "from the earliest dawn of reason I pined for that freedom of thought and action that was then denied to all womankind." News of the convention at Seneca Falls "gave this feeling of unrest form and voice," and she "took action."[91] The intellectually restless Elizabeth Cady Stanton was less patient as she sought and found numerous opportunities to speak out. After her first public speech for temperance in 1841, she assured her friend Elizabeth J. Neall that she had "infused into my speech an Homeopathic dose of woman's rights, as I take good care to do in many private conversations."[92] For many of these women, including Stanton, the most sustained and audible conversation about woman's rights, indeed, their "first lessons of human rights," was taking place within the antislavery movement. Often, as Stanton confessed, the *National Anti-Slavery Standard* and the *Liberator* were "the only woman's rights food I have for myself & disciples."[93] If the Patriot War offered one intellectual moment, a flashpoint, for discussing woman's rights in Jefferson County, other movements offered more enduring opportunities. Given what we know about the awareness of many northern women regarding injustice, it seems likely that the women petitioners did not develop theirs in intellectual isolation, but in community, in exchange, and in comparing notes within a wider world of social activism.

Associational life prepared many middle-class Protestant women to think more expansively about their own civic obligations and to give more explicit consideration to their rights. But the explosion of reform, benevolent, and antislavery organizations that characterized western New York largely bypassed the North Country. In Watertown, elite women and men did participate in some organizational efforts. In 1817 a Bible Society was formed, counting among its officers the town's leaders. Over the next seven years the society distributed 681 Bibles and 457 testaments and had formed town associations. Eighty-four women in Henderson met in 1816 to form a United Female Society and raised $88.74 for foreign missions; within a year women in several other towns had followed their example. The 1840 Watertown City Directory, reflecting the town's more urban status, lists female moral reform societies with some 120 women members, which, like moral reform societies elsewhere, had "for their object, the promotion of moral purity." But Jefferson County's organizations tended to crop up sporadically and were short lived. Even Franklin

Hough, with his insistence on details, concludes simply, "Temperance and other societies have been formed at different times, many of which were soon abandoned."[94]

In the absence of much voluntary activism, the stormy world of partisan politics likely absorbed much of rural New Yorkers' civic attention. In particular, the antislavery Liberty Party offered a forum for activists to discuss both the legal standing of African American men and woman's rights in the context of electoral politics. This may come as a surprise to students of women's history, who have tended not to associate Liberty voters or their party with progressive views about woman's rights. After all, the party itself emerged from a dispute among abolitionists that was, in part, about women's equal participation in the movement. But however much the founders of the Liberty Party sought to ignore distractions such as woman's rights, many of their constituents insisted on a broad and consistent commitment to equality under the law. Some evidence suggests that the awkward coalition of hopeful partisans and orthodox ministers who broke from the American Anti-Slavery Society to form a "new organization" was unable to exercise much control over these local advocates of woman's rights. Indeed, some observers complained that in western New York the party "obtain[ed] 'sweet voices' by being a woman's rights party" while behaving differently elsewhere.[95] Far from the centers of antislavery schism, ministers and politicians seem to have resigned themselves to the reality of women's full participation, and the lines between Garrisonians and new organizationists that were so rigidly defended elsewhere simply blurred as abolitionists set about doing the work of ending slavery in the South and addressing racist inequalities in the North.[96]

Clearly this dissension had an effect. By 1849 a Liberty Party broadside recognized "the right, irrespective of sex, or color, or character, to participate in the selection of civil rulers."[97] Such formal declarations of women's political rights reflected discussions among party activists that began in someone's kitchen or field and ended up in convention halls and newspapers. One such exchange took place in September 1845, when Liberty Party activists responded to William Goodell's recent "Port Byron Address" that advocated expanding the party's platform.[98] A writer to the *Albany Patriot*, while praising the speech's "plain and genuine republican principles," had hoped for more and was "much surprised that the author . . . overlooked . . . extending the right of suffrage to females." "If merely the restricted suffrage of the colored man, is not only contrary to true republicanism, but an actual infringement upon natural rights, (as I believe it is,) then why deny the exercise of this right to women," she asked. "Do not inalienable rights inhere as substantially in one person as another? Do not all profess a capacity for self-government? If not, then the authors of the Declaration of Independence were wrong, when they declared that all governments derive their just powers from the consent of the governed; and republicanism itself is but a name." The letter, signed "One of the Disfranchised," was postmarked Jefferson County.[99]

Intended or not, the irony here is unmistakable. Can anyone really have been "much surprised" by a politician's neglect of women's right to vote in 1845? What was going on up there? Once we get past the assumption that "respectable" women avoided any mention of woman's rights, we must consider the possibility that such talk was rife. Although only six women signed the petition for woman's rights the following year, there is no evidence that they became pariahs as a result. Whether other women chose not to add their names or simply were not asked, some must have shared their views. Jefferson County resident John Haddock described William Angel's wife, Harriet Warner, as "a most charitable, amiable and beautiful Christian lady, [who] was a warm friend of my dear mother." "One of my youthful experiences," Haddock recalled, "was in driving them in a barouche from Watertown to Syracuse, where a woman's convention of some kind was to be held, and to which these two progressive women were delegates."[100] Perhaps Haddock referred to the woman's rights convention held in Syracuse in September 1852. Though their names were not listed in the *History of Woman Suffrage*, both could have been present at City Hall, listening to the "galaxy of bold women" who spoke about women's wage labor, their disfranchisement, and their aspirations. Whether they agreed with the Whig *Daily Journal* that the gathering was "dignified, orderly, and interesting" or feared the cry of "infidel" that came from local pulpits for weeks after, they would have found the event stirring. "My friends, do we realize for what purpose we are convened?" asked Elizabeth Oakes Smith in words that may have rung in her audience's ears for days afterward. "Do we fully understand that we aim at nothing less than an entire subversion of the present order of society, a dissolution of the whole existing social compact?" Certainly some opponents of woman's rights agreed with Smith that the convention was profoundly radical (even that it was a "mass of corruption, heresies, ridiculous nonsense, and reeking vulgarities"), but the Jefferson County petitioners might have been surprised to learn that the rights they demanded involved any such radical subversion. On the contrary, they experienced in their own community a sense of standing, believed themselves entitled to act as full members of their state, and were indignant that anyone thought otherwise. It was in the mainstream conventions of the American political tradition and the political workings of that state—in their own partisanship and in the rewriting of the state's basic laws—that they found the language and the opportunity to say so.[101]

chapter five

Politics and Liberty

"the government and laws under which they live"

A vigorous public discourse about freethought, religion, and female activism offered one framework for considering women's place in the 1830s and 1840s. Newspaper debates about rural girls' education, female judges at agricultural fairs, and a parliamentary battle over woman's rights in neighboring Canada suggested that, close to home, change was in the air. Conflict within the abolition movement over the status of women activists and, especially, a backlash against their public speech infused antislavery newspapers and conventions. But for many upstate New Yorkers in the 1840s, political life was where the action was, offering drama, intrigue, dissension, division, and endless debate. Politics literally lay the groundwork for settlement in northern New York, stabilizing landownership, defining the formal rights and duties of citizens, and providing the language and the mechanisms with which some American women would enter the conversation about their rights. In no sense limited to election day or to those who had the vote, partisan passions reflected a shared sense of purpose within the community; participation in partisan conflict signaled one's concern for (and resentment of) the outside world. Further, in that time and place, the political issue about which Americans disagreed most vehemently was the same one that most exposed the question of woman's rights to public view: antislavery. Indeed, where debate over African Americans' rights and women's engagement in political partisanship meet, the Jefferson County women's political identities and willingness to demand their own rights were forged.

Historians have long associated the rise of the organized woman's rights movement with women's involvement in the antislavery cause. Certainly abolitionists' debates over women's standing in the movement deepened the frustration of many activist women and triggered their insurgent feminism. In cities like Boston and New York, and in the so-called burned-over district towns of Rochester and Utica, it was antislavery women who were most likely to risk demanding new, more radical rights and who most openly entered a contentious political conversation as "citizens."[1] So just as historians expect to locate in religion many women's sense of collective standing, it seemed no wild leap to look for evidence of abolitionist organizing to find possible sources of a bold political stance.

But here, as in so much else, Jefferson County offers mostly silence and little evidence of the fairs, societies, pamphlets, and speakers that signal abolitionist organizing elsewhere. Although the New York City–based *National Anti-Slavery Standard* had agents in Wayne, Ontario, and Cayuga counties, none is listed in Jefferson. Only rarely did an antislavery agent venture so far north. In 1837 Alvan Stewart's eleven-day "Northern expedition" included a Sunday in Antwerp, Jefferson County. Invited by a "noble-hearted congregational minister," he addressed several audiences "on the great evils of slavery" and got a number of subscribers to the *New York Evangelist*. "I notice one thing," he wrote, "wherever the Evangelist has been the family paper, there you will find abolition." The following year the *Colored American* reported that First of August celebrations commemorating the emancipation of slaves in the British West Indies had "come and gone" in Watertown. While there were always stories of escaped slaves who had crossed into Canada from one of Jefferson County's many ports and islands, few permanent organizations seem to have emerged. But occasional reports offer evidence of antislavery organizing in Watertown as early as 1837, when a Jefferson County Antislavery Society was founded. Since the list of the 240 people present has long disappeared, I have no idea if any of the Depauville families made their way to Watertown for the January meeting.[2] A Northern New York Anti-Slavery Society formed in 1843, but it met (in the dead of winter) on Lake Champlain, more than 100 mountainous miles from Jefferson County's easternmost border. It is not even clear how much or how quickly information about that society reached Jefferson County, since the convention ordered its proceedings to be published only in the newspapers of Essex, Franklin, and Clinton counties. Clearly, Jefferson County played only a minor role in the New York State Antislavery Society, for an 1838 list of donations notes that its residents raised only $4.25, in contrast to Oneida's $1,301.37 and even Lewis's $108.80.[3]

But if there are few vestiges of a lasting organization, or of significant ties to a larger movement, there is nothing to suggest that abolitionists were a small and despised faction of their community. Recall Gerrit

Smith's complacency that abolitionist meetings met with a friendly wel-
come in the county's churches.[4] John A. Haddock recalled abolitionists as
"highly intelligent and moral, but utterly impracticable" people who,
inevitably, included some "long-haired cranks."[5] As in much of the North,
white people in Jefferson County would later recollect the antislavery
movement through the gloss of Civil War and Republican Party victories,
and virtually all postwar historians suggest that there was strong and
steady antislavery sentiment in Jefferson County. While fervent abolitionist convictions may have been viewed as extreme or divisive (Hough,
writing in 1854, avoids the topic entirely), the evidence suggests that in
the area immediately around Depauville, antislavery sentiment was
widely shared.

In this setting, too sparsely populated to have much associational life
and with churches largely out of the reach of an established orthodoxy,
antislavery activism, rights talk, and women's civic identities emerged,
and merged, in political life. The Depauville residents were, like other
New Yorkers, a political people, displaying in their partisan wars the
passions that New Englanders devoted to religious conflicts. As their 1846
petition suggests, the six memorialists understood the problems they
faced, as well as the solutions they proposed, as political concerns. Writing
from nearby Otsego County while on a speaking tour through the state,
abolitionist Abby Kelley remarked, "Bigotry and sectarianism, are not so
deeply rooted here, as in New England, but, party ties are stronger; and,
for one, I choose to contend with the latter, rather than the former." James
Edward Alexander, a Scot passing through in 1843, was somewhat taken
aback by the local form political passions could take: "At Depauville and
Brownville," he wrote, in what is virtually the only mention of Depauville
I have found outside county histories, "there were long and earnest arguments among the people assembled at the bar as to the comparative
merits of some new candidates for the offices of Senator, Sheriff, &c., and
dollar bills were freely betted. One man, in the heat of argument, most
irreverently said, 'We'll carry our election in spite of God Almighty.'"[6]
New York's political wars, with their Regencies, Hunkers, Locofocos, and
Barnburners, have long intrigued historians as much as they have confused students. After living in New York for more than a decade, one
participant called its politics "a labyrinth of wheels within wheels, . . .
understood only by the managers." In this setting, "attachment to party"
itself, not simply "class, occupation, residency, and religious denomination," may provide clues to antislavery activism, the significance attrib-

uted to political rights, and people's sense of their place in public life.[7] An analysis of partisan culture that goes beyond "election returns, legislative roll calls, and party nominations" may be especially telling in exploring women's political identities.[8]

If partisan loyalty helps define people's identities as members of a particular political community, so does the willingness of those people to abandon or break up those parties in behalf of a radical idea. Jefferson County's political culture suggests that the approach of northern New Yorkers to slavery, rather than being a distant abstraction or a religiously based crusade, was deeply bound to their parties and their state. Here the opposition to slavery and, even more, the demand for African American men's suffrage, were neighborhood struggles, conversations within residents' own state government and political parties. It is in this context, in which ideas about rights were both universal and intensely local, that we may best understand the commonsense assertion by a few women of their own political standing and of their rights as citizens of New York.

By the Fourth of July, the North Country had thawed, offering as much reason to celebrate in the open air as the anniversary of American independence itself. Although abolitionists were mindful that independence meant little to the enslaved, they hoped that "a day of Independence is coming—if we be faithful,—wherein we may rejoice for all" and so used the occasion to assert their place squarely in the nation's political culture.[9] In Jefferson County the antislavery Liberty Party held its public meeting in 1845 "in a Grove" at Perch River, several miles from Depauville. The estimated 2,000 people who gathered for the event viewed a procession and heard "thanks and prayer to God, the author of our national existence and all our *free* institutions"; a reading of the Declaration of Independence; and a speech by abolitionist William L. Chaplin of Albany. Refreshments followed. But rather than "a dinner at considerable expense, with severe care and labor, as they provided last year," the organizers had decided that the meal would take "a 'pick nic' character, and in kind and quantity such as each individual, company and neighborhood shall see fit to provide for themselves and their friends from a distance."[10] Susan Ormsby and Lydia Osborn, thirty- and forty-two-year-old sisters, and their friends and relatives may well have contributed the "severe care and labor" to the preceding year's event. They almost certainly shared in the 1845 political ritual and community potluck.

It made sense to hold the Liberty Party event at Perch River, for it was the home of Hugh Smith, one of Jefferson County's leading abolitionists. But I did not first learn of Smith or connect him to the petitioners' families through politics. Somewhere along the line, Hugh Smith became friends with a young teacher two years his junior, Bailey Ormsby, who died, unmarried, at age thirty-five. In 1848, when Bailey Ormsby's will was read, it provided, in addition to his property, an intriguing hint about his and probably his family's political sympathies. Susan Ormsby was, as we know, her brother's sole heir. She was also one of two executors. The other person Bailey appointed to the role, a responsibility implying closeness—even intimacy—and certainly trust, was Hugh Smith. Given the intensity of the antislavery commitment and its marked tendency to run in families, this relationship signaled that some or all of the Ormsbys, Osborns, Vincents, Bishops, and Williamses were likely abolitionists.[11]

Hugh Smith's face, in the only photograph I have seen of anyone with even the remotest connection to the petitioners, well-lined and topped by fluffy white hair, is rather sweet and remarkably human for a portrait of its time. In contrast to the other men whose visages appear in John Haddock's 1894 biographical compendium, he seems neither stern nor stuffy, though we are assured that he was a man of "good old Quaker stock." Like everyone else in this story, Smith is an elusive character. He left no published writings and makes no appearance in political accounts. Only Haddock mentions that Hugh Smith was "well known for his decided stand for the abolition of slavery, for temperance and for morality."[12]

Like the families of Lydia, Susan, Hiram, and Bailey Ormsby and the others, Hugh Smith's parents and their seven children arrived in Jefferson County (from Bucks County, Pennsylvania) in 1820. In 1836 Hugh moved to Perch River, a village in Brownville, where he married Charlotte Spicer, the daughter of longtime resident Silas Spicer. Smith and his brother-in-law, Henry, would collaborate in a business "known throughout the northern part of the county, being ever a synonym for honesty and fair dealing." By 1860 the two men lived with their wives, children, boarders, and servants in adjoining and quite prosperous households; reflecting both Smith's position and the Spicers' long-standing commitment to girls' education, Hugh and Charlotte's twenty-year-old daughter, Hannah, still attended school.[13]

But the two families shared more than a common economic interest. Silas Spicer was known as an "active and persistent Abolitionist," and between them the men made Perch River noted locally as a center for reform. Joining antislavery with partisan affairs, they "formed a coterie which was hard to withstand when they pulled together at the polls upon political questions." They served together frequently on countywide Liberty Party committees, including the one that planned the Fourth of July meeting. In addition, Spicer ran on the Liberty Party ticket for state assembly in 1843, and Smith ran for Congress three years later, garnering 763 votes.[14] Like many Quakers and abolitionists, Hugh Smith was less ambitious to gain political office than he was simply political, "a man who took an active and healthy interest in all the political questions of the day." Reflecting, or deepening, his interests in the larger world, Smith served as Perch River's postmaster for several decades. But however respectable they were in their communities, the men took risks for their convictions. Making use of Smith's Bucks County connections, they likely contributed to Perch River's reputation as a "regular depot upon the underground railroad which conveyed escaping slaves to Canada."[15]

If a friendship with Hugh Smith first suggested that the petitioners' families shared his antislavery commitments, other evidence gradually materialized. In February 1844 a "general meeting of the inhabitants of the Town of Clayton" was held in Depauville. Appalled that the United States was about to "present ourselves before the civilized world in the revolting attitude of waging a bloody and protracted war with Christian nations" in behalf of slavery, the meeting opposed the annexation of Texas for "perpetuating the slave power" and referred ominously to the "cup of blood which as a nation we have been so long filling up." No list exists of those who attended this meeting and who "amply discussed" the resolutions before adopting them unanimously. The secretary, however, was Bailey Ormsby.[16] In the fall of 1845 both the *Liberty Press* and the *Albany Patriot* listed the Liberty Party's candidates for statewide and local office and urged voters to make "all proper preparations for the election." In Jefferson County, among the third party candidates for assembly was Joseph Osborne [*sic*] of Depauville.[17] The very few petitions that exist from Jefferson County confirm that the ties among these families included shared antislavery sympathies. When Joseph Osborn signed one in 1850, he did so with his brother Thomas; his brother-in-law Hiram Ormsby; Hiram and Amy's twenty-five-year-old son, Jay; and Abraham Vincent.[18] A handwritten list of Liberty Party subscribers from the late 1840s includes nine names from Jefferson County; H. Smith of Perch River had given $2.00 to the paper, and J. Osborn had given $1.00.[19] This evidence that the Liberty papers were actually subscribed to and read in the Osborn household should not, by now, come as a surprise. After all, the

"Disfranchised" letter writer from Jefferson County had chosen to endorse woman suffrage in the pages of a Liberty Party paper. The ties between Liberty Party activism and woman's rights made visible in the world of partisan politics a conversation that had long been going on in some Jefferson County homes. It was a conversation shaped by rights and obligations that were defined and established by government itself.

Establishing respect for government, not to mention party, was no easy task for those who ruled Jefferson County. Certainly this was not for lack of trying, for local governments set about early to provide structure to life in the North Country. Town officials established penalties for various misdeeds, many of which involved the pernicious Canada thistle, as ornery as their constituents. Towns also offered bounties for killing wolves, crows, and foxes while optimistically electing officers to positions such as "fence viewers" and "deer reeves" as well as overseers of the poor and commissioners of highways.[20] But as with the squatters of Penet's Square, it took some effort to rein in the region as a whole. Only in the most abstract sense was it under the rule of the federal or state governments by the time the Depauville families arrived.

Indeed, an undercurrent of unruliness wafts through stories of Jefferson County's relationship to political authority from its earliest days. Take the embargo of 1808. The restriction on trade with Canada "struck a deathblow to northern New York." American trade and shipping were hurt, farmers lost customers, and Britain continued to attack American ships and sailors. Opposition to the party of Jefferson rose as "the conditions soon grew intolerable."[21] But in the new and sparsely settled county named for Jefferson himself, the situation "naturally led to a spirit of evasion of the laws" as smuggling became commonplace and beating government enforcers was a source of pride. Sitting on the border of a foreign country turned out to be good business for people who lived a great distance from, and who held a relaxed attitude toward, any effective legal authorities. Hart Massey of Watertown, responsible for enforcing the embargo, was helpless, for local farmers "appear[ed] determined to evade the laws at the risk of their lives." Even the weather that winter seemed to conspire against the law's enforcement: "Nature," Massey wailed, "has furnished the smugglers with the firmest ice that was ever known on this frontier."[22] Conflicting loyalties and ironic situations resulted from widespread "political rancor and a practical opposition to a law which they declared unconstitutional and void."[23] Jefferson County residents would recall such resistance with pride; the road from near Brownville to French Creek was called, locally, the "Embargo road."[24] Even the county's local elites seem to have defied the pattern of their class when it came to politics. Like the Federalist landed gentry, they inhabited mansions, donated land for public buildings, and held mortgages and slaves, but Jefferson County's wealthiest men had French ties and French sympathies that likely extended to their partisan loyalties.[25] In partisanship as in religion, it seems, orthodoxy did not exercise much of a grip on Jefferson County residents.

Discontent with government did not mean that people dismissed its powers or disdained its functions. After all, politics in upstate New York began with the problem of getting people and things (cows, wheat, cheese, shoes, cloth, newspapers, and mail) from one place to another, matters of extreme urgency in the far north. Recall the local interest generated and the opportunities offered by the legislature's decision to build the state road. What historians have labeled the Transportation Revolution affected the relationships of women and men to their land, their ability to purchase an expanding array of goods, and their connections to the larger world, as well as their relationships with large landowners and elected officials. Everyone wanted a route—by road, water, or rail—from a particular small farm to a bustling market town to a distant market. For all American farmers talked about small government, everyone looked to the state to help, both in deciding where the routes should go and in establishing private charters that would build them. After all, every pitched political battle in Albany about roads and canals had enormous ramifications, unsettling economies, ending political careers, and launching and erasing both towns and fortunes overnight.

Having experienced the disastrous effect of the Erie Canal (which "signalled," in one historian's words, "a five-hundred-mile funeral procession" for the county's economic hopes),[26] Jefferson County residents frantically sought to benefit from another waterway. Debates in the state legislature over locating, building, funding, and completing smaller canals sustained intense passions in local politics. In 1834 the legislature of New York authorized a study of the feasibility of building a Black River canal, and work began two years later. Suspended several times, the canal project remained a subject of partisan dispute in the mid-1840s.[27] Although devoutly opposed in theory to funding internal improvements, the Democratic *Jeffersonian* indignantly denied that its party had thwarted this one; at the same time, the paper conjured up a community where interest in such political matters was widespread. "The facts are," asserted the writer, "the federalists have a majority in both branches of the legislature . . . and can pass any bill they please. They could have passed that extending the Black River Canal, . . . as every man, woman and child in this section of the state knows."[28] A trickle of bitterness leaks from the record, as when an 1841 convention of towns offered the by-then weak card of a possible war with Canada and urged politicians to "be impelled by patriotic motives, to advocate the construction of a canal through Jefferson county."[29] A full decade later, when the Watertown and Rome railroad opened about a dozen new miles, there was pathos in the *Northern New-York Journal's* announcement that "another link was added to the great chain that connects Jefferson county *with the world.*"[30]

In this setting, politics was not only local but inescapable, a ubiquitous point of reference and source of interest. Even as they built their houses and cleared their first acres, the Ormsby, Osborn, O'Connor, and Vincent men must have been listening to the conversations then under way in Albany and known that decisions made there would shape their own relationship to the state government under which they lived. In the summer of 1821, when a constitutional convention met in Albany, debates over suffrage, independence, and sovereignty were close to home to people with ambiguous claims on their land who were still living in what was essentially a wilderness.[31] Some of them had been born in Vermont, the only state to grant the vote to every man regardless of his ownership of property or ability to pay taxes, and although they had long ago left the Green Mountain state, they surely retained some sense of political entitlement.[32] Just as surely these men talked about whether a man's vote attached to property or to adulthood, for if "the question of who had the vote transfixed mid-century Americans," the Depauville farmers were likely no exception.[33] When they learned that under the new constitution virtually every adult white male citizen would be permitted to vote, they understood that this gave them and their sons a greater voice in political life. I am certain that they approved the change. By the time the state census taker came around four years later, all the men in these households were recorded as eligible to vote. As they settled new farms and acquired new rights, it must have seemed quite literally a fresh start for these newly settled upstate New Yorkers, signers of a new social compact.

Perhaps the Depauville farmers viewed the expansion of suffrage as inevitable, a sign of their own and their state's inexorable progress. Indeed, Federalists who opposed the new rules quickly came to seem irrele-

vant, even quaint. Confronted with the proposal that men without property be allowed to vote, Chancellor James Kent warned darkly that the
1821 convention stood "on the brink of fate, on the very edge of a preci-
pice." After all, "there is a constant tendency in the poor to covet and to
share the plunder of the rich," and "the individual who contributes only
one cent to the common stock ought not to have the same power and
influence in directing the property concerns of the partnership as he who
contributes his thousands."[34] But if the 1821 constitutional convention
signaled the demise of an older political culture, it nevertheless highlights
how each political party portrayed membership in the political community in a language of exclusion and fear, a vocabulary that, as we have
seen, continued to shape the politics of a later time.

New York's leading partisans declared that their parties' differences
were clear and dramatic. Democrats, for instance, depicted their positions
on property, suffrage, and independence as exemplifying the "PEOPLE
against a purse proud overbearing ARISTOCRACY." The commitment to
expanding the suffrage ("the birth-right of every free citizen") soon became liberalism's rallying cry.[35] These supporters of Jacksonian democracy, who dominated upstate New York, eagerly labeled their opponents
"conservatives," tarring them, with some truth, as elites who scorned their
own working-class, urban, and Catholic constituents. But Jacksonians
drew heavily on the rhetoric of exclusion as well. At the 1821 constitutional convention, Martin Van Buren himself insisted that only "house-
holders" should vote and adamantly opposed the "dangerous and alarm-
ing tendency" of a "wholly unrestricted suffrage." It was his "radicals,"
openly racist and exclusionary, who upheld the property limitation on
black male suffrage, while Federalists and, later, Whigs more consistently
advocated for the rights of African American men. By the criterion of
expanding suffrage to the male part of "the people," Van Buren Democrats "had to be dragged, kicking and screaming, into the politically
liberal nineteenth century." No wonder the party's positions were described thus: "Too vague to be an ideological system, too often compromised to serve as official doctrine, and too close to the opposition's to be
precise points of partisan dogma, these attitudes served more as movable
fences than as solid barriers."[36]

I do not mean to suggest that the Democratic Party, which would come
to dominate North Country elections, did not believe in something. Except when they were advocating for improvements on nearby roads and
ports, Democrats claimed that governments should leave people and peo-

ple's business alone. Since a settled society required some rules, they supported a local authority over a distant one, a defense of local control that struck a chord with upstate New Yorkers' own sense of their place in the state, the nation, and probably the world. As some historians have suggested, well after the Revolution, New Yorkers thought of themselves as citizens of New York rather than of the United States.[37] In this setting even Albany seemed a distant establishment, and one not overly sympathetic to Jefferson County's distress.

But if one idea characterized the antebellum Democratic Party it was that of party discipline and loyalty to party leaders. Indeed, many people referred to the Democratic Party itself as a family or, in Van Buren's telling phrase, "a political brotherhood."[38] On every issue of dispute between the major parties, from funding for internal improvements to tariffs to antislavery, Democratic partisans sought to enforce party conformity in the face of real and growing differences among themselves. When those differences emerged in public, they were denounced as betrayal or treason, far worse than simple differences of policy. Thus, when New York's Democratic governor William C. Bouck called in 1843 for funds to complete the Black River and Genesee Valley canals, Democrats, who opposed spending public money on internal improvements, expressed horror at his "open profligacy" and warned of "a ruinous schism in our ranks." Such insistence on unity only increased partisan disarray, for many communities *wanted* such improvements in their own backyards. A few Democrats, notably Michael Hoffman of Herkimer County, recognized that money put into a local project heightened Whig support in that neighborhood and proposed that the issue of spending be laid in the voters' laps. It was Hoffman who, beginning in 1843, led the charge for a constitutional convention that would leave it to voters to revise the state's basic laws.[39]

The issue of slavery and the crisis caused by the move to annex Texas drove a further wedge into the Democratic effort to present a unified front. In upstate New York in the early 1840s, as religious passions along the Erie Canal swept up many New Yorkers in abolition fever, opposition to slavery dramatically broke up and reshaped the party with the Barnburner-Hunker schism. For those whose primary loyalty was to the party establishment, this was nothing short of disastrous: "Party organization has been disregarded," wailed the *Jefferson County Democrat* in 1846, "party ties sundered, and political principles abandoned, at the bidding of faction, and under the promptings of individual feelings and personal malice." Faced with a genuine difference over slavery, its expansion onto free soil, and black men's political rights, Democratic stalwarts could see only treason and disgrace: "We envy not the traitor to the democracy," the paper warned. "Abandoned by his former friends, and leagued with a broken down and unprincipled minority of federalists, . . . the apostate democrat is certainly an object of pity. . . . As a man maketh his bed, so let him lie."[40]

Historians have long looked to the Whig Party for the evangelical, moralizing brand of activism that they associate with the abolitionist movement, as well as movements for temperance, moral reform, and the establishment of Sunday schools. The Democratic Party, with its urban immigrant base, its hostility to religiously based social movements, and its racist rhetoric, was not, most have agreed, sympathetic to the abolitionist cause. Nevertheless, the tide that pulled growing numbers of northerners into the antislavery cause drew Democrats as well. Pennsylvania congressman David Wilmot, who would introduce the proviso that carried his name and so launch the movement against slavery's expansion onto free soil, was, after all, a Democrat. If that tide watered down the absolutism of early abolition, it also left a shattered party system in its wake.[41]

Maintaining party discipline was not, however, a universally held principle. Among rural Democrats such as those who populated Jefferson County, the contradictions between embracing both antislavery and the party of Jackson may not have seemed too troubling to manage. For a few urban Democrats as well, the principles of the Democracy—among them the commitment to allowing people to act without fear of government intrusion—jarred with the growing noise from those who opposed abolitionists' right to speak and petition. William Leggett, editor of the *New York Evening Post*, though hostile to "the whole scheme of immediate emancipation," was burdened with an unusual ability to discern his own and his party's inconsistencies. An advocate of states' rights, he viewed southern newspapers' offer of a reward for the capture of abolitionist Arthur Tappan as an insult to his own state and warned, "Such a proceeding would make abolitionists of our whole two million of inhabitants."[42] He wished to defend "the political rights of the south" but was furious at the southern defense of such "a deplorable evil and a curse" as a positive good. "Slavery no evil!" he fumed. "Has it come to this, that the foulest stigma on our national escutcheon, which no true-hearted freeman could ever contemplate without sorrow in his heart and a blush upon his cheek, has got to be viewed by the people of the south as no stain on the

American character?"[43] By January 1837, frustrated by the "paltry spirit" expressed by his own party, Leggett concluded, *"We are an Abolitionist."*[44] Earlier than many New York Democrats, Leggett abandoned his party's leaders once he was convinced that "every American who, in any way, authorizes or countenances slavery, is derelict to his duty as a christian, a patriot, and a man."[45] But his personal transformation presaged what lay in store for the Democratic Party in the North, where antislavery sentiment encouraged widespread rethinking of political loyalties.

Enough antislavery, free-soil, and antisouthern feeling had emerged by the 1840s in northern New York to establish the Democratic Party there as strongly Barnburner, or Free Soil. Indeed, the national disarray in which the party would soon find itself was due largely to upstate New Yorkers, who proved to be particularly contentious; it was these Barnburner Democrats whom Walt Whitman called "the Undaunted Democracy."[46] "THE REBELLION SPREADS!" shouted the antislavery *North Star* in 1848, welcoming several newspapers, including the Watertown *Democratic Union*, to the Free Soil side. In 1849 a Democratic correspondent to the Liberty Party's *National Era* wrote from Watertown that he had "with very little effort" gotten fourteen new subscribers to the paper —"just such readers as your paper ought to have," he boasted, "genuine 'New York Barnburners,'" adding cryptically, "with the exception of one, with whose name you are doubtless familiar." The writer went on: "To the electors of that region belongs the honor of having given the proudest vote of any portion of the nation, in favor of the great principles of Freedom and Jeffersonian Democracy." Certainly such Whig organs as the *Northern State Journal* relished their opponents' disarray, congratulating the "'unterrified' democracy of the city of New York" for withstanding "the truckling of the Hunker delegates." When Martin Van Buren reluctantly left his party in 1848 to head the newly founded Free Soil ticket, he exemplified northern New Yorkers' growing unease about the Democratic Party's position on the expansion of slavery.[47] Like so many others, he understood that politics had been thoroughly shaken by antislavery activism, as growing numbers of abolitionists had embraced the movement's turn to electoral politics, and even Democrats could no longer pretend that the question of slavery did not concern them.

I am not suggesting, of course, that the impact of the antislavery movement was felt only in the offices of party officials or editors, far less that it appealed only to Democrats. Rather, I hope to confront historians' assumption that a conversation about woman's rights took place only outside partisan life, in the ultraist, nonpartisan wing of antislavery, or, conversely, that those who were involved in the Democratic Party embraced uniformly patriarchal views. In upstate New York, partisan politics not only connected people's farms literally "with the world" but offered them a way to belong to their communities, to express their interests, and to have their views heard. Surely many women (and men) shared the irritation expressed by Susan that men talked too much of "politics, and other everlasting subjects about which they never could come to any satisfactory conclusion."[48] But at a time when questions of representation and suffrage were hotly debated, when Americans expressed a growing and passionate interest in electoral politics, and when the definition of full citizenship was focused more closely on the vote itself, women's identification as full participants in political life takes on special significance.

It is where party loyalties are formed, not only where they end up at the ballot box, that we might get a more textured sense of the political culture in which people live, learn, and communicate. As Jean Baker has pointed out, party loyalties are learned: "No one," she is certain, "was ever born a Democrat."[49] While much advice literature called on mothers to teach their children what were seen as universal themes of good citizenship—including Christianity, patriotism, obedience to authority, and a commitment to the "common good"—party loyalty, too, was preached and practiced in family settings and was surely the subject of newspaper reading, leisure time discussion, and election year debate. Nowhere was this more the case than in upstate New York, where "every man, woman and child" was conversant in political matters.[50]

This was the political culture that shaped a few Depauville women, all of whom were early settlers on their land, came from property-owning families, and were likely sympathetic to antislavery. These women did not see themselves as outsiders to the political system or the political traditions that shaped their community. They would not frame their demand for equal rights in the language of separate spheres, nonresistance, or evangelical religion. They did not address their government as members of families or as subjects of households ruled by men. To these women, it was not a movement, their fellow reformers, their fathers and husbands, orthodox ministers, or the expectations placed on them by domesticity that had excluded or marginalized them or that had failed to "declare and enforce those [rights] which originally existed." Rather, it was "the present government of this state" that had "widely departed from the true democratic principles upon which all just governments must be based."

Timing, of course, played a role in shaping these women's sense of belonging as well as their political principles. Here, as in so much else, Jefferson County's remoteness helped define their community's place in the political world. By the time Jefferson County was well settled and farm women had time to engage in political activities, the early days of abolitionist passion and schism had passed and support for antislavery was nearly respectable, not to say universal, throughout much of the North. Indeed, by 1855, when the town of Adams hosted a "grand Anti-Slavery Jubilee" to commemorate the First of August, half-fare train tickets on the Watertown-Rome line were available, a tradition that had been established for state agricultural fairs years earlier. Even then, the region seemed out of the way to "many of the old 'Radicals' from all parts of the country" who were present. The widely traveled Frederick Douglass bemusedly (and in dialect) described the ignorance of the "uninitiated": "One old man said to the writer, 'what is the matter? . . . Some of your great folks birthday you are goin to keep I s'pose?' . . . After narrating the history of the West India Emancipation, he remarked, 'That's news to me, living away back in the country, I'n never found that out. Go it! I'll help you.' "[51]

Abolitionism was most visible and most pervasive in far upstate New York in the region's vibrant and contentious political life. This was aided, of course, by the arrival of the Liberty Party in 1840, which determined to draw antislavery voters to an electoral strategy even as it signaled the emergence of antislavery thought itself in partisan life. The party's reputation has suffered ever since at the hands of historians of both abolitionism and politics as well as historians of women. To defenders of Garrisonian tactics of moral suasion, an electoral strategy for ending slavery seemed a capitulation to partisan compromise, a defeat to those who had concluded that the Constitution sanctioned slavery—and who believed of their former allies that "Politics have made [them] mad."[52] For political historians, the Liberty Party simply failed, since it never gained enough votes to be more than a spoiler and was more significant in breaking up parties than in garnering office.[53] Women's historians have tended to dismiss the party as one concerned entirely with the activities of men, among them the orthodox ministers who sought to bar women from full participation in abolition. We have, by and large, assumed that advocates of woman's rights emerged only from the Garrisonian wing of the movement. Elizabeth Cady Stanton implicitly recognized the quandary. As a supporter of women's full rights in the movement, Stanton "found [herself] in full accord with the other ladies." Yet, like her husband, she confessed, "I am in favour of political action, & the organization of a third party," and she found herself awkwardly at odds with many of the women in antislavery's inner circle.[54]

But far from the sectarian battlefields of Boston and New York City, in places where there were simply too few people to indulge in schism and too little orthodoxy to enforce it, abolitionism and partisan politics had long been fused. As early as 1837, several years before the Liberty Party would make electoral politics central to the movement's goals, Jefferson County abolitionists had resolved "that we will, in right of citizenship, petition the State Legislature, to extend to the colored population of this State, equally with the white, the privileges of trial by jury, and of suffrage."[55] Although most men in the county continued to vote Democratic, the Liberty Party's presence was strong.[56] In 1840 Gerrit Smith gained 59 Jefferson County votes (far fewer than Oneida's 351 but more than the 37 in Lewis) for his Liberty Party ticket for governor against the antislavery Whig, William Seward. Perley G. Keyes gathered 205 Jefferson County votes in his bid for state senate the following year on the "Abolitionist ticket."[57] While no Jefferson County delegation seems to have attended the Liberty Party convention in 1843, in 1844 the county remained among the top ten Liberty Party supporters in the state.[58]

The nearer we look to the Depauville women's own households, the more striking the Liberty Party's strength. In 1846 several hundred men voted for Liberty Party delegates to the constitutional convention about to assemble in Albany. Fifty-five men from Clayton—more than from any other town—gave their votes to Hugh Smith, George W. Knowlton, and Aaron W. Porter.[59] More than 100 Clayton men voted that November for the Liberty Party candidate for Congress, Hugh Smith (763 ballots were cast for him countywide). Magnifying this further reveals still more local divisions and, relatedly, solidarity, for the political differences between Clayton's first and second electoral districts were profound. The first district, encompassing the homes of all the petitioners' families, was a veritable bastion of antislavery feeling where 88 men voted for Hugh Smith that year. Only 17 men in the second district followed suit. A similar pattern would emerge that fall in the referendum over granting equal suffrage to black men. In the first electoral district 155 men (an astonishing 76 percent of those who voted) supported "equal suffrage to colored persons," while 50 did not. In the adjacent second district, the vote was 46 to 141 against, a 25 percent positive vote that was well below the county as a whole, where 38 percent of voters endorsed political rights for African American men.[60]

Partisan passions ran high in upstate New York, but sorting out their meaning on an individual or community level is far more complicated. I cannot say for certain how Abraham Vincent or Hiram Ormsby voted in 1846. Still, such a strong third party presence indicates both where a voter stood on a particular issue and that he was willing, usually accompanied by some neighbors and friends, to abandon his former partisan ties and, perhaps, embrace controversial ideas. While the Liberty Party was strongest in abolitionist Gerrit Smith's home county of Madison, in few places was its presence as formidable as in the Depauville neighborhood in which the petitioners' families lived. The Ormsbys, Osborns, Vincents, and Bishops were literally surrounded by an abolitionist community of which they were very much a part.

There is very little evidence of the former political loyalties of these particular families. The dominance of the Democratic Party, the nature of Jefferson County, and the striking antislavery voting strength in Clayton, however, suggest that at least some of them were rebellious Democrats, committed to antislavery as well as to many of the tenets of their former party. The strength of Freewill Baptists in the area and among the petitioners' families further supports this view, since members of this denomination commonly "abandoned their traditional Democratic political allegiances" to support political antislavery. Certainly Jefferson County fits Jonathan Earle's description of likely free-soil strongholds as "poorer, farther from the mainlines of immigration and transportation, . . . [with] fewer ties to the revivals of the Second Great Awakening and . . . more solidly Democratic." Free-soil politics, Earle asserts, carried great appeal in what he aptly dubs the "passed-over district" of upstate New York.[61]

Liberty Party supporters certainly counted adherents of both major political parties among their friends and neighbors. Silas Spicer, for one, had been a Whig before he became a prominent Liberty Party activist. Joseph Osborn probably had been, too, since before becoming a Liberty man he had been "strongly prejudiced in favor of a Tariff," and it was the Whigs who upheld "the gospel of protection."[62] But their former neighbor Alpheus S. Greene was a faithful Democrat who had been "prominently identified with Judge Perley Keyes in the old 'Watertown Regency,'" and perhaps some had voted for him.[63] Although Judge Keyes died in 1834, a few years later a Perley G. Keyes was listed as an abolitionist and, by the 1840s, a local Liberty Party activist, serving on an 1845 committee alongside Hugh Smith.[64] As the rise of the Liberty Party shows, the Democratic Party may have ruled much of the time, but it was unable to exercise much control over the upstate political conversations and partisan loyalties that infused daily life.

Whatever the timing of Jefferson County's abolitionism and its entrance into local partisan battles, the years 1845 and 1846 were dramatic ones. By the mid-1840s, talk of politics and partisan dissent was everywhere, as people met to discuss the rights of African American men, property rights, and the basic laws of New York. As the Liberty Party struggled over its own principles, it became a forum for a conversation about women's right to full membership in the party and the state. While the Liberty Party might have been founded with an "extremely limited . . . agenda for gender reform" and recognized women's political roles only in "the context of increasing social pressure to redefine women's . . . rights" in the late 1840s, some evidence suggests that sympathy for woman's rights was present all along.[65] In 1839, in the heat of antislavery schism, Appleton Howe wrote privately to Amos A. Phelps about the offer to serve as a vice president of a "new organization," the Massachusetts Abolition Society. Appleton "regret[ted] exceedingly that it should be thought important or expedient to exclude Ladies from the business meetings of the Society. This to me does not seem *fair* or equal. . . . It . . . savours a little too much of that *spirit* which it is the object of the Society to overthrow. . . . [It] argues more aristocracy of feeling than is consistent with what I consider Orthodox in Abolition. It is a species of Gag law unworthy of those whose object is to make all men free. . . . These are my views in brief," Howe concluded. But since he was convinced of the importance of an antislavery party, he declared, "I shall not make these objections paramount."[66]

Explicit defenses of equal rights for women surfaced only rarely in the Liberty Party press. More evident was a widespread tolerance of women's active participation in political antislavery—and little of the outrage and hysteria that characterized the abolitionist schism only a few years before. Two months before the woman's rights meeting at Seneca Falls, the Liberty League convention met in Buffalo to choose a slate of candidates for president and vice president of the United States. Among those not chosen was Lucretia Mott, who received five votes for the vice presidential slot. "As the ladies present . . . were invited to vote," explained the writer, "the door was of course considered open by some for the nomination of a female Vice President." The reporter added, apparently without irony, that "if the door of the Constitution had been equally open, . . . she might have had an unanimous vote, as there is not the slightest doubt that she would honor the office quite as much as any man who ever filled it."[67] Several years later, the New York Liberty Party included on its slate for the party's state executive committee Mrs. Laura Rice of Madison County and Mrs. Douglass Williams of Erie. Among the resolutions passed by that convention was the following: "That in the eye of true civil government, woman is the equal of man, and her rights identical with his rights." By the time Antoinette Brown addressed the Liberty Party convention in 1853, Frederick Douglass could describe her as "a member of the Liberty Party, [who] gives it the aid of her presence and counsel, serves on its committee, and really means what she says, when she demands the right to vote." "With her," Douglass asserted, "the right to vote is no abstraction, a right to be asserted not exercised."[68]

When open discussions of woman's rights do appear, they offer yet another glimpse into a household whose conversations we first imagined upon reading the 1846 petition. In October 1845 Joseph Osborn of Depauville wrote the *Albany Patriot* what was, as far as I know, his only letter to a newspaper. In it he raised several points about William Goodell's Port Byron speech on the Liberty Party's "exalted 'one-idea,' (the equality and brotherhood of all mankind)." "By the bye," Osborn observed mildly in conclusion, "friend Goodell has neglected to present in the Address some important matters that genuine republicanism must recognize." Prominent among these was "the enfranchisement of females." "The public mind at present may not be prepared to consider this subject," he admitted, "but when the great *one idea* of the Liberty party is understood and *properly appreciated*, the equality of mankind will mean something more than a mere rhetorical flourish." One day, Osborn was sure, "the right of the governed to choose their governors will be acknowledged."[69]

Since this appeal came on the heels of the letter by "One of the Disfranchised" two months earlier and shared that writer's disappointment that Goodell had "neglected" to endorse women's right to vote, readers of the *Patriot* may have wondered what was happening in the far north of their state. In any case, the editors apparently felt pressed to discuss the subject and so reprinted an article from the *National Press*. It is a masterpiece of equivocation. Noting that delegates to the upcoming constitutional convention "will be chosen solely by men, and the other sex will have, neither directly nor indirectly, any voice in the selection of delegates," the article acknowledged that women "are strictly an unrepresented class." "We are not now complaining of this exclusion," the writer backtracked hurriedly. "We are not now urging for their admission, in some form, to a direct influence over public affairs." Still, the writer waffled again, "it would not do to say, that because women never have had any share in our public affairs, therefore they never are to have." "Observe that we are here simply stating matters of fact," continued the author nervously, "without claiming that the condition of things . . . is necessarily wrong. But we may say, and perhaps without fear of contradiction, that it is a state of things, the right and necessity of which ought not to be taken for granted."[70] Perhaps they were pleased to see this discussion take place, but the Ormsby, Osborn, and Vincent women must have been disgusted by the article's vacillating and its petulant "fear of contradiction." Still, discussion was precisely what letters such as Joseph Osborn's and petitions such as that signed by six women of Jefferson County would guarantee.

I wish I could have glimpsed Susan Ormsby's and Lydia Osborn's faces as they read the article in the *Patriot*. But it is not difficult to imagine the talk in these Depauville farmhouses during the months leading up to the 1846 convention. These were politically alert and engaged people, friends and relatives who had spent many hours discussing the happenings of the day, individuals whose very lives and farms had been shaped directly by the political compact with which they struggled. One of the men had run for local office on a third party ticket, something he would have been unlikely to do without the support and sympathy of his wife, brothers, and friends. Surely some of the women had helped with campaigns, cooked for Liberty Party outings, and encouraged brothers and neighbors to vote their antislavery consciences. They had participated in partisan battles, and if none of them had actually written as "One of the Disfranchised," they had certainly read the letter. I have no doubt that Joseph Osborn had the encouragement of his wife and his sister-in-law when he decided to support woman suffrage in a letter about other partisan concerns.

For several years the fervor and fury that New Yorkers devoted to politics had centered on whether to hold a state constitutional convention, and newspapers were abuzz with the idea. That convention would provide an opportunity for New Yorkers to talk publicly about some of the state's, and these households', most burning concerns: suffrage for black men, property rights for married women, the rights of tenants, the financing of roads and canals, and the protections against state debt. Susan Ormsby and Lydia Osborn, sisters who shared daily chores, family crises, and political conversation, must have read the plans and proceedings of the convention with great interest, and no doubt they exchanged views. Just as their father, Elias, must have known when an earlier convention expanded voting rights to the state's white men, and as African American New Yorkers were asserting in their own convention resolutions, these women understood that a constitutional convention opened a rare opportunity for debate. The denial to "the female portion of community the right of suffrage and any participation in forming the government and laws under which they live" fell within the "province of civil government," the women knew. This "just cause of complaint" could only be addressed there as well. As members of a particular political community —one composed of people who did not expect to win an election but who nevertheless believed in the promise of republican government—they knew that discussion propelled an unpopular idea. One of them must have said first what others were thinking: that since other people's political rights were going to be discussed, it was high time to demand their own.

chapter six

The Convention

"modifying the present Constitution of this State"

On Saturday, August 8, 1846, six women from Jefferson County wrote and signed a petition to demand that their state recognize their full and equal rights as citizens. Like many of their neighbors, they had surely been following the constitutional convention closely in the newspapers. Although the antislavery *Albany Patriot* complained about the convention's slow progress and scoffed that the delegates (so many of them "*cute* lawyers") "looked hot and sweltering—oppressed by heavy dinners and the dignities of public station," the paper nevertheless kept a reporter on hand.[1] The Osborn household received both the *Patriot* and the *Liberty Press*, and by early August, with the delegates at work for more than two months and no end in sight, Lydia, Joseph, Susan, Bailey, and their friends may well have shared the papers' skepticism that the convention would result in so much "wordy, frothy talk."[2]

When they sat down to write their petition, the women must have felt confident that they would get someone to submit it to the convention. But it is hard to know with what blend of reluctance, sympathy, and sense of duty Alpheus S. Greene agreed to present the petition for women's full rights to his colleagues, many of whom, he must have known, would laugh. ("What a time for courting, love matches, etc., an election will be when that petition succeeds," hooted the reporter for the *New-York Daily Tribune*.)[3] There is nothing in the record to suggest whether or how much Greene minded being teased. Yet the women's decision to ask Alpheus Greene to present their petition and his agreeing to do so were probably made on the basis of personal, not political, ties. Of the three delegates from Jefferson County, Greene was, as far as I can tell, the only one they knew. He was a part of the petitioners' world, and if he did not support their claims, he would at least have acknowledged their right to enter the conversation.

In 1846 Alpheus S. Greene was an unmarried physician in his late fifties.[4] Like the women whose petition he presented—indeed, like nearly all of his constituents—Greene had migrated to Jefferson County from someplace else. His own path was becoming well traveled. Born in Rhode Island, Greene moved with his parents and siblings to Newport, a town bordering Russia in Herkimer County, before uprooting once again and heading north. In 1817 he purchased some eighty-two acres of land on Perch River in Brownville; he added fifty-seven more in 1828 and apparently settled down.[5] Whether he had known the Ormsbys or Osborns prior to his move I do not know, but in 1820 he lived two households down from Phineas Osborn. Greene practiced medicine in Brownville for more than a decade, through the time that Phineas's son Joseph married Lydia Ormsby and others of the Depauville families grew up, bore children, and settled down. He may well have been present at their births and deaths; he surely knew them.

Although Alpheus Greene was a well-respected country doctor (he had been elected to the Jefferson County Medical Society in 1817), his life soon took on a more public character.[6] In 1823 he became a judge of the common pleas court and in 1826 and 1828 was elected to the New York Assembly. Only in 1829, when he accepted the appointment of postmaster in Watertown, did he move to that city, although he may have continued to own and rent out his Brownville land. He served as postmaster for more than a decade and participated actively in Democratic Party politics. He was also one of three signatories to an 1841 appeal by the Watertown Temperance Society for an alcohol-free celebration of the Fourth of July, the second time this "novel experiment" was tried.[7] Six years later Greene served as the president of the Jefferson County Temperance Society, a group that apparently met with some local success, reporting that the "taverns in Depauville had discontinued the sale of spirits" and that Clayton's voters were "against license, probably four to one."[8] In addition to serving on various public boards, Greene, like the members of his family who remained in Brownville, was a "zealous and active member of the Baptist church."[9]

As postmaster, sitting in the basement of the American Hotel on the corner of Washington and Arsenal streets in Watertown, Greene was literally in the center of the action. No doubt he heard a great deal of local news and opinion; as the local agent for various newspapers, he would have been well informed about debates taking place in the world of agricultural reform, religious organizations, and state and national politics. Indeed, his arrival in Watertown coincided with an intense campaign against operating the U.S. post office on Sunday. Along the Erie Canal, a competing stagecoach line, vowing to observe the Christian Sabbath, began operation that year only to fail soon after. Watertown's post office opened on Sunday for one hour in the early morning, in the middle of the day, and in the late afternoon.[10]

For a man with so public a career, Alpheus Greene left little in the historical record to signal his opinions on the important issues of the day. Still, what evidence there is suggests that he was a fellow of moderate views. As a Democrat in the Jackson years, he was surely uncomfortable with efforts to impose religious sanctions on public institutions and individual behavior. His temperance activism, for example, is tinged with unease. The 1841 appeal for a dry Fourth of July celebration promised to "do nothing intentionally to mar the happiness or infringe the liberty of those who prefer ancient customs," since "to such customs they have formerly paid their vows."[11] A party loyalist, Greene likely identified with Democrat Hiram P. Hastings's opposition to any effort "to coerce temperance by law." "I do not wish to purchase spirits or wine at the taverns or groceries," wrote Hastings, "but others differ from me in this respect, and as long as they do no wrong, I have no right, and the public have no right, to prohibit the sale of either to them."[12] Whatever his own political convictions, Greene's election to the constitutional convention reflected the high regard in which he was held as a doctor, a Baptist, a member of the Democratic Party, and a public servant. It must have been with a sense of pride and purpose that he headed for the state's capital and took seat number twenty-nine in the second row of the assembly chamber.

The constitutional convention that opened in Albany in June 1846 was a four-month spectacle: part philosophizing, part policymaking, and part theater. Throughout the land, men were gathering to revise state constitutions, adapting the governments established a generation earlier to the economic changes and legal reworkings that had occurred in the years since.[13] After the War of 1812 and the Panic of 1819, Massachusetts (1820), New York (1821), and Virginia (1829–30) initiated comprehensive reconsiderations of their governmental principles. In some states, the effort to get a new constitutional convention was more protracted than the process of revision itself; New Jersey, after nearly fifty years of debate, called a convention, revised its constitution, and ratified a new one in a six-month period in 1844.[14] But even in those states that had adopted new constitutions in the 1820s, some constituencies demanded yet another rethinking of their basic laws, and the first generation born since the American Revolution set about doing that work.

Antebellum state constitutional conventions, which prescribed the formal limits of membership in the political community, were important sites for discussions of the rights and obligations placed on citizens and, indeed, for defining full membership in civic life itself.[15] Although they have often been acclaimed for expanding white male suffrage and heralding the age of the "common man," none of these efforts at constitutional revision unambiguously enhanced democracy. No state granted women the right to vote, and several placed new limitations on Americans who had formerly cast a ballot. In particular, by the late 1830s and 1840s, whether they had embraced or merely surrendered to universal white manhood suffrage, politicians were increasingly forced to grapple with the citizenship rights of black men, and they did so with disgraceful consequences. Pennsylvania, which had boasted the most expansive suffrage in its 1776 constitution, passed a constitution in 1838 that explicitly disfranchised African American voters. In Ohio a deeply divided and particularly virulent constitutional convention of 1850–51 debated the right of African Americans even to petition the assembly.[16] The right to vote for a state's rulers, which many equated with "the right to *express my opinion*," was a subject of rancorous debate.[17]

Not only old states but new ones and territories applying for admission as states gathered men together to write constitutions. In Wisconsin (1846), Michigan (1850), and Minnesota (1857), delegates expressed an intense interest in defining citizenship. Minnesota's voters, for example, included "persons of Indian blood, and persons of mixed white and Indian blood, who have adopted the customs and habits of civilization." Some states, such as Wisconsin, permitted immigrant men who had declared their intention to become citizens to vote. Most striking was that "every state that entered the union after 1819 prohibited blacks from voting" even as many older states curtailed black men's long-held rights.[18]

The process of calling for a state constitutional convention was, typically for New York, complicated beyond description by partisan politics. While a bloc of Democrats originally sought to revise the state's basic laws, with the Whigs jumping on their bandwagon in 1845, it is hard to sort through what the different factions thought a new constitution might contain. Democratic Party leaders fought among themselves over nearly every issue, including the need for constitutional change, property reform, internal improvements, and, most divisively, the expansion of slavery into new territories—squabbling that weakened any chance of partisan unity in the convention itself.[19] Still, when the call for a constitutional convention finally emerged from the impenetrable tangle of New York's partisan posturing, it came from both parties, and Democrats dominated the proceedings.[20]

The demand for a new constitution centered on such issues as courts, canals, legislative districting, and public debt, as well as on efforts to tailor the rights of citizenship, including both property and voting rights. The 1821 constitution had long been inadequate to deal with the expansion of New York's economy and the complex systems of credit and debt, and much legislative revision had already taken place. Still, by the 1840s, courts were bogged down in litigation resulting from new commercial transactions. Internal improvements brought expanded trade, but the loans that funded New York's canals had nearly bankrupted the state, causing the preceding governor, William Seward, to tax New Yorkers to pay off the debt. Many believed that only a constitutional amendment could keep the state's future borrowing under control. This issue was far from abstract for Jefferson County's farmers, who watched their region's fortunes decline steadily as they waited year after year for the Black River canal to be finished.

If the state government in Albany seemed distant and unresponsive, banks were worse, for farmers considered them responsible for "the frenzied creation of credit."[21] Readers of the Democratic press in particular blamed banks (along with the "prevalent impatience to get rich faster than one's neighbors") for the 1837 financial crisis.[22] True, there were not many banks nearby. The Jefferson County Bank was first incorporated in 1816 and failed three years later; subsequent efforts were erratic and small. But this lack of financial institutions nearby merely reinforced the notion that banks represented an impersonal elite bent on "ruining farmers." A sense of frenzy reached even distant rural areas, as "titles flew from hand to hand, credits piled upon credits, book fortunes rose and vanished overnight, until in the sad reckoning brought by panic and depression the whole mad structure fell apart." In the context of these economic changes, farmers viewed all corporations with distrust, and many supported a revision of the laws of incorporation that would limit their charters.[23]

But if economic changes were the most urgent reasons to revise the state's laws, land reform, black male suffrage, and married women's property rights also generated a great deal of heat. To some, the prospect of opening these doors threatened utter chaos; to others, it must have been exhilarating. With nearly 2 million acres and some 10,000 farms under lease, a violent anti-rent rebellion had reached a peak in 1845, as embattled tenant farmers failed to get relief through traditional legislative enactments.[24] Politicians were eager to find a way to ameliorate the hardships faced by tenant farmers at the same time that they wanted to protect landlords' property rights, however anachronistic. For Whigs, the goal, if not the means, seemed clear: "The constitution will be purged of whatever of feudalism remains in our form of government," editorialized Thurlow Weed, "and the elements of discord will pass away."[25] Democrats were plagued by this issue, as they tried simultaneously to challenge feudal relations and to insist that government had nothing to do with it.

African Americans also had high hopes for a new constitution. The rhetoric surrounding voting rights for black men in New York is convoluted, with all sides claiming to support greater democracy. But the story of who could vote and who could not is simple enough. New York's first state constitution of 1777 established that any man who had a $50 freehold or who rented a $5 tenement could vote for his congressional representative; he needed $100 to vote for governor or state senator. Alerted to the fact that this requirement did not explicitly bar black men from voting, Democratic delegates to the 1821 constitutional convention extended suffrage to greater numbers of white men while passing a stiff property requirement of $250 for African American voters. Some African American men thus lost their vote, and the vast majority remained voteless. Only 298 black men out of a population of 39,701 African Americans could vote.[26] (In Jefferson County only 2 African American men could vote in 1825; this number had increased to 6 twenty years later.)[27] "Little public outcry" resulted at first from black men's exclusion, although black New Yorkers eagerly, and no doubt angrily, awaited a reversal of their disfranchisement.[28]

By the 1840s the climate for African Americans had grown steadily worse in the North, as states imposed new restrictions on black voting, property ownership, and residency requirements. At the same time, an antislavery movement had placed African Americans' rights inescapably on the political agenda. Through the late 1830s and early 1840s, while antislavery petitions were being gagged in Congress, black abolitionists, led by Henry Highland Garnet, Charles Reason, and George Downing, petitioned New York's legislature. They surely hoped that some progress would result from the "political revolution"[29] of William Seward's victory over Democratic incumbent William Marcy in the 1838 governor's race, accompanied by a sizable Whig majority in the state legislature. A combination of events, including the financial crisis of 1837, forestalled reform. But the few years of Whig dominance in the state opened tiny cracks for African American political activism and some renewed optimism that New York's politicians would act on "the light of reason, the principles of Christianity, and the dictates of living and eternal right" in granting black men the ballot.[30] For abolitionists, the prospect of a constitutional convention offered the chance to abolish completely the "most odious and contemptible" racial restrictions on male citizens' political rights.[31]

Joining questions of property, law, and representation, the issue of married women's property rights promised to surface as well. Throughout most of the United States, traditional notions of marital unity decreed that wives could not own, buy, sell, or inherit property, nor could they sign contracts, sue, or be sued. These restrictions on married women's commercial activities had been opposed before but were made more urgent by the changing economy. In 1836 Workingmen's Party assemblyman and free-thinker Thomas Herttell had requested that a committee investigate married women's property rights both to remedy burdens on debtors and to protect wives from profligate husbands. A year later Herttell introduced a bill "to Restore to Married Women 'The Right of Property' " that was later published as a woman's rights pamphlet. Far broader than the bill that would finally pass—in Herttell's bill, wives would have had a legal right to their wages—his proposal offered an explicit feminist challenge to those who wished to modernize the laws of landownership without tampering with male authority over land itself. By 1846 a much wider range of New Yorkers was impatient to see a constitutional revision of wives' legal standing.[32] Thus, in his *Essays on Human Rights*, Elisha Hurlbut, a Democrat, advocated strongly for a new constitution while also signaling that the issue of woman's rights would be unavoidable in negotiations over property and credit. To Hurlbut, the law of marital property was "a most apt illustration of this species of injustice," whereby "the law creates a right arbitrarily, and without a shadow of foundation in nature." Insisting that "man surrenders not a solitary natural right, when . . . he enters into the social state," Hurlbut asked, "Why then should woman, by . . . entering the married state, be required to surrender any of her natural rights?"[33] For advocates of property and marital law reform, a convention opened new possibilities for change. For opponents, this Pandora's box thrust into political discourse precisely the disruption they feared.

New Yorkers seem to have been willing to take the risk, for on November 4, 1845, they voted overwhelmingly to call a convention to revise their state's constitution.[34] But it is not entirely clear what they hoped to achieve. "While all admit the importance of the consequences that may hang upon the labors of the Constitutional Convention," fretted the *Jefferson County Democrat*, "how few are there who have come to a full decision as to the alterations desirable in our organic law." Of even greater concern was that "appearances indicate that there is but little feeling upon the subject among the masses." Of course, almost as soon as the votes were counted and the process of selecting delegates had begun, accusations of partisan maneuvering, all of which were probably true, burst from the pages of Whig and Democratic newspapers. Sarcasm reigned. Having listed the county's three Whig candidates for delegates, the *Jefferson County Democrat* remarked, "pledged to uphold monopolies and class legislation, and to oppose restoring to the people the right of directing for what purposes their money shall be drawn from them by taxation, with what effect these gentlemen will appeal to tax payers and hard-laboring men for their votes remains to be seen."[35] Although Whigs, under the skillful leadership of John Young, had engineered the call for the convention, more Democrats won election as delegates.[36]

Those who believed in securing or expanding the rights of tenant farmers, African American men, and married women would be deeply disappointed by the new constitution. But these issues made for a stormy spring and promised an exciting convention. The prospect of addressing the issue of black male suffrage made Democratic newspapers especially nervous. "The principal object of the Whigs who have participated in the movement for a Convention," warned the *New York Morning News*, "has been to procure the right of suffrage for the Negroes to the same extent that it is enjoyed by white citizens." Whig editors, some of whom openly opposed slavery, did not disagree. As the *New York Tribune* modestly put it, "On the one side stand Equality, Reason, Justice, Democracy, Humanity; on the other are a base, slavery-engendered prejudice and a blackguard clamor against 'Niggers.'" Rehearsing its rhetoric for the convention itself, the Democratic press retorted that this was not really about suffrage but about "whether we shall endeavour to overcome the great laws of nature, which do not permit two distinct and uncongenial races of men to mingle together in harmony or in mutual self-government."[37] Hiram Hastings explained his party's "democratic" logic of both abolishing property requirements and excluding African Americans from voting even as he illuminated the Democrats' growing fault line. "I, for one, am opposed to all aristocracies, and all property tests, for blacks or whites," he wrote. "The negro race must all be allowed to vote or none." Fearing that the "country members of the Convention may underrate the danger," Hastings warned that urban voters "cannot shut our eyes to the danger and disgrace" of "political amalgamation."[38]

When Jefferson County voters went to the polls on April 28, 1846, to choose delegates, there were three candidates each from the Whig, Democratic, and Liberty parties. For abolitionists, the central issue was which of the candidates could be counted on to vote for equal suffrage for black men. "The Whigs are setting traps," insisted the *Albany Patriot.* "They bait with 'colored suffrage,' and they care as much about the bait, compared with the game, as other trappers." Concerned, not unreasonably, that the Whigs' main goal was "the *annihilation of the Liberty Party,"* antislavery activists argued over the effectiveness of a third party ticket.[39] In Jefferson County, third party sentiment was relatively firm, and George W. Knowlton, Aaron W. Porter, and Hugh Smith garnered several hundred votes as Liberty delegates.[40] Fifty-five men from Clayton, more than from any other town and likely with Ormsbys and Osborns and their friends among them, voiced their support for African American men's political rights with those votes. Once the votes were counted, however, both the Whigs and the Liberty Party had lost, and three Democratic delegates, Elihu McNeil, Azel Danforth, and Alpheus Greene, prepared to represent Jefferson County in Albany.

For New Yorkers who relished political drama, the atmosphere was already stormy when 128 delegates and numerous secretaries, reporters, messengers, and visitors crowded into the state capitol on the first day of June. For all the partisan maneuvering (a caucus of forty-nine "Radical Members" of the Democratic Party had already met on Saturday, with "a very numerous attendance of citizens in the lobbies and galleries"), there must have been a sense of pomp and of history.[41] As they took their seats in the "old capitol," an impressive four-columned building completed in 1808 and recently restored, every delegate understood that he worked in the shadow of the jurists and political thinkers who had written the 1821 constitution. They may well have agreed that they were "an able group but hardly as distinguished as the men who had gathered for the same purpose in 1821," with none of the state's most noteworthy politicians among them.[42] Only two, Whig James Tallmadge and Democrat Samuel

Nelson, had served as delegates to the 1821 convention. Most of the delegates were in their thirties and forties, with an average age of about forty-seven. Stephen Allen, a mechanic from New York City, was, at seventy-five, the oldest; the youngest delegate, Lorenzo Shepard, a Greene County native who had settled in New York City, was twenty-five. (For some reason, the convention documents listed other data as well: at 305 pounds, David Munro was the heaviest delegate, and William Conely, a scant 110 pounds, was the lightest.)[43] Forty-six delegates listed themselves as farmers (though a few were also merchants or physicians), forty as lawyers, and four as both.[44] They were, obviously, all white and all male, and yet among the issues that divided them were those that challenged white men's standing as the exclusive owners of property and rightful makers of laws.

Given the slowness with which news traveled and the all-too-frequent dullness of the debates, it is remarkable how much the convention was in the public eye and, presumably, on its citizens' lips. Layer upon layer of proceedings emerged, as reporters wrote competing accounts of each day's events, usually paraphrasing speeches in the third person. Some version of these reports was immediately printed in the Albany papers, which delegates, after a long day of talking, read and discussed, often at Delavan House, where Alpheus Greene boarded.[45] At his next opportunity to speak, a delegate might elaborate on or apologize for what he viewed as a misrepresentation of himself in that day's paper, leading to an almost real-time dialogue between newspapers and delegates, as well as among delegates themselves, even as the convention proceeded.[46]

No one doubted that women were interested in the convention. As historians have shown, women were present both rhetorically and physically at political events, and this convention was no exception. A dispute surfaced early about whether to appoint a doorkeeper for the "ladies' gallery." Apparently the crowds were so large that "ladies coming to this house, desiring, anxiously and commendably, to hear the debates and witness the proceedings, had been crowded out of their legitimate seats, in the front of their gallery." George Patterson opposed paying three dollars a day for a doorkeeper, certain that a posted sign could inform men that the women's gallery was "so designated by the legislature." Laughter suffused the debate: about which of the delegates knew best the wishes of the local women, about who among them had earned "the admiration of the ladies," and about who had, or wished to have, the seats with the best view of the women. There was some pleading with the delegates to observe "the spirit of gallantry, if not of justice." On one level a foolish give-and-take among men, the dispute underscores that women (including "many ladies from the country . . . who did not know where the appropriate gallery for them to sit is located") would want to listen to them talk. Understandably, some delegates grew impatient. Ansel Bascom, for one, doubted that "there would be a very strong disposition among the ladies to witness these proceedings, unless the work changed, nor was he desirous that the trifling, technical character of the matters which had been debated should be thus witnessed." But for all the arguing that would ensue that summer about women's standing in law, no one questioned whether women had a place (indeed, a "commendable" one) in the audience.[47]

Serious issues of policy soon emerged, as delegates grappled most urgently with the state's ability to borrow money and fund internal improvements. But they also dealt with the rights of foreign residents, the balance of power between urban and rural areas, land reform, suffrage for African American men, and property rights for married women. Floating through many of these issues were the questions of property and suffrage. For more than fifty years, politicians had struggled to determine the source of the suffrage itself: Was it ownership of land or control of a household? Was it a matter of being white or of paying taxes? Did a man represent the will of his family and other nonvoters with his vote? Whether suffrage was a right, a privilege, or a tool simply commandeered by those who already had it was a persistent theme.

The question of property was central, although its hold on the political imagination was loosening. Being able to protect one's property was, in theory, the birthright of Americans and at the very heart of citizenship. Debates over voting had long centered on who owned property, what kind, how much, and whether the ballot could be safely entrusted to those without it. Indeed, women's political status differed so fundamentally from men's in part because the patriarchal family "was responsible for separating the right to property, which republicans equated with individual liberty, from the legal status of married women."[48] Additionally, in a seriously illogical twist of republican ideology, unmarried women landowners could not vote. But by 1846 a large number of citizens, all of whom were white men, whose independence was compromised by debt or tenancy, could vote. Among this group were thousands of Hudson Valley tenants who were even then rising up against the feudal relationships between themselves and their landlords. It may have been tempting for politicians to treat these men as peasants. The harsh reality was that they had to recognize them as voters.

The question of tenants' rights and landlords' interests infused the convention debates. But if delegates were under pressure to put an end to the smoldering rebellion, there was no consensus on how to do this. Whig Ambrose Jordan of Columbia County believed it "inconsistent with the spirit and genius of our institutions that men should hold their farms, on which they were to sweat and toil, subject to the superior domination of a lord."[49] Charles Kirkland of Oneida opined that land tenures "tended to degrade the character of the tenants" and, while not wishing to violate individuals' property rights, hoped to "induce the landlords to part with their lands to those who occupied and tilled them." But most delegates agreed with Democrat John W. Brown, who, after declaring himself deeply committed to solving the "hardships of these tenants," concluded that "there was no such mode" for doing so.[50] The new constitution would prohibit future leases of more than twelve years' duration but would fail to resolve the ongoing crisis with leases dating from colonial times.

That voters can wield their votes promotes reticence, if not respect, on the part of politicians. Indeed, delegates evinced a nervous regard for the demands of non-elite (and enraged) white men. They felt no compulsion to display even superficial politeness toward African American New Yorkers; on the contrary, their hostility was both open and ugly. In talking about a proposal to allow only chosen jurors to elect justices of the peace, John Hunt, a printer representing New York City, argued that allowing "unfit" jurors "tends to degrade the democratic element of our judiciary, precisely as the extension of the elective franchise to an inferior, barbarian, or servile race, would degrade those who might exercise it in common with them, and impair its value." He dismissed the notion that his views might be considered antidemocratic: "While democracy is opposed to all false and aristocratic distinctions," he asserted, "it recognizes all distinctions that are real, and that exist in the nature of things." Enoch Strong remarked sardonically that Hunt's proposal was "very novel" even if "the gentleman was something like, at least, a century behind the age."[51] Neither Strong nor his colleagues objected on the record to Hunt's racism.

Inevitably the subject of voting rights for black men arose more directly. When the delegates met to debate phrasing suggested by committee number eleven, "Men are by nature free and independent, and in their social relations entitled to equal rights," Whig Ansel Bascom proposed adding the words "and political" after "social." This change, which all present understood as a move to establish black men's equal suffrage, was swiftly rejected. Isaac Burr, a sixty-five-year-old Whig surveyor from Delaware County (whom the *Albany Patriot* applauded for having "voted for Mr. Birney in 1844"), immediately moved to substitute the paraphrased words from the nation's most sacred text, "Men are created equal and are endowed by their Creator with certain inalienable rights, among which are life, liberty and the pursuit of happiness." The chair declared him, and his irony, out of order.[52]

But the challenge of debating black men's political disfranchisement was inescapable that summer, in Albany as in much of the North. When a proposal to grant political rights to "every white male citizen of the age of twenty-one years" was read aloud, Whig Benjamin Bruce immediately moved to omit the word "white," and Isaac Burr had the platform he wanted. He declared, with sarcasm and wit, that the constitution of 1821 "took a step toward the dark ages" by restricting the vote on the basis of race. He urged his colleagues not to "take still another step in that direction by continuing this odious provision." Bruce followed, drawing on black men's military service, England's abolition of slavery, the experience of Massachusetts (where black men had always voted), the nation's founding documents, and biblical authority itself to argue against disfranchising any (male) citizens.[53]

All this was, opponents claimed, so much philosophical ranting. Democrat John Russell declared righteously that the voters had trusted their delegates to behave "safely and wisely," not to advance "visionary philosophical theories concerning the best natural state of society." As a practical matter, he went on, many people (including women, "the entire half of society paying a large portion of the taxation to support society" and men under twenty-one) were justifiably denied political rights. Caution, he insisted, was necessary, lest black suffrage "would invite . . . a dangerous proportion of another race of men" to their state.[54] The fear that their state would be "overrun with runaway slaves"[55] was not unique to New Yorkers. Four years later, delegates to an Ohio constitutional convention would propose banning African Americans from migrating to their state, and in 1851 Indiana legislators voted by a large majority to restrict black migration to theirs. Illinois reinforced a similar exclusion in 1862, and several legislatures, including those in Connecticut, Wisconsin, and Minnesota, voted against black suffrage as late as 1865.[56] But such charges could not still the debate, which exposed delegates' assumptions about whether the body politic did, or should, include African American men.

Debates about suffrage forced delegates to be explicit about who the "we" were in the constitution, for these deliberations were drenched with notions of "us" and "them." Russell, so openly hostile to black male . suffrage, represented St. Lawrence (bordering Jefferson), a county that, in his words, "has no blacks, and never had a slave" and whose citizens "abhor slavery." But " 'Our own free race' has there cleared the face of mother earth of its primeval forests, and have rendered it habitable for civilized man. They have there founded social institutions adapted to their wants. . . . They want no co-partners . . . who come fresh from an inferior race of men, for ages debased by the claims of servitude." He went on to elaborate on the degeneration of "civilization" that would result from racial mixing. Such views were not, of course, the monopoly of rural New Yorkers. John Hunt of New York City regarded the effort to extend suffrage to black men as a great danger. "We contend for self-govern-ment," he insisted, in a speech that would become extraordinarily ugly. "We hold that no man who is not a partizan [sic] of the republic's self—who is not a bona fide citizen, shall have any voice in the state." African Americans, he asserted, were "irreclaimable aliens."[57]

It fell to John Kennedy, a paint dealer representing New York City, to report the opinion of committee number four on the elective franchise. All sides had been heard, he noted, including "a delegation from the colored population." He and his committee advocated democracy and progress, he assured the convention, and so had concluded that property requirements were "the last vestige of an odious, cruel and unjust condi-tion" and should be abolished. A black man, he went on smoothly, "should be either excluded altogether from a participation in government, on account of his race; or admitted into full connexion for the sake of his humanity." He himself believed that suffrage was a privilege, not a right, as evidenced by women's and children's disfranchisement; it was up to the assembled delegates to grant or withhold that privilege.[58]

Those who knew Kennedy must have guessed where he was headed, but his growing heat can take the reader by surprise. Suddenly, after ranting against the "gross proposal" that black men vote alongside white, he began to list his own antislavery credentials. In a stunning attack on William Lloyd Garrison (and a striking revision of history), he told how, in his native Baltimore, he had been part of a movement (colonization) that would have ended slavery had not a "pitiless ruffian forced his way into our midst, urged on by fanaticism . . . and ruthlessly endeavored to compel the slaveholder to do that which he was about to do of his own free will."

Kennedy's enmity toward abolitionists was surpassed only by his contempt for African Americans. His lecture about human physiology, the permanence of racial hierarchies, and black people's "degradation" and "vice" outlined why he thought only white men should be allowed to vote.[59]

Antislavery delegates were quick to respond to Kennedy's assault, and some noise ensued. In a rare editorial aside, reporters Bishop and Attree noted that "there was considerable excitement and much confusion, during which it was impossible to hear distinctly what transpired." Efforts to halt debate failed, and passionate speech-making continued. Federal Dana, a Madison County Whig, dissected Kennedy's claim of sympathy with African Americans with cold contempt, concluding, "from such friends, well may my colored brother exclaim, . . . 'Good Lord, deliver us.' "[60] Democrats such as Conrad Swackhamer, who opposed all property requirements on principle, agreed with Kennedy that "the colored race were either entitled to vote on the same terms with the whites, or not at all." Swackhamer's own constituents, whom he seems to have assumed were all white, "were of [the] opinion that the colored man was not capable." Whether or not most delegates shared Kennedy's extreme racist views, Bruce's proposal to omit the word "white" from the article on political rights was defeated, 37 to 63. Of the three Jefferson County delegates, Greene and Azel Danforth voted with the majority, leaving only Elihu McNeil to stand firmly for black men's suffrage.[61] The news of Greene's vote must have distressed Lydia and Joseph Osborn and Susan and Bailey Ormsby; I have no idea if it surprised them.

The issue of black men's voting remained an open wound, triggering passionate and painful debate as several delegates, mostly Whigs, fought word by word against the restrictions based on race. Predictably, some descended to nitpicking over biblical precedents; the tower of Babel, Noah's ark, and the curse of Ham were all revisited. Even the dry tone of the proceedings cannot hide the exasperation in Federal Dana's voice when he admitted his inability "to successfully oppose the learned and Biblical orator who had preceded him," but he "could not . . . see the bearing of the gentleman's arguments on the question, as to the right of the colored man to vote." Resigned, he entered the argument about the origins of "the wickedness of man." Whig George Crooker groused about delegates' pontificating about the divine source of their own suffrage. "Whence, sir, do we derive the power to deny to that oppressed race the enjoyment of that sacred right?" he asked. "Have not they just as much right to deny it us? It is might and power alone that gives right."[62]

The question of African American men's voting could tear apart the convention, not to mention further divide the Democratic Party, and everyone knew it. William Taylor, Democrat of Onondaga, thus proposed that the delegates avoid risking the defeat of the whole constitution by "submitting the question [of black men's suffrage] to the people, that they might have an opportunity of deciding of themselves."[63] Disguising this move as democratic, the constitutional convention declared itself too deeply divided to reach a decision and turned the issue over to the voters, knowing it would be defeated.

Philosophical differences as to the meaning of citizenship, the laws of nature, and the Bible all entered the debate about married women's property rights as well, though here partisan divisions were more blurred. On June 10, Democrat John Bowdish, a thirty-eight-year-old merchant and farmer from Montgomery County, introduced a resolution authorizing a committee to look into "the expediency of giving to females the right to hold and transfer, after marriage, all property real and personal, acquired by them." Less than three weeks later, James Tallmadge of Dutchess County submitted a committee report that proposed that "all property, real or personal, of the wife, owned by her before marriage, and that acquired by her afterwards, by gift devise or descent, or otherwise than from her husband, shall be her separate property."[64]

The question of a wife's right to separate property and her obligation to pay her husband's debts was inescapable in an economy based on credit and debt. Rural New Yorkers, in particular, might have been expected to support laws making land simpler to buy, sell, and inherit. The financial panic of 1837 merely confirmed that even the most rural New Yorkers "lived amidst an intricate network of speculation, credit, insurance, stocks, and wages which was subject to cycles of boom and bust."[65] Even delegates most stubbornly opposed to reform knew the world had changed; that was, after all, why they were there. So, with hindsight, the debates about married women's property reform seem unreasonably frantic, exhibiting the inflated nervousness of men who wanted their state's constitution both to sustain an old society and to reflect new realities. But both opponents and supporters of married women's property rights understood that the right to hold property, so long associated with independent citizenship, would alter women's status as citizens. They recognized, even when they did not admit, that property reform threatened a larger transformation in women's status, possibly legitimating a broad-based challenge to men's authority as husbands.

The debate about married women's property rights ranged as widely in its arguments as in its advocates. Supporters included, predictably, Whigs such as Ansel Bascom, Ira Harris, and A. W. Young, but also Conrad Swackhamer, the young mechanic and assemblyman from Kings County who spoke so vehemently against granting black men the vote. For some, protecting women's property was a pragmatic issue. Whig Charles Kirkland worried about the burdens placed on women by "worthless husbands." Robert H. Morris, a Democrat and former mayor of New York City, disdained the notion that "the harmony of a family consisted in the man's pocketing all the cash" and offered numerous examples of once comfortable wives reduced to poverty by dissolute husbands. Ansel Bascom tried to appease opponents by promising that the proposal "aims to secure the rights of men, too."[66] The realities of the new economy, supporters stressed, as well as the occasional difficulties of married life, required new rules to protect women and secure property.

It was a Democrat who submitted the most radical analysis of the relationship between this proposal and society's broader inequities. An "obscure young man," Conrad Swackhamer offered a class analysis that dismissed the claims of black New Yorkers while it exhibited a deep sympathy for those white women who did not enjoy the privileges of middle-class domesticity. Historian Marvin Meyers views Swackhamer's "harangue on corporate privilege as the root of all social evil" as anachronistic but admits that it "allowed him to touch a reality which eluded the speeches of his fellow delegates: the facts of poverty and social immobility, not as the special curse of immigrants and Negroes, not as the sad material for charitable rescue operations, but as the continuing condition of a large class of urban laborers and mechanics."[67] Swackhamer's was a strong indictment, and he placed the blame squarely on the shoulders of the government he was there to remake.

Almost alone among the supporters of reform, Swackhamer admitted that there were "larger ramifications" to the debate.[68] That single women were "taxed without representation, all knew. That the reward for their labor was much below what was received by males, none would deny. That they were spurned from society, if entangled in but one of the thousand snares which were thrown in their rugged and unprotected path of life, was too painfully true." Government itself was to blame: "While vast sums of money had been appropriated for the higher institutions of learning, for the education and refinement of young men," Swackhamer declaimed, "comparatively nothing had been done for the instruction and

embellishment of the female mind." Men's selfishness "occasioned un-
pleasant emotions" in Swackhamer, though he hoped none of his colleagues doubted that "females were mentally and morally equal to
males." Indeed, over the course of the debate Swackhamer offered many
of the points that would be made in favor of woman's rights over the next
decades: "this portion of the community," he raged, was "excluded from
the halls of legislation,—taxed without representation—despoiled of their
property—deprived of an equal share of education, and confined to the
menial drudgery of the domestic." Confident that "the neglect and oppression of females was a sure evidence of an absence of civilization and
christianity," he harangued the assemblage about a system that, in his
view, virtually enslaved wives.[69] In Swackhamer's plea, intriguingly both
anachronistic and forward looking, we hear an echo of Fanny Wright and
New York's tailoresses more than a decade earlier, evidence that their
message had not vanished entirely and that support for woman's rights
did not emerge only from the antislavery milieu.

Proposals for married women's property laws resonated for these men
as citizens but also as husbands, sons, and fathers. For them, no less than
for women, politics was personal. Why else did the reporters who tran-
scribed the proceedings list—alongside each delegate's residence, place of
birth, age, occupation, and ancestry—his marital status? Some delegates
who wanted to change the law confessed to a personal interest in protecting their wives' or daughters' property. Ira Harris, a widower, supported
the bill "as a father, anxious to secure to his own the benefit of the little
that he might have then."[70] Others snidely mentioned that the bill's major
opponents were bachelors. Fifty-five-year-old George Simmons, for one,
seemed rather hurt by "the propensity of gentlemen to make themselves
merry over his 'solitary and alone' condition, whenever he undertook to
talk about the domestic relations."[71]

Whatever significance property ownership carried in a convention hall,
women's legal status and the political meanings of marriage carried more.
In the traditional view, marriage bound women legally to their husbands
and authorized husbands, acting as citizens, to represent the interests of
their families. For liberals, marriage was better understood as a civil
contract in which men and women assumed mutual obligations but that
did not erase their independent legal standing. For opponents of reform,
however, the notion of married women controlling separate property, of
becoming independent actors in a commercial society, betrayed the underpinnings of the social order itself. Many critics were apprehensive

about larger "domestic trouble" should such a separation of marital property come to pass.[72]

Democrat Charles O'Conor's stand on married women's property rights reflected a consistent, staunchly conservative political philosophy. A lawyer whose expertise lay in commercial and corporate law, O'Conor participated in several highly publicized trials, some in defense of slavery. Throughout the convention, O'Conor advocated the narrowest possible view of membership in the political community and the rights it entailed. Neither "the ladies" nor free African Americans, he insisted, had rights the convention was bound to respect; they "constituted the subjects of government, and not the members of the political body." When the question of married women's property came up (in spite of his best efforts to table it),[73] O'Conor argued passionately that granting property rights to married women would lead inexorably to the dissolution of marriage itself. It promised a change too painful to contemplate: the full equality of women and thus the utter breakdown of American society. "If there was any thing in our institutions that ought not to be touched by the stern hand of the *reformer*," bellowed O'Conor, a bachelor inclined to lofty rhetoric about domestic tranquility, "it was the sacred ordinance of marriage." So vociferous and drawn out was the debate that by October, O'Conor would whine that he wished the convention would "devote a little [time] to the rights of men as well as the rights of women."[74]

Some of O'Conor's attacks were simply inflammatory, rhetorical charges that linked married women's property rights to irreligion, sexual immorality, and France. This was old news. Supporters of married women's property rights had long included admirers of France, evidence (as members of an 1844 New York legislative committee put it) that should such a reform pass, "we shall rival France and some of the other continental nations in the laxity of our morals."[75] To understand the dangers of wives owning property, O'Conor insisted, one had only to "look at the state of society in the nations of continental Europe" and "to pause and deliberate before they fixed permanently in the fundamental law, this new and dangerous principle."[76]

What did Alpheus Greene make of this debate? Surely the women who entrusted Greene with their petition knew that he was no radical, but the record offers few hints. Throughout the proceedings he sat between Democrats Arphaxad Loomis of Herkimer County, who feared that married women's property rights were "of too much difficulty and delicacy" to be inserted into a constitution, and William Maxwell of Chemung, who supported the measure.[77] At night he ate and slept in a boardinghouse packed with delegates from both parties, where discussion continued. He observed members of his own party disagree vehemently, but he made no speeches on the issue. At the convention his votes on issues that articulated the nature of citizenship are ambiguous, and he almost never spoke for the record. As I have noted, he voted against the proposal to delete the word "white" from the definition of voters and largely adhered to his party's goal of removing property qualifications from white, but not black, male voters. In an attempt to find a middle ground between universal manhood suffrage and the harsh exclusion of African American voters, he did vote to reduce the property qualification for black men from $250 to $100, a proposal that failed, 42 to 50.[78]

In addition to presenting the women's petition, Alpheus Greene offered one other proposal: to establish a literacy requirement for voters. Whether this revealed Greene's innate elitism, the complacency of someone from a highly literate region, or merely a lapse in political judgment, I do not know, but the idea garnered only a half-dozen votes in its favor. In its defense, however, Greene offered a view of representative democracy that hints at his sense of obligation to his female petitioners. Each voter, in his view, represented five or six people who could not vote. "These persons have claims upon the voter," he insisted. "Their rights are to be affected by the vote he casts. They therefore have a right to demand that the voter should be intelligent."[79]

Greene's votes on women's property rights were more liberal than those on black men's suffrage. In this and in spite of Charles O'Conor's indignation, he stood with a large segment of the Democratic Party. Indeed, a leading advocate of married women's property rights in the state assembly in the early 1840s had been John L. O'Sullivan, the editor of the *Democratic Review*. Firm in its support, the *Review* in 1846 would count among the few defects of the proposed constitution its failure "to secure to females the right to hold, transfer or devise property as fully after as before marriage."[80] (A dozen years later the editor and proprietor of the *Democratic Review* would be none other than Conrad Swackhamer.) For whatever reason, Alpheus Greene's unmarried state did not cause him to wax sentimental about marriage as it apparently did Charles O'Conor. Perhaps his four sisters had disposed Greene favorably toward women's independent property ownership. Certainly the family counted among themselves their own defenders of woman's rights, for one of

Greene's nephews would marry a woman who was "an unfaltering advocate of temperance, of the duty of giving the ballot to women, and of every cause that shall lift up the poor and oppressed."[81] On October 2 he alone among the Jefferson County delegates voted to allow married women to own and control their separate property. The resolution passed, 58 to 44.[82]

There the debate should have ended. The *Evening Post*, a Barnburner Democratic paper, immediately applauded this "great and important change."[83] But three days later, Charles O'Conor, after persistent lobbying, asked that the vote be reconsidered. It had been raised in a "sudden manner," he declared, that had "prevented full discussion." He was certain that "due reflection would induce a majority to reverse the former vote."[84]

Indeed it did. As debate resumed, opponents of reform stressed that the article was risky and rash. In spite of pro-reform efforts, support began to slip, as a few more delegates came to agree that permitting wives to own property was too drastic a reform to make part of the "inflexible constitutional law of the land." On October 5 the convention delegates reversed their earlier decision by a vote of 50 to 59, leaving married women's property rights to a later legislature. Alpheus Greene was either absent or abstained.[85]

Resistance to married women's property rights was both simple and emotionally compelling. Allowing married women to own, buy, sell, and inherit property was a slippery slope, a Pandora's box that "once opened . . . would throw relations between the sexes into total chaos."[86] If you grant women certain rights associated with full citizenship, the logic went, they will come to accept them as normal and want more. Everyone knew, as John Adams had suggested long before, that rights were sneaky things. Jews, religious liberals, and freethinkers were not content with simple tolerance; they wanted to run for office, challenged the public funding of clergymen, and asked to have their testimony heard in court. African American men who lived in states that had abolished slavery were not satisfied; they wanted civil protections, fair trials, access to jobs, and a vote. Tocqueville knew this as well: "Once a people begins to interfere with the voting qualification," he wrote, "one can be sure that sooner or later it will abolish it altogether . . . for after each new concession the forces of democracy are strengthened."[87] Impatient with the pace of reform, Elisha Hurlbut threatened as much: "If man will legislate no more wisely, let woman be heard upon this point," he wrote; "she hath suffered enough from the barbarous tyranny of the common law."[88] Try as they might to defend marriage (Ansel Bascom insisted that women's legal disabilities "arose from a violent construction that the law put upon the marriage contract," rather than a problem with the contract itself), men on both sides knew that these doors, once opened, were hard to shut. "Where will it all take us?" queried legal writer John F. Hargrave in 1847. "To women on juries, in the militia, serving on posses?"[89]

Yet there is evidence that on the issue of married women's property rights, convention delegates may have lagged behind their constituents. For many Americans, the idea of wives owning their own property may not have seemed so outrageous. Among the early supporters of reform was Sarah Josepha Hale, the editor of *Godey's Lady's Book*, who believed that the old law "degrades the woman to the condition of a slave" but was careful to reject any identification with "women's rights." Outside the convention halls there was "a broad awareness of and dissatisfaction with married women's disabilities" in law. Several states (beginning with Mississippi, whose 1839 statute focused on property in slaves) had begun to pass laws to protect wives' property, though these did not extend to their wages. Although New York's legislative committees prevented a full vote on the issue before 1848, national journals held the public debates that politicians avoided, and these seemed to reflect a widespread recognition that marriage laws had become anachronistic. Within two years of the convention, even arguments about "France, French women, and French civil law" did not evoke sufficient fear to delay passage of this particular law, although those epithets remained effective in thwarting other changes in women's status.[90]

In the face of such rhetoric, many supporters of reform embraced the strategy of drawing lines around demands they declared unthinkable. What Sarah Josepha Hale defensively disdained as "women's rights" included, of course, the right to vote. As early as 1828, Caleb Cushing had denied that he was setting his foot on a slippery slope when he endorsed reform of married women's property rights. Suffrage, he declared, was out of the question, as was "any extravagant standard of legal privilege." "The constitution of nature . . . has . . . settled the question," Cushing wrote complacently, "whether the female sex should exercise political franchises equally with man."[91]

At the 1846 constitutional convention the question of woman suffrage arose, noisily and repeatedly, as a rhetorical device. As we have seen in earlier conventions, the very absurdity of the idea was urged as evidence that suffrage was not a natural right that had to be granted to black men. When Levi Chatfield of Otsego, a leading radical Democrat, wished to add the words "without regard to color" to a statement on rights, Charles O'Conor asked jokingly whether he would amend it further to include "age *or sex*!" Delegates and observers laughed. The record does not indicate whether Chatfield was being sarcastic when he retorted, "Oh, certainly." Whig Alvah Worden got the discussion back on track, suggesting nervously that "this amounted to the recognition of a principle that no man dare to deny, but it was of no practical use."[92] (Worden would be "practical" again in October when he changed his "aye" to "nay" and thus helped defeat married women's property reform. One cannot help but wonder what his wife, Lazette, who was judging products at the state agricultural fair, thought of this vote.)

Delegates on both sides used the specter of women's full citizenship to frame their arguments about African American men's claims. John Kennedy, who "did not design to be understood as advocating any farther extension of the elective franchise," noted nonetheless that white women, "our own flesh and blood," should receive the vote before "the Ethiopian race." As for the notion of extending the suffrage to black men, "Nature revolted at the proposal."[93] A "staunch and reliable Liberty man," Democrat David S. Waterbury took the opposite view, that the extension of the suffrage did not necessarily open the door to women: "The wives and children of all white citizens were protected in their rights and privileges by husbands and brothers," he maintained. "Where do you find any one to stand up for the colored man? Not one."[94] If suffrage were indeed a natural right, as some delegates declared, then logically it would have to be extended to all: "Wherefore the qualification of 21 years of age?" cried Whig Horatio Stow as proof that suffrage was, instead, a privilege. "Wherefore the qualification of male citizenship? . . . Why not allow it to all of both sexes, and all conditions and ages, whether alien or citizen, if it was a matter of absolute right?" "If the people were sovereign, . . . wherefore . . . do we exclude females and children of a certain age, &c., from voting?" asked Democrat Benjamin Cornell, concluding that the experiment in black suffrage "had failed to produce any other effect than to mislead the public mind as to their citizenship" and should be abandoned. At the New York convention only Robert Morris, having argued that electors, while "not the whole body of the people," were expected to represent that entire body, recommended that the suffrage be extended to "the widow who had property to protect."[95]

What did these arguments say about women's place in political life? The early, silly squabble over the "ladies' gallery" might be taken as a symbol of what these politicians knew: women had interests at stake, and they were watching. Declaring that in voting each man represented himself as well as "five unqualified citizens," one delegate argued that the female population of "one million two hundred and ninety-three thousand, three times the number of your whole electoral body" had a strong interest in the convention's outcome. "They have as deep an interest in this government as you," he asserted, "—nay, a deeper interest. If your laws prove dangerous to liberty, you can unmake the work of your own hands. You are clothed with the power of the ballot box. . . . They are voiceless, powerless, defenceless." Charles O'Conor disagreed about the nature of representative government and drew on a rather astonishing analogy to describe women's place in American politics. "The electors of this State did no more represent all these classes of persons, than did the Emperor of Russia, the Sultan of Turkey, or any other despot, represent the people of his country." He went on: "We represent the free white citizens of the State over 21 years of age, and those negroes who happen to have $250 worth of real estate. . . . We control the Indians because they are fewer in number—the negroes for the same reasons—and the fair ladies because we have chosen to deprive them of the right of representation."[96] Far from demonstrating that woman suffrage was under serious consideration by politicians in 1846, these arguments foreshadow post–Civil War debates by suggesting that antebellum legislators understood (and manipulated) the relationship between enfranchising women and enfranchising African Americans in multiple ways. More often than not, the issue of women's citizenship was raised to foreclose, dismiss, or simply ignore the question of women voting for themselves.

The issues of land, wives, and black male suffrage were thus intertwined rhetorically throughout the convention debates, entangled with proposals that represented a new and dangerous threat to property, family, and the state. Judging by the extremism of the rhetoric at the convention, the issues of black men's suffrage and women's property rights made some delegates sweat; certainly the temperature in the hall seemed to rise whenever these subjects came up. It was not that these men actually feared losing to women their hold on political authority, economic prerogatives, and their right to govern, but the question had been raised, forcing some to insist that the prospect remained unthinkable, beyond consideration. That they *had* to consider it, "if only to justify their conservatism effectively," had become inescapable.[97] There is a sense throughout these proceedings of a storm threatening that would unleash a dangerous new discussion of the status of women as wives and as citizens.

Of course, the gauntlet had already been thrown among them, and by an unlikely hand. Alpheus Greene may have returned home to Jefferson County in late July and remained there for two or three weeks; he was present at the convention for a vote on Friday, July 24, and does not appear on a roll call again until August 15. The petition he carried to the assemblage on that Saturday is dated August 8 (the same day that David Wilmot presented his famous proviso to Congress and thus launched a movement for free soil). Perhaps the women simply took the opportunity of Greene's visit to write a long-planned petition. More than likely they had all seen the Albany memorial then in circulation and discussed it among themselves. Perhaps Greene was cornered by one or more of them, as Elizabeth Cady Stanton had "tackled" her neighbor Ansel Bascom to appeal for his support.[98] A man not given to extremes, Greene could not have missed the inflammatory nature of the women's demands; maybe he tried to convince them to moderate those demands or to lighten the petition's tone. Nevertheless, on Saturday, August 15, on the sixty-third day of the convention, immediately following the prayer by the Reverend Mr. Rawson, Alpheus S. Greene stood up to present a petition by six women of Jefferson County. That it was printed in its entirety suggests that Greene read the document aloud, a departure from the usual practice. Upon Greene's motion it was sent to committee number four to be discussed or, just as likely, ignored. But the complete petition and its signers' names found their way into Bishop and Attree's version of the convention debates. Thus the grievance of a half-dozen women was registered, offering a dissenting view of citizenship and belonging and insisting on debate.[99]

Presenting a petition could mean little or a great deal to a politician; a petition itself could reflect a modest plea or a controversial demand. By the 1840s, John Quincy Adams's and other politicians' insistence on submitting antislavery petitions in the face of the congressional gag rule already threatened to destroy the party system and disrupt relations between North and South. Such controversial appeals were generally proferred by men who sympathized with the cause or, at least, insisted on the right of the people to petition on its behalf. A. W. Young of Wyoming County, who presented New York's 1846 convention with another petition for woman's rights, was himself a staunch supporter of black men's voting rights and married women's right to hold property, but these were not necessary qualifications. Indeed, on occasion a delegate admitted that his views conflicted with the petition he proferred. Thus Conrad Swackhamer presented a memorial "relative to Negro suffrage" with the remark that "he might differ from the sentiments contained in the memorial," but "as it came from a very respectable inhabitant of his village, it was entitled to a consideration."[100] Often politicians agreed to present petitions that were petty or irritating or politically inexpedient. A delegate might do this out of conviction or simply from a sense that his duty to his constituents included literally placing their words in front of men they did not know.

However little we know about the interaction between six Jefferson County women and Alpheus Greene, we do know this: several women among his former neighbors thought they were entitled to enter a conversation about women's status in their state's laws, and he agreed. Presumably they followed the convention debates in the press; perhaps one or more of them even sat in the gallery among other "ladies from the country." Quite likely, as women (and men) living in the far rural north of their state, the first and second generation of property-owning families on newly settled and newly purchased lands, simpler land sales and married women's property rights made common sense. Associated with the Liberty Party, they and most of their neighbors supported black male suffrage as well. In a climate where suffrage for black men and property rights for married women were so explosive, these women expressed not only a pointed and personal anger, but the conviction that their standing in their community gave them the right to demand "equal, and civil and political rights with men."

For all the arguing and posturing, the constitutional convention ended with remarkable consensus, even complacency. One hundred four delegates approved the proposed constitution, with only six, including the irascible Charles O'Conor, voting no.[101] The parallel campaigns for constitutional ratification and for unrestricted black male suffrage began even before the convention adjourned. Gerrit Smith at once expressed his "feelings of shame, sorrow, indignation, alarm" at the proposed constitution. "A deep and cruel wrong has been devised against the fifty thousand colored people of this State," he intoned. Witness Pennsylvania, which "stripped her colored people of the right to vote, [and thus] made, as the sequel proved, all the other rights of that afflicted people an open and easy prey."[102] As black Philadelphians described it in 1853, the "sequel" to disfranchisement was grim indeed. Having been "calmly and unjustifiably robbed . . . of those rights we had enjoyed . . . for forty seven years," they were now "assaulted on the public streets, our wives, mothers and daughters insulted, and . . . arrested and dragged before a magistrate. . . . Forced from our places of business by a population incapable of comprehending the freedom of our institutions . . . ever ready to crush out the light of our souls."[103]

So-called equal suffrage, to no one's surprise, was soundly defeated by New York voters.[104] Predictably, more men in areas with a strong Liberty Party presence voted in its favor. In Oswego County, equal suffrage got 57 percent of the vote. Jefferson County as a whole polled only 38.1 percent for black male suffrage, but that figure was nearly doubled in the first district of Clayton.[105] By the late 1850s, the property restriction on black suffrage in New York was one of only two remaining in effect (Rhode Island had one against foreign-born residents), though other states maintained taxpaying qualifications.[106]

Anger and insult leaped from the political writings of black New Yorkers over the next several years. For African American abolitionists who were committed to a nonvoting stance, disfranchisement presented a dilemma. In an 1849 article ("Away with the $250 Suffrage!—Equal Rights, and Nothing Less!"), an angry "J. C." exhorted "Proscribed New Yorkers" to "arise from your slumber! Shake off your lethargy!" "For my part," he confessed, "I will not vote, though possessed of one. . . . I scorn the act—spurn the bribe. Nevertheless, we go heart and hand for equal political privileges: the right to vote or not, and let each exercise his influence . . . according to the dictates of his conscience." S. R. Ward, although writing to a newspaper that "eschews all political action," exhorted the "Four Thousand Colored Voters of the State of New York" to vote for Gerrit Smith against Martin Van Buren in 1848. "You are voters," he reminded them, "in spite of that tyrannical, despotic clause, . . . which makes the enjoyment of the Right of Suffrage, in our case, dependant [*sic*] on a property qualification."[107]

Married women's property reform met with greater success, though it was gradual and piecemeal and affected ownership of land rather than wages and unpaid labor. The reform essentially gathered into the community of property owners those women (middle class and married to farmers) already likely to consider themselves members of the civic life of their state. But what opponents of married women's property rights feared did happen: the debate over married women's property made the question of women's political rights impossible to ignore. Over the next two years petitioning and writing on the topic intensified, with an unmistakable increase in sarcasm on the part of women petitioners themselves.[108] In 1846, however, the demand for woman suffrage, referred to either as a rhetorical argument against black male suffrage or as a frightening implication of permitting wives to own property, was ignored.

If Alpheus Greene's career was conventional, the end of his life was not. Only three years after the constitutional convention, Greene became insane, "a calamity worse than death, for although existence had not ceased, he had ceased to live." Forced to watch his "intellect gradually fade away," his friends and relatives placed him in the decade-old State Lunatic Asylum in Utica (at his own expense), where he "returned to the helplessness of infancy." After his death, Greene's nephew, John G. Webb, swore in a poignant deposition that he "removed said Alpheus S. Green from Jefferson County after he began to lose his mind . . . [and] that on his arrival at Utica he found him so much bereft of reason that it was advised by medical men that he be placed in the said asylum where he remained about 18 months prior to his death." A wide range of afflictions led people to the asylum, with "ill health" ranked highest among the causes of insanity and "religious anxiety" generally not far behind. But although annual reports note that patients published a newspaper and placed their products in competition at state agricultural fairs, the reports offer no information about individuals, nor do they provide any clues to the treatment Greene received or the company he kept. Certainly the Utica asylum had "pledged to avoid corporal punishment, chains, and long periods of solitary confinement," but care and cure, if not brutal, were erratic.[109] When Greene died there on January 25, 1851, he was one of forty-eight inmates who would pass away that year. He left his heirs, mostly siblings, more than $2,000 each and a number of books and other personal belongings. The inventory of books testifies to a well-educated if conventional man interested in medicine, theology, and travel. Some of the titles recall a time only five years earlier when there was not yet evidence, at least in the public record, of Greene's mental decline: two volumes of convention documents, a copy of the convention journal, yet another version of the "Convention of 1846," and three volumes of the revised statutes of the state of New York.[110]

Concluding Thoughts

"sufficiently plain without argument"

Several overlapping conversations were taking place in the summer of 1846, conversations that concerned the privileges of citizenship, the relationship of property to rights, and the meaning of full membership in the state and nation. This book has moved between discussions that occurred in state assembly rooms and those in farmhouse kitchens by being attentive to a small group of people who considered themselves entitled to participate in both. Rather than offering a single argument, I have tried to rethink political culture while keeping the global and the local, so to speak, in one frame. The insights of scholars who have explored the connections between gender and nation building have deeply informed this work.[1] But it is the local itself that gives meaning to the Jefferson County petitioners' story, for it is from their concrete daily experience, not abstractions, that these women understood and articulated their own political identities. At the very least, the fact that my investigations led me to discover their antislavery commitments reinforces the regional specificity of this story, for their political identities emerged from a distinctly northern experience of which they were keenly aware. Although they called upon a national rhetoric of rights ("all governments must derive their just powers from the consent of the governed"), they did not appeal to a national citizenship, nor did they address a national audience. They did not blame the federal government for having "widely departed from the true democratic principles" that they endorsed or hold it responsible for having "ungenerously . . . withheld" their rights. Rather, they spoke directly to the government of their state, and particularly to the men assembled to rewrite its constitution, for those "rights, which they as citizens of the state of New York may reasonably and rightfully claim." Investigations into nation building, and definitions of citizenship that focus on formal and national rights, can miss the very personal nature of these women's sense of belonging. That assumption of membership, especially when contrasted with their unequal status as citizens, underscored the women's conviction that their opinions mattered and that they were entitled to act.

As everyone who participated in these conversations about rights and belonging knew, talk is cheap, but ideas are dangerous things. Taken to their extreme, the most frightened participants declared, ideas could threaten the laws not only of the state but of God and nature. Those who resisted permitting nonbelievers to offer testimony in court understood this, as did politicians who insisted on the practice of opening legislative sessions with prayer. Thus were married women's property rights so vociferously opposed by delegates to New York's constitutional convention. Conservatives declared that the social order itself would be endangered if wives were allowed to own, buy, and sell property in their own names.

In part, this argument was difficult to refute in a hall full of middle-aged men because it was so emotionally compelling, so ardent in its defense of the known, the unquestioned, and the beloved institutions of hearth and home. It was also true. To change the legal status of married women meant stepping off a small (or perhaps a large) cliff. It meant following both the simple logic and the radical implications of Thomas Herttell's defense of married women's property rights: "Is not a female a 'member of this state,' as well as a male?" he asked his fellow legislators in 1837. "Is not a married woman as important a member of this state, as an unmarried woman?"[2] It was absurd for reformers to promise that this was the only, tiny change they would consider; they had to have known better. Those who advocated that married women be permitted to own and contract for property had no idea where even a modest demand for equality would end or what their world would look like if women became equal citizens. Eager to establish that married women's right to property fell within the boundaries of respectable reform, they insisted that theirs was a small and nonthreatening proposal. Their opponents, drawing on a strategy that sought to contain an idea whose consequences they determined too terrible to imagine, declared any movement toward women's equality out of the question.

What is declared out of the question has been of central concern to this book. The demand for women's "equal, and civil and political rights with men" challenged the commonsense belief that men's rule was natural, normal, and just, even as it offered evidence that women considered themselves members of standing in political life. The very existence of the petition points to an ongoing discourse that has ebbed and flowed through the nation's history, forcing, at some moments, even the most politically and religiously orthodox individuals to defend what they desperately wished to consider a given. What is described as impossible, unthinkable, or unimaginable is itself an ideological construction that needs to be repeated and reinforced only in response to actual challenges. However much these demands for silence on certain subjects seem absurd in retrospect—they failed, certainly, to quell the growing discussion about or advances toward women's more equal citizenship under the nation's laws—they did continue to shape the boundaries of those discussions in ways that affect efforts at social change to this day.

The story of the Jefferson County petition—and the anxious assertion that the ideas it expressed were unimaginable—makes certain demands on us. It insists, for instance, that we listen closely when people pretend that words have not been spoken or demand that they not be heard. Students of woman's rights will recall the 1840 World Antislavery Convention in London, site of the infamous exclusion of female delegates and of the meeting between the young Elizabeth Cady Stanton and Quaker abolitionist Lucretia Mott. As Stanton recalled, it was in this context that they "resolved to hold a convention . . . and form a society to advocate the rights of women." The formal silencing of the women, and their commitment to being heard in spite of it, has become a central piece of the creation story of the movement for woman's rights. But another silencing took place as well. According to Stanton, Massachusetts legislator George Bradburn objected vehemently to ministers' dominance of the convention and argued that "if they could prove to him that the Bible taught the entire subjection of one-half of the race to the other, he should consider that the best thing he could do for humanity would be to bring together every Bible in the universe and make a grand bonfire of them." Lysander Spooner, writing after Bradburn's death, recalled instead that Bradburn boomed that "if it were proved that the New Testament sanctioned American slavery, he would 'repudiate its authority' and 'scatter its leaves to the four winds.'" But whether Bradburn had spoken against sexual inequality or slavery on that occasion, his irreligious words themselves were beyond the pale of public speech. His statement, recalled Spooner, "so shocked some of the pietists present that it was omitted from the published reports of the debates."[3]

Outside antislavery conventions as well, some sought to bar words that they declared too dangerous to hear. As in London, a tradition of exclusion served them well, as they questioned not only the validity of certain ideas but the respectability of their advocates. Several delegates to the Ohio constitutional convention of 1850–51, for instance, argued that petitions on behalf of or signed by African Americans should be excluded from discussion because either their language, their signers, or the issues they raised were unrespectable and therefore signaled a lack of respect for the convention itself. Framed as a matter of decorum, this discussion focused explicitly on who could participate in political debate. Indeed, Mr. Sawyer, whose ears most flamed at having to hear petitions for black civil rights read aloud, announced, "There are some things that I hold that even a *white* man has no right to petition for."[4]

But you can only table or silence what has been proposed. Convincing people, including oneself, that an idea is unspeakable takes work. Sustained by a political culture that linked woman's rights both to irreligion and to sexual chaos, politicians described the demand for legal equality for women and men as ridiculous, as blasphemous, and as outside the laws of nature. Why a half-dozen ordinary and otherwise invisible women could, in the face of this, imagine political life differently is at its core a question of how small communities of thinkers and activists buffer themselves against insult and thus how intellectual change becomes possible.

Whatever the sources of their views and their confidence, these six women believed and said that their status as citizens had been unfairly diminished by the laws of their state. Just as the "founding fathers" had declared themselves the originators of the social compact that became the United States, the Jefferson County petitioners used the opportunity of another constitutional convention to claim full rights in their own civic community. Within that world, they believed that they had standing, in the formal sense of that term: the right or capacity to bring suit, to make a claim. The Jefferson County women likely did not see themselves as foolhardy, for they seem to have risked little, and if they stood apart from their neighbors in the intensity of their views, they were certainly not outsiders. Unlike Elizabeth Cady Stanton, whose struggle against the stifling limitations of small-town domesticity has shaped the story of feminism ever since, these women seem to have rebeled less against the particular circumstances of their domestic lives than against laws that declared them unequal partners in their civic ones. Supported by at least some husbands and brothers, as well as by a larger community of antislavery activists, they took for granted their right to express their opinions and make their demands in the wider world.

So much of this conversation must be left to our imagination, given the dearth of historical materials on hand. Throughout the process of writing this book I have searched and longed for letters, diaries, and family histories that would give me further clues into what made these six Jefferson County women think and act as they did. I have wondered whether they were unusually assertive or talkative or furious. I have tried to imagine them as individuals, articulate and cranky. Was Lydia Osborn, who lived with her Liberty Party husband, the center of the action? Or did her unmarried sister, Susan Ormsby, perhaps in collaboration with their brother Bailey, start it? What did Eleanor Vincent, the mother of nine, imagine about her daughters' futures when she placed her name at the top of the petition? Did Anna Bishop's husband, Luther, a Swedenborgian, embrace woman's rights as a logical extension of other socially progressive concerns? Did their daughter, Cynthia, also a minister's wife, or their evangelist son, John, squirm at their mother's radicalism? Should we read into Nahum D. Williams's absence from local antislavery petitions that he was more conservative than his neighbors, or did he simply miss the meeting? Did they write the petition at one sitting, did they argue, did they seek more names? Having read a few of their words across time, I have wanted more.

I would be happy with rumors. But among their descendants with whom I have corresponded, many of whom are extremely knowledgeable about their families' histories, none had heard of the petition or that their family trees included rebels. Different views of this silence have emerged. One descendant of Amy Ormsby's had long heard that her male ancestors treated their wives as partners, giving them full control over their estates, something she viewed with an equanimity characteristic of her own era. Another Ormsby descendant, a man, considered that the circumstances of "pioneer" life inevitably made women feminists. In contrast, one local genealogist was of the opinion that the women would have been embarrassing to their families; having early feminists among the skeletons in one's closet, she believes, would be like having an ancestor born out of wedlock.[5] With all due respect, I incline to the view that these women were forgotten because they were ordinary, that their families did not single them out because they fit in. If their action was unusual, even within their antislavery community, their views were unremarkable.

The petition of the six women of Jefferson County offers a valuable window into their lives, their community, and the sources of nineteenth-century political identity. It is, like any window through time, a distorted one, for this is not the story the women themselves would have told. The lives of Lydia Osborn, Susan Ormsby, Eleanor Vincent, and their friends did not center on a set of demands put down on paper on a summer Saturday sometime in their middle years. However important and inspiring and exasperating that summer's events were, it was just a moment in lives filled with hard work, family, conversation, friends, and politics, and there are no clues to indicate that they imagined how stunning it might seem from a distance. Certainly writing the petition did not transform their lives, for all six women remained close to home. None of them attended either the Seneca Falls or the Rochester convention in 1848 or, as far as I can tell, any other woman's rights events. Indeed, even when nearly every other county in upstate New York hosted a woman's rights convention, the organized movement bypassed Jefferson.[6] Still, I doubt that their petition was their final word on their rights.

Let us return to Joseph Osborn. The man has remained virtually invisible to history; indeed, probably because he and Lydia had no children, his brothers' descendants did not know he existed on their family tree.[7] But he was, like the others in this story, deeply embedded in his family and community, buying and selling land from friends and relatives, witnessing their sales, and living near his four brothers, two sisters, and their parents. Osborn's communal responsibilities included involvement in antislavery politics, and his name appears alongside those of family and friends on petitions to Congress as well as on a list of Liberty Party candidates for office; doubtless he supported African American men's right to vote. An echo of a more personal talent emerges from the record as well. Just as the constitutional convention was concluding its business in Albany in late September 1846, a Jefferson County antislavery convention met in Dexter village. On the first morning, the crowd listened to a "Liberty song by J. Osburn"; in the afternoon he sang "A Liberty song, 'We're Coming' "; and he sang again that evening.[8]

Given what we have been taught to expect, it is even more remarkable that Joseph Osborn publicly declared his support for woman suffrage half a year before his wife, sister-in-law, and friends wrote their petition. The "enfranchisement of females," he believed, would ensure that "the equality of mankind will mean something more than a mere rhetorical flourish."[9] His support may have taken a more personal form as well, reminding us of the connection, for men as for women, between what we have called private and political life. On June 5, 1848, twenty years before he died, Joseph Osborn wrote his will. I have no direct evidence of what motivated him, childless at age forty-one, to do so. Indeed, the will had little effect on what Lydia Osborn's standing as a widow would be. But the timing is suggestive. Osborn wrote and filed his will exactly two months after New York's Married Women's Property Act had finally been made law. It rather wordily gave his wife, Lydia, "all my real estate, and likewise all my personal property to be hers exclusively, to do with, and dispose of as she may think proper." He added, somewhat redundantly, that he "nominate Constitute and appoint [her] sole Executrix of this my last will and testament." The will was witnessed by an intimate group: Lydia's unmarried siblings, Bailey and Susan Ormsby, and Joseph's brother James accompanied the Osborns on their late spring outing to the county clerk's office in Watertown.[10] I do not know whether they had any clue that Bailey would live only a few more months—it seems unlikely, since Bailey did not write his own will until November. But I imagine that they discussed subjects other than death that day and that they saw their trip as a small political victory—and that they sang liberty songs.

The words of politicians are far more numerous, but understanding them nevertheless demands some imagination. Twenty years earlier, possibly before Joseph and Lydia Osborn had ever discussed the rights of women, Littleton Tazewell, a delegate to the Virginia constitutional convention of 1829, wondered whether "intelligent men" meant by the term "universal suffrage" to include "all the men, all the women, and all the children of the community?" Scoffingly, he answered his own question: "Such an absurdity never entered into the head, even of '*a reformer*,' however '*hardened his heart might have become by experimenting on the rights of man, to ascertain how large a dose of French principles might be administered without causing their destruction.*'"[11] But was a demand for woman's rights actually unthinkable? Was it reasonable for a Pennsylvania legislator in 1872 to refer to woman suffrage as "this startling innovation, this pernicious heresy"?[12] Of course not. That so much work had to be done to place the advocates of woman's rights outside the boundaries of religious or sexual respectability proves as much. Nor does it seem likely that only women endorsed their right to vote, though Stanton, for one, made much of women's reluctance to express their views around their husbands. Soon after the woman's rights movement had been launched,

[163]

Elizabeth Oakes Smith recalled a political meeting in Portland, Maine, at which the "women dashed into politics with a zest," "every woman was partisan," and all met with only friendly support. "Not a man there," she recalled cheerfully, "read the handwriting of suffrage on the wall."[13] But maybe they did read it. Maybe they welcomed it. Surely a few women and men, among them people who had thought about and advocated the rights of African Americans, considered women's equal treatment under the laws of their state as simply among the rights that citizens "may reasonably and rightfully claim."

Yet however self-evident legal and political equality may have seemed to them, and seems to us, the argument had to be made and reshaped and adapted and made again. Over the course of the nineteenth century, voting itself increasingly replaced property, racial heritage, and class standing as the primary marker of citizenship. Perhaps it was this change, as well as all the talk about married women's right to property, that forced growing numbers of Americans to begin to picture an electorate that included the female citizen. Many of them, having long understood female citizenship in terms of marriage and religion, sought to depict women as both voters and the embodiment of middle-class Christian sexual virtue, to make woman's rights seem palatable by keeping in one frame the representation of female religious and sexual purity with that of the female citizen.

The relationship between women's religious obligations and political rights would not vanish with the emergence of a movement for political equality. Indeed, the pervasiveness of religious thought remained part of the intellectual landscape from which women demanded recognition as full members of the nation.[14] "Three facts stand in the way of Woman's being helped by the Ballot," wrote the Reverend J. D. Fulton in 1869, "God, Nature, and Common Sense." "It is essential," he continued, "that we inquire reverently and earnestly, on which side is God." Calling feminists un-Christian remained a prevalent charge, and one that was largely impossible to answer without rejecting its very terms. "Look at the facts," Fulton went on. "Who demanded the ballot for woman? They are not the lovers of God, nor are they the believers in Christ, as a class."[15] Like the idea of women owning property a few years earlier, woman suffrage was not only wrong or disruptive; it was unrespectable and, therefore, dismissed. Rhetoric about the terms under which women "belonged" to the nation explains but also complicates the political and religious culture that woman's rights supporters would face. Late in the nineteenth century, efforts to defend woman's rights on the basis of advocates' own religious and sexual respectability, while perhaps strategically under-standable, only reinforced these exclusions.

But this was never a neutral or inevitable way to imagine women as full citizens. Indeed, describing something as "unthinkable" works as a rhetori-cal strategy in part by exacting precisely such compromises from the advocates of change. Certainly it was an effective tactic in convincing many proponents of woman's rights, or beneficiaries of women's expanding possibilities, to inch away from the frightening or disruptive implications of their own position and seek a middle ground. Women preachers in the 1850s and 1860s, for instance, who were increasingly attacked for stepping outside their biblically ordained role, "tried to reassure clergymen that they were not radicals who questioned women's divine subordination to men, but pious Christians whose voices deserved to be heard."[16] Similarly, over the course of the nineteenth century, some woman suffrage activists agreed to a limited suffrage on school boards or advocated literacy require-ments in exchange for granting more educated women the vote. An appeal to more conservative women seemed to require that suffrage rhetoric take on a more "respectable" cast. Leading suffragists, including Elizabeth Cady Stanton, faced with the "insult" of black men's suffrage and feeling aban-doned by male abolitionists after the Civil War, made racist appeals in defense of the prerogatives of white and native-born women. The next generation of middle- and upper-class leaders, more distant both from the movement to end slavery and from the rhetoric of republicanism, assured politicians that woman suffrage would not threaten white supremacy or encourage radical activities. In spite of widespread support for woman suffrage among union members, immigrants, and African Americans, leading suffragists often "railed against the 'slum vote' that defeated woman suffrage referenda" and "stood in silent protest at naturalization ceremonies and considered supporting voting restrictions for black and foreign-born Americans." Those who most vigorously opposed woman suffrage were also those most fearful of an "excess of democracy." The Daughters of the American Revolution, for instance, were active in anti-suffrage campaigns.[17] Faced with their opponents' fears, middle- and upper-class suffragists insisted that women voters would enhance the Christian vote, would lessen partisanship, or would diminish the power of working-class, immigrant, and radical men. Most agreed that women voters would make politics better, cleaner, more domestic, more polite, more religious, or more white.

The Jefferson County women did not so much as hint at religion, maternity, or feminine morality in defense of women's political equality, nor did they stake their right to speak on their own respectability. They never suggested, as others did that summer, that clergymen were their natural allies or that the disfranchisement of ministers was a comparable injustice. Though they knew perfectly well that there were "arguments both numerous and decisive in support of our position," they declared only the "self evident truth" that they had been denied the rights they had "inherited" as citizens. Perhaps in retrospect their petition seems rather innocent, their plea for simple justice not yet defeated by tactical considerations, and their defense of their own belonging a sign of naive privilege. But there is another way to read this. These women lived in a tiny rural community that could draw 2,000 people to a Liberty Party event. They lived in a place whose voters would overwhelmingly endorse African American men's political rights. In that setting, women's full and equal citizenship may indeed have seemed too obvious to require much debate. As they stepped into the larger political conversation taking place in their state, their simple declaration of their rights and their refusal to produce many arguments on its behalf may well have been an ironic pose. They knew that the men to whom they appealed were already torn, as were their political parties, by arguments about slavery and the rights of African Americans, and that what they took for granted locally as "a self evident truth" was far from universal. So they acknowledged, by their refusal to moderate their demands, that they stood within a long-standing political tradition of those who, demanding to be heard but not expecting to win, can say what they think.

The Jefferson County story is one tiny glimpse into a process that is ongoing: how an idea repeatedly declared unthinkable gets raised among a small group of people, is launched into public debate, and becomes part of a conversation about the rights and responsibilities of the nation's citizens. Along the way, of course, claims to full membership in the political community change shape, as an idea becomes familiar and as people struggle to define and defend their own respectability, and thus their right to make demands on those in power. Just as suffragists would later insist that it was women's very difference from men, and especially their experience as mothers, that made them particularly suited to cleanse and reform the nation's political life, many twentieth-century women have appealed to the state "as mothers," prayed to political authorities on behalf of their children, and staked their claim to representation and resources on the basis of their feminine influence. The contradictions in claiming sexual difference as a justification for sexual equality has long pervaded and, in some sense, defined Western feminism.[18] But in the process of making democracy safe for women, the nineteenth century's obsession with religious and sexual morality provided us with categories of exclusion and habits of thinking about civic belonging that are still in use today.

Part of this process of political and intellectual change might seem familiar today. In the 1970s, opponents of the Equal Rights Amendment (ERA) declared ominously that its passage would open the door to same-sex (then called homosexual) marriage. ERA advocates, by and large, insisted that it would not, that such an outcome was unthinkable. It is impossible to ignore how this more recent conversation echoes the one over women's legal rights. Thirty years ago, the notion that the laws of marriage constituted one aspect of the entrenched discrimination against gay men and lesbians was obvious among activists but was barely visible on the agenda of a movement that confronted laws against sodomy, familial rejection, public invisibility, housing and employment discrimination, violence, and outright hatred. Further, in seeking to affirm a sexually liberatory culture, members of radical communities and liberation movements tended to dismiss the state's role in legitimizing sexual and domestic relationships; marriage was widely understood, as Su Docekal recently recalled, as "a pillar of conventional, bourgeois society." The issue rankled and positions were taken, but few imagined that it would soon be openly debated, with enormous policy implications, within the American legal and political system.[19]

Times have changed. Marriage has emerged as a grassroots battleground between civil rights and belonging, on the one hand, and a defense of "eternal" family arrangements (a "definition of marriage that has come to us from custom, tradition, every society, every culture, every nation in all of recorded history as one man and one woman"), on the other. Like the demand for women's political rights, the notion that people of the same sex should be allowed to marry seems as obvious to some Americans as it does blasphemous to others. With that older story in mind, the opposition sounds remarkably familiar. "This is not about religion," insisted a Massachusetts state representative in 2004, adding that "we all have gay and lesbian friends and colleagues and family members." "It's not about a bible. It's not about civil rights. It's not about civil law. It's about natural law with me, the law of nature."[20] Revising the laws of marriage to include gay and lesbian couples, these politicians are declaring, is not simply unworkable or unacceptable or unwinnable; faced with a rhetoric of rights, they have declared it unnatural and unthinkable.

I do not want to be understood here as endorsing a triumphalist approach to history. Quite the contrary. For if the outcome—the inclusion of gay and lesbian couples in the definition and benefits of marriage accorded by the state—has come to seem inevitable, the conversation itself, again like the demand for woman's rights, continues to invoke traditions of exclusion as well as equality. The demand for same-sex marriage was, after all, shaped by the 1980s, a deeply conservative time, when the rise of the religious right and the AIDS crisis imposed a new anxiety about and defense of "family values." Real needs, with previously unconsidered implications for public policy, emerged in force. Few young gay men had thought much about hospital visitation rights before the disastrous outbreak of AIDS. Thus a movement for sexual liberation blended into one that equates full citizenship with marriage and parenthood and that insists urgently that gay men and lesbians are "everywhere," "safe," domesticated—not so different, after all, from what the nineteenth century would have called "virtuous" or "respectable." Indeed, from the massive same-sex marriage industry to the proliferation of gay-friendly religious institutions, dramatic steps toward inclusiveness have redrawn the very boundaries of respectability. None of this is to dismiss or trivialize the many meanings of true acceptance and legal rights. It is, however, to acknowledge that amidst these dramatic changes "hovers a deeply conservative appeal to family as the basis for social legitimacy and political enfranchisement," one that associates rights with conformity to a new domesticity and so excludes others from full membership in the political community.[21]

Rejecting marriage as the basis for full membership in the nation, a critique and analysis that seems barely to have survived the conservatism, the consumerism, and the rise of religious fundamentalism in American politics, still has much to recommend it. Coupledom, Lisa Henderson argues, should not constitute the "measure of maturity—to say nothing of the legal foundation of rights and benefits, from property and tax law to immigration."[22] There remain better or worse, and more or less just, outcomes to this debate, as there were to the seventy-year movement to gain legal and political rights for women. Other choices could have been, and still can be, made—to demand full legal equality, certainly, but also to demand a separation of all state and federal benefits from one's domestic standing, to rethink the antisexual political culture that Americans exemplify, or to fight the expansion of religious rhetoric in American politics and thus shake off the remnants of "sanctity" in our laws. Through each of these conversations, we could reject old habits of exclusion, of boundary making, when we talk about rights and civic belonging.

The conversations that took place in upstate New York in the 1840s are, like so many conversations taking place today, about belonging: about who is "us" and about why our rights depend so heavily on denying them to others. Just as a Protestant consensus helped describe the boundaries of women's political respectability in the nineteenth century, and as the role and image of women continues to define who is "not us" in numerous national contexts, so the struggle over same-sex marriage invokes sexual respectability as part of a renegotiation of people's full membership in the nation. This conversation forces us to reexamine, on the many levels of family, workplace, community, state, and nation, a view of citizenship that is "broadly defined to refer to the status bestowed on those who are 'full members of a community,' . . . [and that] goes beyond the legal rules that govern an individual's relationship to the nation-state to include the social relationships between individuals and the state and between individual citizens."[23] Those relationships still turn, in part, on reasserting boundaries of respectability whose political meanings hold great resonance over time. But we are also reminded by this small and untidy story that once individuals have had an idea and have opened or reopened or merely kept ajar a door, it is difficult to close it, as small groups of people insist upon possibilities once declared unimaginable. If we express in enough corners of these public conversations our conviction that there are enough rights to go around and reject a rhetoric that declares certain categories of ideas out of bounds, we may come to believe that the logic of full and equal human rights is "sufficiently plain without argument."

Notes

ABBREVIATIONS

BFF
  Bishop Family File, Genealogy Department, Flower Memorial Library,
  Watertown, N.Y.

JCD
  Jefferson County Deeds, Office of the County Clerk, Jefferson County,
  Watertown, N.Y.

JCHS
  Jefferson County Historical Society, Watertown, N.Y.

JCSC
  Estate and Administrative Probate Papers, Jefferson County Surrogate's Court,
  Watertown, N.Y.

NARA
  National Archives and Records Administration, Washington, D.C.

Smith Papers
  Gerrit Smith Papers, Microfilm Collection, Special Collections Research Center,
  Syracuse University Library, Syracuse, N.Y.

CHAPTER ONE

1. Foucault, *History of Sexuality*.
2. Trouillot, *Silencing the Past*, 73, 90, 91.
3. Irwin, *Angels and Amazons*, 82.
4. Bishop and Attree, *Report of the Debates and Proceedings*, 646. For an early (and, I now know, sometimes inaccurate) essay about the petition, see Cogan and Ginzberg, "Archives."
5. Stanton, *Eighty Years and More*, 149.
6. During the Cold War, civil rights activists effectively denied or minimized the role of earlier Communist Party activists in imagining a nonsegregated society. Similarly, as Daniel Horowitz has shown, Betty Friedan's story of her recognition of the "problem that has no name" recalls Elizabeth Cady Stanton's assumption that nineteenth-century feminism stemmed from an individual experience of isolation and discontent. Just as Friedan glossed over the left-wing roots of her inquiry into the "woman question," so many nineteenth-century woman's rights

activists ignored both the freethought and working-class roots of feminism, as well as earlier abolitionists' demands for the vote. See Kelley, *Hammer and Hoe*; Horowitz, *Betty Friedan*.

7. See Croswell and Sutton, *Debates and Proceedings*, 480. See also Bishop and Attree, *Report of the Debates and Proceedings*, 284, 763.

8. "New-York Constitutional Convention," *New-York Daily Tribune*, August 17, 1846. For the standard report of proceedings, see *Albany Evening Journal*, August 15, 1846, and *Daily Albany Argus*, August 17, 1846.

9. Lincoln, *Constitutional History of New York*, 2:231. As a result of the *Signs* essay, notice of the petition picked up in time for the seventy-fifth anniversary of the Nineteenth Amendment. See Golden, "Feminism Roots Found in the North."

10. Wellman, "Women's Rights, Republicanism, and Revolutionary Rhetoric in Antebellum New York State," 354–55. On how the *History of Woman Suffrage* has shaped the historiography of the woman's rights movement, see DuBois, "Making Women's History," and Tetrault, "Memory of a Movement."

11. Hough, *History of Jefferson County*.

12. "Affidavit by John G. Webb," Estate of Alpheus S. Greene, JCSC.

13. "Declaration of Sentiments," in Stanton, Anthony, and Gage, *History of Woman Suffrage*, 70–73.

14. Brown, "Negotiating and Transforming the Public Sphere."

15. Isenberg, *Sex and Citizenship in Antebellum America*, xiii.

16. The list of works on woman's rights and politics is lengthy. A classic account, first published in 1959, is Flexner, *Century of Struggle*. See also Paula Baker, "Domestication of Politics"; DuBois, *Feminism and Suffrage*; Hewitt, *Women's Activism and Social Change*; Ryan, *Women in Public*. More recent works include Anderson, *Joyous Greetings*; Hoffert, *When Hens Crow*; Newman, *White Women's Rights*; Terborg-Penn, *African American Women in the Struggle for the Vote*; Zaeske, *Signatures of Citizenship*.

17. Keyssar, *Right to Vote*, xx.

18. "Judicial Account of Burton G. Whitney," Estate of Susan Ormsby, JCSC, 1800O-115.

19. See Boylan, *Origins of Women's Activism*; Ginzberg, *Women and the Work of Benevolence*; VanBurkleo, *"Belonging to the World"*; Varon, *We Mean to be Counted*.

20. *Godey's*, founded in 1830, boasted a circulation of some 63,000 by 1851; see Finley, *Lady of Godey's*, 47.

21. Boydston, Kelley, and Margolis, *Limits of Sisterhood*.

22. Zaeske, *Signatures of Citizenship*, 6, 142.

23. Barry, *Susan B. Anthony*, 97–104; quote is Stanton's, p. 97.

24. See, for example, Mary Vaughan's letters to the *Lily*, in Cott et al., *Root of Bitterness*, 208–12.

25. Petition of the Women of Harrisville, Ohio, NARA. Thanks to Susan Zaeske for bringing this petition to my attention and supplying me with a copy.

26. Federal Writers' Project, *Proceedings of the New Jersey State Constitutional Convention of 1844*, 438.

27. Bishop and Attree, *Report of the Debates and Proceedings*, 763, 284.

28. *National Anti-Slavery Standard*, October 1, 1846, 72. I have quoted here from the *Albany Patriot*, July 15, 1846, which the *National Anti-Slavery Standard* copied.

29. *Albany Patriot*, July 15, 1846.

30. Fairfield, *Federalist Papers*, 111−12.

31. Most of the personal information has been pieced together from deeds, wills, cemetery inscriptions, and federal and state census records (which are notoriously inconsistent as to age). I have found no church records for Depauville churches. The federal census was taken every ten years, and New York's state census was done every five. Unfortunately I have been unable to locate the relevant sections of the 1845 New York State census. Very scattered genealogical records and occasional obituaries exist, such as "Bible Records" [Aaron Bishop] in BFF; these have provided valuable bits of information. Debbie Quick of the Historical Association of South Jefferson provided me with a copy of "Obituary of Amy Ormsby," *Jefferson County Journal*, January 20, 1885. The work of genealogists in making information available online has been extraordinary; see <www.rootsweb.com/~nyjeffer> and <www.usgennet.org>. Among the online data are listings of local cemetery inscriptions, occasional vital records, and some census data, as well as scanned copies of county histories and maps. In visits to Jefferson County I have seen and confirmed some of these families' gravestones, including those of Vincents, Williamses, and Osborns (Depauville cemetery) and Zerviah Williams (Corbins Corners).

  The Family History Center of the Church of Latter-Day Saints and its genealogy website are invaluable resources for acquiring state and local information on microfilm. Their records include voluminous Daughters of the American Revolution records of family Bibles, various indexes to wills and estates, marriage and death records, and court records. That few of these yielded specific information about the six women in Jefferson County or their families is no reflection on this extraordinary collection.

  A note about spelling: the spelling of names and places varies widely in nineteenth-century documents. Eleanor O'Connor Vincent is listed as Ellanor, Elinor, and O'Conner; Alpheus Greene appears often as Green; Osborn, as Osburn and Osborne; etc. I use the most common or most standard spelling and have avoided using *sic* when the spelling appears differently in the record. The section of Clayton they lived in is spelled "Depauville" (after Francis Depau) in most places; only the 1855 map of the area spells it "Depeauville" (see map 4).

32. Nahum D. Williams may have been one of the first white children to have been born in Jefferson. The 1855 New York State census lists him as fifty-one years old and records Jefferson County, N.Y., as his place of birth.

33. JCD, S2/556−57. The timing of Nahum's marriages is unclear. Zerviah's gravestone in Corbin cemetery may list the death year as 1842 at thirty-one years old. And the 1840 census indicates that a woman between the ages of thirty and forty lived in the household.

34. Flexner, *Century of Struggle*, 77.

35. JCD, 92/244−45.
36. For example, Phineas A. Osborn, Joseph's brother, married Ann Frame (1806−55), and Halladays were related to Hiram and Amy Ormsby.
37. Cogan and Ginzberg, "Archives," 436.
38. Faragher, *Sugar Creek*, 56−60, suggests a similar pattern of association. However, the Jefferson County settlers did not experience an "isolation [that] robbed women of the company and companionship of female peers" (112). Other historians have also noted the importance of family networks in "generat[ing] the distinctive configuration of rural society" (Osterud, *Bonds of Community*, 52).
39. This pattern continued through the next generation. For example, Thomas Osborn (Joseph's brother) was married to Harriet Patchin, another neighbor. When their daughter Lovina died in 1888 at age sixty-four, her last name was Vincent.
40. See Hal S. Barron, "Staying Down on the Farm: Social Processes of Settled Rural Life in the Nineteenth-Century North," in Hahn and Prude, *Countryside in the Age of Capitalist Transformation*, 335.
41. "Final Account of Lydia A. Williams," Estate of Nahum D. Williams, JCSC, 1800W-110.
42. Hough, *History of Jefferson County*, 430.

CHAPTER TWO

1. Quoted in Stanton, Anthony, and Gage, *History of Woman Suffrage*, 65.
2. Quoted in Zagarri, "Rights of Man and Woman," 223.
3. Kerber, *No Constitutional Right to Be Ladies*, xx.
4. Even here, the exceptions were numerous and complex and signal the boundaries of full belonging in the nation. In 1834 a controversy occurred over the passport application of free African American Robert Purvis. See Winch, *Gentleman of Color*, 262. Interestingly, later disputes over granting passports to free African Americans involved the secretary of state, former senator John M. Clayton, after whom the town of Clayton was named. See *Albany Atlas*, July 27−September 4, 1849.
5. See Rogers M. Smith, *Civic Ideals*; Kerber, *No Constitutional Right to Be Ladies*; Cott, *Public Vows*; Grossberg, *Judgment for Solomon* and *Governing the Hearth*; Hartog, "Abigail Bailey's Coverture" and *Man and Wife in America*.
6. Kerber, *No Constitutional Right to Be Ladies*, 9; Zagarri, "Rights of Man and Woman," 228.
7. Kerber, *No Constitutional Right to Be Ladies*, 9, xxiii.
8. Ibid., 24. Writing to the *New-York Weekly Museum*, a "Lady" worried that merely discussing "equality of right" would "excit[e] an insurrection in the female world" (Zagarri, "Rights of Man and Woman," 237).
9. Boydston, "Making Gender in the Early Republic," 242, 246, 241.
10. Scott, *Only Paradoxes to Offer*, 3.
11. Landes, *Women and the Public Sphere in the Age of the French Revolution*, 7. See Pateman, *Disorder of Woman* and *Sexual Contract*; Hesse, *Other Enlightenment*; Phillips, *Engendering Democracy*.

12. Kann, *Republic of Men*, 82.

13. Perley, *Debates, Resolutions, and Other Proceedings*, 149.

14. For a discussion of the disfranchisement of propertied women in New Jersey, see Klinghoffer and Elkis, "'Petticoat Electors.'"

15. See Barbara Taylor, *Mary Wollstonecraft and the Feminist Imagination*.

16. Zagarri, "Rights of Man and Woman," 203, 205.

17. *Proceedings and Debates of the Virginia State Convention of 1829–30*, 383–84, 438.

18. *Yankee and Boston Literary Gazette*, March 5, 1829, 77.

19. Jones, *Treatise on the Right of Suffrage*, 48; Mansfield, *Legal Rights, Liabilities and Duties of Woman*, 128.

20. Quaife, *Convention of 1846*, 219.

21. See Hoff, *Law, Gender, and Injustice*, 170–74.

22. *Journal and Debates of the Constitutional Convention of the State of Wyoming*, 365–66.

23. *Mechanic's Free Press*, August 8, 1829.

24. See Ginzberg, "'Hearts of Your Readers Will Shudder.'"

25. *New-Harmony Gazette*, November 23, 1825, 69.

26. "Address of Sarah Monroe" and "An Address Delivered Before the United Tailoresses Society," in Cott et al., *Root of Bitterness*, 119–21.

27. Boston *Evening Transcript* quoted in Dublin, *Women at Work*, 91; "daughters of freemen" references, 93–94.

28. Quoted in Dublin, *Women at Work*, 117.

29. "Backwoodsman," *Albany Patriot*, May 14, 1845.

30. [Warner], *Inquiry*, 9, 13, 189. This is sometimes attributed to Theodore Frelinghuysen, but the Library of Congress catalog (and penciled notation in New York Public Library copy) identify it as Warner's work.

31. Mr. Young, in L. H. Clarke, *Report of the Debates and Proceedings*, 236. For each state's early oaths, see Neil H. Cogan, *Complete Bill of Rights*. Until the early nineteenth century New York State also restricted Catholics from seeking office.

32. Perley, *Debates, Resolutions, and Other Proceedings*, 72.

33. Quotes are in Feldman, *Please Don't Wish Me a Merry Christmas*, 187; Borden, *Jews, Turks, and Infidels*, 39. See Eitches, "Maryland's 'Jew Bill,'" and Brackenridge, Worthington, and Tyson, *Speeches on the Jew Bill*.

34. *Atwood v. Walton*, 7 Con. 66, quoted in *American Jurist and Law Magazine* 3 (April 1830): 389; *People v. Ruggles*, 8 John. 290, 293 (1811) (NY State Supreme Court). I am indebted to Sarah Barringer Gordon for bringing several of these cases to my attention. For an excellent discussion of these and other cases, see her "Blasphemy and the Law of Religious Liberty."

35. Bishop and Attree, *Report of the Debates and Proceedings*, 1055.

36. Indeed, liberals argued that tolerance did not equal full acceptance of all sects: "Can any person . . . believe, that were there a *Shaker* society in Albany . . . their *ministering elder* [would] be permitted to perform any of his religious duties in the Legislature? Can it be imagined that the Legislature meant, under any

circumstances, to give a *call* to *Shaker* chaplains?" (*Free Enquirer*, May 19, 1832, 236).

37. Tocqueville, *Democracy in America*, 1:305–6. Even without religious oaths, Mr. Iredell of North Carolina exclaimed confidently in 1788, "it is never to be supposed that the people of America will trust their dearest rights to persons who have no religion at all, or a religion materially different from their own" (Neil H. Cogan, *Complete Bill of Rights*, 64).

38. [Warner], *Inquiry*, 121.

39. See Kolmerton, *American Life of Ernestine L. Rose*; Suhl, *Ernestine L. Rose*.

40. *Racine Advocate*, quoted in Quaife, *Struggle over Ratification*, 492.

41. See Zagarri, "Rights of Man and Woman."

42. See Ginzberg, " 'Hearts of Your Readers Will Shudder' " and " 'Pernicious Heresies.' "

43. Having "Jews, Turks, and Infidels" exemplify the political threat of non-Christians also provided a shorthand with which to condemn religious outsiders within the United States, such as Mormons. See, for example, Tyrrell, *Woman's World / Woman's Empire*, 140–41.

44. L. H. Clarke, *Report of the Debates and Proceedings*, 303.

45. Isenberg, *Sex and Citizenship in Antebellum America*, 87.

46. Rupp, *Worlds of Women*, 58. The emergence of a Western discourse against veiling is a fascinating story in this context. See Ahmed, *Women and Gender in Islam*, chap. 8.

47. "Woman," *Ladies' Repository*, April 1841, available online at Making of America <http://www.hti.umich.edu/m/moagrp/>.

48. John Neal, "Rights of Woman," *Brother Jonathan*, June 1843, 183.

49. Bishop and Attree, *Report of the Debates and Proceedings*, 551.

50. *Proceedings and Debates of the Virginia State Convention of 1829–30*, 459.

51. *Updegraph v. Commonwealth of Pa.*, Supreme Court (1824), 11 Serge. & Rawl. 393, 398–99, 408.

52. *Debates of the Convention to Amend the Constitution of Pennsylvania*, 540.

53. In Kerber, *No Constitutional Right to Be Ladies*, 25.

CHAPTER THREE

1. Landon, *North Country*, 1:206; Meinig, "Geography of Expansion," 140. See also Hough, *History of Jefferson County*, 25.

2. Haydon, *Upstate Travels*, 164.

3. Hough, *History of Jefferson County*, 3.

4. These were the same years that Sugar Creek, Illinois, saw its first white settlers, a process described in Faragher, *Sugar Creek*. In some ways, the settlement of Jefferson County more closely resembled that of Otsego, New York. But whereas William Cooper first viewed his landholdings in 1785 and had sold land, laid out streets, and settled there by 1790, Depauville remained unsettled for another generation. By 1820, Alan Taylor writes, "Otsego was no longer a promising, frontier county, but an aging rural district transformed by twenty to thirty years

of hard labor with axes, saws, oxen, and fire." "Densely settled" and "mature," the county was already experiencing significant outmigration just as Jefferson County's farms and towns were being cleared. See Alan Taylor, *William Cooper's Town*, 386, 387. On other settlements of upstate New York, see esp. Osterud, *Bonds of Community*.

5. Hough, *History of Jefferson County*, 127, 124.

6. Lyman Ellis settled in Ellisburgh about 1797, Noadiah Hubbard did so in Champion around the same time, and Jacob Brown had established Brownville by 1799. Much of the information about Jefferson is from Hough, *History of Jefferson County*; other resources include Higgins, *Expansion in New York*; Landon, *North Country*; Ellsworth, "Settlement of the North Country." Seemingly absurd predictions were common. According to Hough, one group in the town of Champion, emboldened by whiskey, were talking, "and one more sanguine than the rest, hazarded the prediction, *that there were those then living, who would see a weekly line of mail stages pass through the town*" (Hough, *History of Jefferson County*, 129). But already by 1804, Daniel Gould was carrying the mail to Jacob Brown's home weekly; by 1812, stagecoaches operated on a regular, if muddy, basis in several communities on the lake and inland. See Ellsworth, "Settlement of the North Country," 194.

7. Jefferson and St. Lawrence Counties, *1810 and 1820 Federal Population Census Schedules*. Quote is in Landon, *North Country*, 1:219.

8. Hough, *History of Jefferson County*, 30-31.

9. Brownville was established several years before the county itself. Orleans and Lyme were taken from parts of it in 1818, and then another section became Clayton in 1833. Information on Depauville's history as a neighborhood of each of these comes from William Gillette (or Gillet), *History of Depauville* (1905). Written for the Jefferson County Centennial, this now appears on <www.rootsweb.com>; as a pamphlet, *Depauville* (1905; repr. 1993); and as a supplement to *The Thousand Islands Sun Vacationer*, August 27, September 3, 10, 1997. Also see Hough, *History of Jefferson County*, 143-45.

10. Fitch, *Watertown Directory*, 13; Hough, *History of Jefferson County*, 113. In 1815 James Le Ray wrote Ethal Bronson, "As it appears that the Blessings of Peace are to be again our Lot, I am about to renew an Undertaking which the War had stopt in its beginning. In the year 1812 I obtained from the Legislature a grant for a Turnpike from Chaumont, to Cape Vincent, and one from Watertown, to Indian River" (February 17, 1815, Archive Box on Early Roads, JCHS). Faragher notes similar timing in Illinois; see *Sugar Creek*, 33.

11. Hedrick, *History of Agriculture*, 181. In 1819 William Darby reported that trade along the St. Lawrence was much greater than most Americans thought; see *Tour from the City of New York*, 76-77.

12. Boydston, "Woman Who Wasn't There," 189; James Le Ray de Chaumont, *An Address*, 12.

13. Hedrick, *History of Agriculture*, 181; Peterson, *Democracy, Liberty, and Property*, 125; James Le Ray de Chaumont, *An Address*, 13.

14. Stilwell, *Migration from Vermont*, 114. New England's loss of population and increase in large farms mirrored New York's growth. Faced with steady population decline, Vermont claimed a first place of dubious value. "No other state in the entire Union," remarked Stilwell dryly, "has sent forth so large a proportion of its people to aid in the establishment of newer commonwealths" (64). By about 1820, Vermont was "so to speak, bankrupt" (151). For a different approach to Vermont's outmigration, see Barron, *Those Who Stayed Behind*.

15. Hardin, *History of Herkimer County*, 434.

16. Ibid., 26.

17. The county's "population increas[ed] from 15,000 in 1810 to over 34,000 in 1820" (Landon, *North Country*, 1:206). For the act authorizing these roads, see Hough, *History of Jefferson County*, 316–17. By 1820, 278 companies in New York had been chartered to construct and operate a planned 6,000 miles of roads; see Meinig, "Geography of Expansion," 156.

18. "Old State Road." See Oliver W. Holmes, "The Turnpike Era," in Flick, *History of the State of New York*, 270, 272; Hough, *History of Jefferson County*, 322–34.

19. On pre-Revolutionary disputes over French, English, and Indian landownership, see Ellsworth, "Settlement of the North Country," 181–82; Meinig, "Geography of Expansion," 141. See also Hough, *History of Jefferson County*, 153, 196–97.

20. Gates, *Farmer's Age*, 30. See also Halsey, *Old New York Frontier*, 338.

21. Fox, *Yorkers and Yankees*, 18.

22. Hedrick, *History of Agriculture*, 40; Macauley, *Natural, Statistical, and Civil History*, 3:427, 428.

23. Quoted in Fox, *Decline of Aristocracy*, 126.

24. Powell, *Penet's Square*, 116. This was also the largest sale ever made by the state. See Ellsworth, "Settlement of the North Country," 189.

25. Quoted in Alan Taylor, *William Cooper's Town*, 113–14 (spellings and brackets are Taylor's); Hough, *History of Jefferson County*, 45.

26. Hough, *History of Jefferson County*, 39–44, includes the Fort Stanwix treaty in its entirety. For the most detailed account of Penet's Square, see Powell, *Penet's Square*; on how French residents in New York gained and then lost the right to own land, see 128–34.

27. Massey, *Links in the Chain*, 10.

28. Moore, "Some French Influences," 126–28.

29. Quote in Hough, *History of Jefferson County*, 57. Former president John Adams, no Francophone, congratulated Le Ray on founding the Jefferson County Agricultural Society. "Thirty-nine years ago, I little thought I should live to see the heir-apparent to the princely palaces and garden of Passy, my fellow citizen in the republican wilderness of America," Adams wrote; see ibid., 404.

30. Scharer, "African-Americans in Jefferson County," 7.

31. Landon, *North Country*, 1:271; Powell, *Penet's Square*, 167, 171, 157; Hough, *History of Jefferson County*, 62.

32. Hough, *History of Jefferson County*, 209; A. G. Marshall, "Historical Sketch of Orleans Township," JCHS, 2.

33. Macomb's tract number 4, on which some of the settlers would eventually settle, was surveyed in 1796 by a team of men who created 1,000 sites, each of 440 acres; see Hough, *History of Jefferson County*, 55–56. As Andro Linklater has shown, it was the land survey that made the possession of land and, therefore, the development of communities, a reality; see Linklater, *Measuring America*. Laurel Thatcher Ulrich describes a similar pattern of squatters and surveyors, among them Martha Ballard's husband, in *Midwife's Tale*, e.g., 212–17. A chain of 100 links equals 22 yards.

34. Hough, *History of Jefferson County*, 136; Garand, *Historical Sketch of the Village of Clayton*, 17.

35. Linklater, *Measuring America*, 169; Hough, *History of Jefferson County*, 136, 209. According to Faragher, *Sugar Creek*, 43, 54–55, by the time surveyors arrived in 1821, "emigrants had already begun the process of transforming Sugar Creek into an American farming community" and the population of Illinois had passed 13,000 *before* the arrival of legal titles to land.

36. Of course, this renaming was part of a long tradition of asserting ownership of land. Pieces of far northern New York had been owned by the Onondagas, Oneidas, and Mohawks, most of whom had long left the area. The state of New York, as the new colonial power, renamed these places; many were changed again to reflect the ambitions of a more local gentry.

37. A. G. Marshall, "Historical Sketch of Orleans Township," JCHS, 1.

38. Hough, *History of Jefferson County*, 210–12; Massey, *Links in the Chain*, 10.

39. Massey, *Links in the Chain*, 10; Hough, *History of Jefferson County*, 212–13; Powell, *Penet's Square*, 175.

40. Massey, *Links in the Chain*, 117.

41. JCD, P2/357–59; Higgins, *Expansion in New York*, 148.

42. A copy of this broadside is in Gates, *Farmer's Age*, 32.

43. Cornelia (named in 1823) became Clayton when the first town meeting was held at the home of Isaac L. Carter in June 1833; see Hough, *History of Jefferson County*, 135–45. William Angel offered the name Clayton, after "an ardent Whig and a man whom he much admired," senator and, later, secretary of state John M. Clayton of Delaware; see *Clayton on the St. Lawrence*, JCHS, 9, 11. See also Frank D. Rogers speech in Coughlin, *Jefferson County Centennial*. On Depauville store, see French, *Gazetteer of the State of New York*, 357.

44. *Watertown Eagle*, March 20, 1853, in Hough, *History of Jefferson County*, 138.

45. Fitch, *Watertown Directory*, 8; Landon, *North Country*, 1:137. Farmhands got $8–11/month; mechanics, $12–16. These costs are also cited in Gates, *Farmer's Age*, 34.

46. JCD, P2/357–59.

47. Hough, *History of Jefferson County*, 79.

48. The work and dangers of clearing land were enormous. Mrs. Gallt in Herkimer County, "always afraid" that her husband or son would be hurt, "would listen whenever a tree fell and they had a signal, after the tree came down and they were all right, they would pound on the log with the axe three times so she would

know they were safe" (Conklin, *Through "Poverty's Vale,"* 131). Solon Massey recalled that Watertown's first deaths were those of men crushed by falling trees; see column dated May 24, 1850, in Massey, *Links in the Chain.* Early settlers referred to girdled trees as "widow-makers" (Faragher, *Sugar Creek,* 64). On potash, also called "Black salts," see Alan Taylor, *William Cooper's Town,* 108–9; Powell, *Penet's Square,* 149; Ellsworth, "Settlement of the North Country," 198; Landon, *North Country,* 1:129. On potash's role in soap production, see Tryon, *Household Manufactures,* 236.

49. *Life on the Border Sixty Years Ago,* quoted in Ellsworth, "Settlement of the North Country," 206–7; Conklin, *Through "Poverty's Vale,"* 11.

50. The Vincents, Ormsbys, and Osborns accumulated not more than 100 to 150 acres over a period of decades. Most observers agreed that a farm this size, if efficiently worked, could support a family better than one twice as large. Farms in New England, for example, averaged just under 100 acres. See Alan Taylor, *William Cooper's Town,* 72. Agricultural journals commonly complained that farmers bought too much land.

51. Fathers in Oneida County's founding generation (1790–1820) commonly provided some land to older sons and left the parental farm to the youngest. This seems to have been true in the Ormsbys' case, although Bailey was only fifteen when his father Elias died in 1828. See Ryan, *Cradle of the Middle Class,* 28–29.

52. In the Jefferson County Historical Society, a small leatherbound book lists the tax assessments for the town of Orleans for 1824. State of New-York, *Census* (1825), indicates how many of the acres were improved. Vincent's first deed is dated June 2, 1834, JCD, P2/357–59. In addition to Vincent, the book lists other men old enough to have owned land: Phineas A. Osborn with 80 improved acres; Phineas Osborn with 60; Elias Ormsby, 40; John Smith, 27; and Benjamin Vincent.

53. JCD, S2/556–57. This may have been land that Susan Ormsby inherited from her brother in 1848. See "Inventory and Real Estate Appraisal," Estate of Susan Ormsby, JCSC, 1800O-115.

54. JCD, 104/402.

55. JCD, D3/574–55.

56. JCD, K2/223–24.

57. Hiram Ormsby purchases, JCD, W2/590–92, D3/575–76, L3/421–23, 92/494–95, 92/495–97; sale to Williams, JCD, F3/114–15, and to Woodin, JCD, T2/372; Osborn purchase, JCD, N2/74–75; Williams purchase, JCD, S2/555–56.

58. Quote is from sale by Fox to B. Vincent, 1835, JCD, R2/181.

59. Hough, *History of Jefferson County,* 96–97.

60. T. Wood Clarke, *Émigrés in the Wilderness,* 169; Landon, *North Country,* 1:271; A. G. Marshall, "Historical Sketch of Orleans Township," JCHS, 11–12.

61. Landon, *North Country,* 1:272; Hough, *History of Jefferson County,* 142.

62. *Watertown American,* February 2, 1837, in T. Wood Clarke, *Émigrés in the Wilderness,* 173–75. The farm was purchased by Bishop Dubois, who opened St. Vincent De Paul, a Catholic seminary, on the grounds. Considered "too remote,"

the seminary soon moved to New York City, where it ultimately became Fordham University. See Hough, *History of Jefferson County*, 213–14.

63. See Jacob Katz Cogan, "Look Within."

64. The wording of this stipulation varies only slightly; this one is from an 1824 sale by John and Zurviah Bishop to Luther Bishop, JCD, U/491–92. See Hurlbut, *Essays on Human Rights*, 167.

65. Hurlbut, *Essays on Human Rights*, 166.

66. Boydston, *Home and Work*.

67. Kelly, *In the New England Fashion*, 9.

68. Mary Ryan describes a "corporate family economy" in Oneida County whose interdependence across generations and between the sexes would have seemed familiar to the Jefferson County families. Still, settling a full generation later and engaged in a later market economy and intellectual culture, they may not have established the "patriarchal" relations that Ryan proposes for Oneida. See Ryan, *Cradle of the Middle Class*, 31.

69. Kelly, *In the New England Fashion*, 12.

70. Jensen, *Loosening the Bonds*, 128.

71. Ibid., e.g., 84–87. Jensen notes that producing butter in large quantities for sale "took increased time from [women's] more traditional duties, especially the preparation of cloth" (87).

72. Information about the ownership of domestic animals and the produce on the farms is in State of New-York, *Census* (1825). Jensen claims that the average mid-Atlantic farm in 1850 had about six dairy cows; see *Loosening the Bonds*, 96. Faragher, *Sugar Creek*, considers an eighty-acre farm with "several score of hogs, a dozen head of cattle, oxen, and milch cows, a small flock of sheep, and assorted poultry" about average and able to support a decent living (98).

73. Gates, *Farmer's Age*, 264; *Cultivator*, January 1844, 86; Darby, *Tour from the City of New York*, 121; *Cultivator*, April 1846, 132. See also *Cultivator*, February 1846, 70.

74. Thomas F. Gordon, *Gazetteer of the State of New York*, 65; Hedrick, *History of Agriculture*, 184.

75. See, for example, Hedrick, *History of Agriculture*, 214.

76. *Cultivator*, February 1837, 199–200. I have been unable to find out if he was related to Anna [Carter] Bishop.

77. Gates, *Farmer's Age*, 303–4; *Cultivator*, May 1836, 47; *Monthly Genesee Farmer*, May 1, 1837, 69; *Cultivator*, February 1837, 199–200. Major Edmund Kirby, in an *Address Delivered Before the Jefferson County Agricultural Society*, 15, assured his audience that silkworm production was "perfectly simple."

78. Declaring wild speculation dangerous, agricultural editors' "words of caution . . . generally came after the contagion had reached ridiculous heights," and in any case, the editors had often promoted the enthusiasm in the first place. See Demaree, *American Agricultural Press*, 60–61, quote on 63.

79. *Cultivator*, March 1844, 100; Emmons, *Agriculture in New-York*, 2:297–98; *Working Farmer*, June 1850, 95.

80. Emmons, *Agriculture in New-York*, 3:2, 129; French, *Gazetteer of the State of New York*, 104–7.
81. State of New-York, *Census* (1855), refers to a household's "neat cattle" and does not distinguish between beef and dairy cows.
82. Osterud, *Bonds of Community*, 33.
83. "Inventory," Estate of Lydia Osborn, October 23, 1875, JCSC, 18000-91. On the motley assortment of cows preferred by dairying households, see McMurry, *Transforming Rural Life*, 18–19.
84. "Difficulty in Producing Butter," *Cultivator*, January 1847, 30; *Cultivator*, June 1838, 79.
85. Gates, *Farmer's Age*, 242. According to Gates, New York State produced 22 percent of the butter (242) and 46 percent of the cheese (244) made in the country.
86. *Lewis County Republican*, quoted in *Working Farmer*, December 1850, 221.
87. Massey, *Links in the Chain*, 40.
88. Conklin, *Through "Poverty's Vale,"* 55–56. Halsey, *Old New York Frontier*, also contains vivid descriptions of these early labors; see, e.g., 392–99.
89. On domestic manufacturing in particular households, see State of New-York, *Census* (1825), Brownville, and (1835), Clayton.
90. That year the county produced 54,470 yards of fulled cloth, 77,082 of unfulled cloth, and 144,758 yards of thin cloth; see Tryon, *Household Manufactures*, tab. 12, p. 171; tab. 15, p. 288. See also 202–6.
91. Tryon, *Household Manufactures*, 249. See Faragher, *Sugar Creek*, 208–9.
92. Conklin, *Through "Poverty's Vale,"* 99–100.
93. McMurry, *Transforming Rural Life*, e.g., 235. Tryon, *Household Manufactures*, describes these processes in detail; see, e.g., 206–14. See also Boydston, *Home and Work*, esp. 94–97.
94. Tryon, *Household Manufactures*, tab. 16, p. 304; tab. 18, p. 316. Aggregate county-wide figures on agricultural and household production are included in French, *Gazetteer of the State of New York*.
95. *Cultivator*, April 1836, 30; *Journal of the New-York State Agricultural Society* 1, no. 4 (August 1850): 49.
96. McMurry, *Transforming Rural Life*, 66–67. Hal Barron describes men working alongside one another in a similar context on a farm of comparable size in rural Vermont; see *Those Who Stayed Behind*, 53–56.
97. Estate of Timothy O'Connor, JCSC, 18000-83.
98. By 1860 Abraham Vincent had three children still living at home, and his farm was assessed at $1,400 in real estate and $500 in personal property.
99. JCD, 132/632–33; JCD, 162/237–38. The location of particular parcels of land is difficult to sort out. But the land that Eleanor Vincent purchased in 1856 is likely that designated as "L. Vincent's" on the 1864 map of Clayton (see map 5). Since both the 1860 and 1870 censuses show the Vincents living in Lyme, they may have moved to a new home on the land she next purchased, consisting of 36.9 acres, and given or sold Leonard their other land. Nahum and Lydia Williams are also listed in Lyme in 1860, so it is also possible that the town boundaries changed once again.

100. JCD, 181/517; JCD, 245/119–20; U.S. Bureau of the Census, *Ninth Census*. Whitney offered both properties at public auction, the parcels having been appraised at $1,250 and $250, respectively; the highest bid for the farm was $970, to be paid in cash by the current tenant, Fred V. Haas. See Estate of Susan Ormsby, JCSC, 1800O-115.

101. Estate of Nahum D. Williams, JCSC, 1800W-110.

102. "Final Account of Lydia A. Williams," ibid.

103. See Barron, *Those Who Stayed Behind*, e.g., 78–79, 93.

104. *Jeffersonian*, February 17, 1841, and various issues, including throughout January 1841. Magnetism piece in *Jeffersonian*, May 10, 1841.

105. *Albany Atlas*, esp. April 3, 1849.

106. Conklin, *Through "Poverty's Vale,"* 138; "Influence of Agricultural Journals," *Cultivator*, April 1849, 109–10; *Albany Atlas*, April 16, 1849.

107. Estate of Timothy O'Connor, clipping in the *Albany Evening Journal*, JCSC, 1800O-83; Estate of Nahum D. Williams, clipping in the *Albany Evening Journal*, JCSC, 1800W-110; Estate of Joseph Osborn, clipping in the *Albany Evening Journal*, JCSC, 1800O-106.

108. Stanton to Anthony, April 2, 1852, in DuBois, *Elizabeth Cady Stanton, Susan B. Anthony*, 55.

CHAPTER FOUR

1. Hedrick, *History of Agriculture*, 199.

2. Hough, *History of Jefferson County*, 166. In 1824 John Bishop purchased 150 acres on what became known as Bishop Street. He sold 50 acres to his son Luther (who was by then married and the father of two children). Luther and his brothers soon added adjoining land, often buying and selling among themselves. See JCD, U/491–92; BFF. Luther's father was likely the John Bishop who, with 138 others, signed the Declaration of Subscribers on April 12, 1776, to oppose British hostility "against the United American Colonies" and who served in New Hampshire's 6th Company of Colonel Baldwin's regiment. See Randall, *History of Chesterfield*, 51–53, 91. Anna Bishop's father, John Carter, was also a Revolutionary veteran and may have been one of many who first saw northern New York during the war.

3. JCD, 92/244–45.

4. BFF; obituary of Sylvester Bishop from *New York Reformer*, November 8, 1860, BFF. The obituary refers to him as an esteemed Depauville minister in the Methodist Episcopal Church. The family Bible refers to Luther as a Baptist. In John Fletcher Bishop's periodical *The Revivalist*, "Baptist" and "Methodist" seem to be used almost interchangeably to refer to evangelists of whom the author approved. See *The Revivalist*, May 1859, 120 and contents. The only known copy is at the Southern Baptist Theological Seminary; Christy Davis made it available to me.

5. Hough, *History of Jefferson County*, 170; quote is in obituary of Sylvester Bishop, BFF.

6. Gaustad, *Historical Atlas of Religion*, 37; Hatch, *Democratization of American Christianity*, 184; Matthews, *Toward a New Society*, 43.

7. *The Beacon*, March 11, 1837, 187.

8. "Modern Religion," *The Telescope*, July 7, 1827, 21. See also Dr. Thomas Cooper, "Arrogant Pretensions of the Orthodox Clergy," *The Beacon*, September 26, 1840, 356.

9. There is no way to know, but women in the Baptist congregation likely heard the news in 1844 when the General Conference of Freewill Baptists formally barred women from exercising political authority within the church. Nor do I know whether the Millerite revivals of the mid-1840s, with their strong support for female lecturers, made their way to the far North Country. See Brekus, *Strangers and Pilgrims*, 289, 318–19.

10. Hedrick, *History of Agriculture*, 271.

11. Brekus, *Strangers and Pilgrims*, 77.

12. Hough, *History of Jefferson County*, 132–33, 127; *Journal of the Rev. John Taylor*, 680.

13. Hough, *History of Jefferson County*, 133.

14. "A Narrative of the State of Religion," *American Missionary Register*, June 1823, 189.

15. Hough, *History of Jefferson County*, 76, 106–7. See also Haddock, *Growth of a Century*, 573.

16. Conklin, *Through "Poverty's Vale,"* 126.

17. Wellman, *Grass Roots Reform in the Burned-Over District*, 65; American Baptist Home Missionary Society, *Third Report of the Executive Committee* (1835), 15. In contrast, the society sent two agents to Upper Canada, sixteen to Illinois, and thirteen to Indiana.

18. He may be related to Alpheus Greene, one of whose sisters married a Webb. Greene's nephew was John G. Webb, also a devout Baptist.

19. American Baptist Home Missionary Society, *Eleventh Report* (1843), 31, 56 (the Lefargeville association had 3,241 members, and the Jefferson Union had 418). As late as 1851 the *Home Missionary* reported the appointment of a missionary to Chaumont, Jefferson County; see *Home Missionary*, May 1851, 20.

20. Alan Taylor, *William Cooper's Town*, 212–14, 227.

21. Hough, *History of Jefferson County*, 394.

22. On the role of dissenting sects in antebellum reform, see Hewitt, *Women's Activism and Social Change*. Brekus points to far greater tolerance of women preachers among Freewill Baptists, Methodists, and African Methodists than among more orthodox churches; see *Strangers and Pilgrims*, 16. Freewill Baptists had openly endorsed abolitionism by 1837, having declared slavery "sinful" two years earlier; see McKivigan, *War against Proslavery Religion*, 43–44.

23. *Albany Patriot*, January 1, 1845; "Prospectus," *The Revivalist*, May 1859.

24. Sweet, *Religion on the American Frontier*, 72, 17.

25. Obituary of Amy Ormsby, *Jefferson County Journal*, January 20, 1885.

26. Hough, *History of Jefferson County*, 144.

27. Gaustad, *Historical Atlas of Religion*, 79–81. On an 1850 map, a dark blotch over Jefferson and St. Lawrence counties (indicating twenty-five or more congregations) signals a Methodist stronghold. See ibid., fig. 64, p. 78.

28. *The Revivalist*, May 1859, 120 and contents.

29. Ellis et al., *Short History of New York State*, 307; Ahlstrom, *Religious History*, 1:584–87.

30. Rose, *Transcendentalism as a Social Movement*, 166–67.

31. Quoted in Marty, *Pilgrims in Their Own Land*, 333.

32. Ahlstrom, *Religious History*, 1:584.

33. Ellis et al., *Short History of New York State*, 11–12.

34. *Albany Patriot*, November 20, 1844.

35. Foreword by Louis C. Jones in Ellis et al., *Short History of New York State*, ix.

36. Hough, *History of Jefferson County*, 39–41; Powell, *Penet's Square*, 72, 93. The Reverend P. S. Garand, the bishop of Ogdensburg, saw in the signatures by "four squaws" along with those of men "proof that the Iroquois had already emerged from the state of savagery to the milder stage of barbarism." "In the savage state," he explained, "inheritance is only in the female line and women alone can sign away real estate." For Garand, Iroquois men's claim to *any* authority marked progress toward full male ownership of land. See Garand, *Historical Sketch of the Village of Clayton*, 11.

37. A. G. Marshall, "Historical Sketch of Orleans Township," JCHS.

38. Wagner, *Sisters in Spirit*, quotes on 44, 32, 37.

39. Referring to its state's 1839 passage of the first married women's property act, the Mississippi Bar Association noted that the law "embodied and was suggested by the tribal customs of the Chickasaw Indians, who lived in our borders" (quoted in ibid., 75).

40. In 1839, when Benjamin and Polly Vincent sold land, Benjamin signed with "his mark" (JCD, I3/102–3). Luther Bishop's mother, Zurviah, signed with her mark in 1824 (JCD, U/491–92). So did longtime neighbor Lucy Corbin (JCD, D3/574–75). District schools, with ungraded classes and rudimentary curricula, were held from four to six months of the year; see Hedrick, *History of Agriculture*, 198.

41. Obituary of Amy Ormsby, *Jefferson County Journal*, January 20, 1885.

42. "Judicial Account of Burton G. Whitney," Inventory, Estate of Susan Ormsby, JCSC, 18000-115.

43. The first female school is mentioned in Massey, *Links in the Chain*, 30. See also Hough, *History of Jefferson County*, 378, 389.

44. *Emma Willard and Her Pupils*. The Cady sisters are on 147–49, and Lazette and Frances Miller, the future Mrs. Worden and Mrs. Seward, are on 82.

45. The main source on Zeruvia Porter Weed is *Faith and Works*.

46. Tocqueville, *Democracy in America*, 2:111. Mott, *American Journalism*, 194, says that before the 1830s, "more than ninety per cent of the mails consisted of newspapers." Further, newspapers propelled other political matters, since as Mott

points out, "poor mail service was the great popular leverage for 'internal improvements,' and the dependence of newspapers on the mails enlisted many of them in this cause."

47. Kelly, *In the New England Fashion*, 85.

48. Annette, "Mis-Education of Farmers' Daughters," *New Genesee Farmer and Gardener*, July 1840, 109.

49. "Farmers' Daughters," *New Genesee Farmer and Gardener*, August 1840, 199, 128.

50. "Education of Farmers' Children—No. 1," *New Genesee Farmer and Gardener*, February 1841, 32; *Cultivator*, February 1849, 45.

51. See Demaree, *American Agricultural Press*. Farmers differed in their attitudes toward the agricultural press. See, for example, Faragher, *Sugar Creek*, 96–98.

52. R. G. Pardee, "Good and Bad Management," *Cultivator*, January 1850, 57.

53. Susan, "Small Comforts" from the *Farmer's Cabinet*, in *New Genesee Farmer and Gardener*, April 1840, 63.

54. Gates, *Farmer's Age*, 321. See esp. *American Agriculturist* and *Working Farmer*, April 1849.

55. Gates, *Farmer's Age*, 312–14. See also Barron, *Those Who Stayed Behind*, 33.

56. *American Agriculturist*, January 1850, 10; Demaree, *American Agricultural Press*, 38. See also, for example, "Things Necessary to the Successful Pursuit of Agriculture," *Cultivator*, July 1850, 233–34.

57. Barron, in *Those Who Stayed Behind*, 36, argues that farmers who remained in rural Vermont applauded agricultural reform. By 1849 the *Genesee Farmer* concluded that "the absolute rule of this class of farmers [opposed to 'mental training'] is drawing to a close." Quoted in *Albany Atlas*, February 6, 1849. See also Emmons, *Agriculture in New York*, 3:v.

58. Gates, *Farmer's Age*, 348–49; Demaree, *American Agricultural Press*, 43–45; Vincent Le Ray de Chaumont, *Address*, 21.

59. Demaree, *American Agricultural Press*, 161–63, quote on 161. The *Ohio Cultivator's* editor M. B. Bateham married Louisa Jane Lovell, an 1846 graduate of the Oberlin Ladies Department, who became ladies' editor. After Louisa died, Bateham married another Oberlin graduate, Josephine A. P. Cushman; she took on the column and wrote on topics such as woman's rights.

60. *Cultivator*, May 1844, 153, and April 1844, 134.

61. Annette, "Female Readers—Farmer's Daughters," *New Genesee Farmer and Gardener*, March 1840, 48; Demaree, *American Agricultural Press*, 176–79, quote on 175.

62. Susan, "Small Comforts" from the *Farmer's Cabinet*, in *New Genesee Farmer and Gardener*, April 1840, 63. Other articles about such practicalities as cisterns did follow. See, e.g., *New Genesee Farmer and Gardener*, October 1840, 146. See also, *Cultivator*, November 1839, 165, and September 1845.

63. *Cultivator*, July 1845, 216.

64. "Jefferson County Dairy Farming," *American Agriculturist*, November 1850, 332.

65. *Genesee Farmer*, July 1857, 208–9.

66. *Cultivator*, September 1844, 289–90; October 1844, 327; September 1845, 282.

67. Ibid., August 1846, 244.

68. Ibid., August 1847.

69. John Neal, "Rights of Woman," *Brother Jonathan*, June 1843, 184.

70. Stanton, Anthony, and Gage, *History of Woman Suffrage*, 462–63.

71. Ibid., 464–65.

72. *Albany Patriot*, January 1, 1845.

73. Gates, *Farmer's Age*, 340. Its weekly edition, begun in 1841, had a circulation of some 200,000 by 1860. See Mott, *American Journalism*, 269.

74. Quoted in Mott, *American Journalism*, 302.

75. Hough, *History of Jefferson County*, 519.

76. Greer, *Patriots and the People*, 3. For accounts of these events, see also Hough, *History of Jefferson County*, 519–29; Guillet, *Lives and Times of the Patriots*; Ellsworth, "Settlement of the North Country," 203; Coughlin, *Jefferson County Centennial*. See also *The Patriot War*, part of a 1947 radio series "Memories of Northern New York," JCHS. Vermonters also supported the rebellion. See Stilwell, *Migration from Vermont*, 182; Ellis et al., *Short History of New York State*, 216–17.

77. Hough, *History of Jefferson County*, 519.

78. Ellsworth, "Settlement of the North Country," 203.

79. See also Enos Martin, in Coughlin, *Jefferson County Centennial*; the number 200,000 is from Ellsworth, "Settlement of the North Country," 203.

80. Coughlin, *Jefferson County Centennial*, 31; Haddock, *Growth of a Century*, 344. Haddock (p. 347) lists the names of the Jefferson County volunteers, as does Landon, in *North Country*, 1:301–21.

81. Earle, *Jacksonian Antislavery*, e.g., 52, 65–68. King committed suicide in 1865. See Harriet A. Weed, *Life of Thurlow Weed*, 475.

82. Hough, *History of Jefferson County*, 527, and Haddock, *Growth of a Century*, 347, differ slightly on the numbers. See Ellsworth, "Settlement of the North Country," 204–5.

83. Landon, *North Country*, 1:301.

84. Guillet, *Lives and Times of the Patriots*, 86, 178.

85. Hough, *History of Jefferson County*, 526–27. See also *Jeffersonian*, August 9, 1841. Others were drafted by the U.S. government to help quell the rebellion and received 160 acres of land for their service.

86. Greer, *Patriots and the People*, 358–59. The Canadian crisis of 1837 had partisan ramifications in New York, weakening the Democratic Party along the border, although the Democrats soon returned once the tumult had quieted. See *Silas Wright*, 171; Benson, *Concept of Jacksonian Democracy*, 137 n. 21.

87. Greer, *Patriots and the People*, 210.

88. Ibid., 205; *La Minerve*, February 3, 1834. Interestingly, while none openly defended women's right to vote, one legislator said that a law prohibiting the practice was simply preferable to "an accusation of impropriety (*impudicite*)." I am grateful to Benedicte Monicat for translating these papers.

89. Landon, *North Country*, 1:159.
90. Ellsworth, "Settlement of the North Country," 195.
91. Stanton, Anthony, and Gage, *History of Woman Suffrage*, 88.
92. Stanton to Elizabeth J. Neall (November 26, [1841]), in Ann D. Gordon, *Selected Papers of Stanton and Anthony*, 24–25.
93. Stanton, Anthony, and Gage, *History of Woman Suffrage*, 460; Stanton to Neall, in Ann D. Gordon, *Selected Papers of Stanton and Anthony*, 25.
94. Hough, *History of Jefferson County*, 393–96, quotes on 396; Fitch, *Watertown Directory*, 29.
95. *National Anti-Slavery Standard*, September 14, 1843. Michael D. Pierson argues that Liberty Party newspapers reflected the party's relatively conventional views of gender relationships. While I do not doubt his findings, I want to stress instead the role of the Liberty Party press as a forum for a larger conversation about woman's rights. See Pierson, *Free Hearts and Free Homes*.
96. This is a vast literature. See esp. Kraditor, *Means and Ends in American Abolitionism*; Friedman, *Gregarious Saints*; Hansen, *Strained Sisterhood*; Mayer, *All On Fire*.
97. Liberty Party broadside, February 20, 1849 (handwritten date), in Smith Papers, film no. 709, reel 76.
98. Goodell, *Address*.
99. *Albany Patriot*, September 24, 1845.
100. Haddock, *Growth of a Century*, 531. In 1839 both Haddock and Angel served as officers of the branch of Watertown's Female Moral Reform Society connected with the Methodist church. See Fitch, *Watertown Directory*, 29.
101. Stanton, Anthony, and Gage, *History of Woman Suffrage*, 542–43 (*Daily Journal*, September 13, 1852); 522–23 (Smith); 854 (*Daily Star*, September 11, 1852). For the full report of that convention, see 517–46.

CHAPTER FIVE

1. Zaeske, *Signatures of Citizenship*, 91–92. Also see Hewitt, *Women's Activism and Social Change*.
2. *Colored American*, September 23, 1837, and August 18, 1838; *Friend of Man*, February 22, 1837. The meeting was held in the Second Presbyterian Church in Watertown, with P. G. Keyes as secretary.
3. *National Anti-Slavery Standard*, March 30, 1843; *Friend of Man*, September 26, 1838. There are two printed petitions, signed by women and men, from Smithville, Jefferson County, in 1839; see Petitions from Smithville, NARA.
4. *Albany Patriot*, January 1, 1845.
5. Haddock, *Growth of a Century*, 23.
6. *National Anti-Slavery Standard*, April 27, 1843, 186; Haydon, *Upstate Travels*, 159.
7. Oliver Wolcott, quoted in Benson, *Concept of Jacksonian Democracy*, 3; Jean H. Baker, *Affairs of Party*, 11. This historiography is too vast to list, much less to

comprehend, within the boundaries of the current work. In addition to Benson's work, classics include Fox, *Decline of Aristocracy*; Schlesinger, *Age of Jackson*. For more recent works, see esp. McCurdy, *Anti-Rent Era*; Huston, *Land and Freedom*.

8. Jean H. Baker, *Affairs of Party*, 12.

9. *National Anti-Slavery Standard*, July 11, 1844. On abolitionists' use of the Fourth of July, see Waldstreicher, *In the Midst of Perpetual Fetes*, 310-15. Frederick Douglass famously spoke on the question, "What to the Slave is the Fourth of July?" (*Oration*).

10. All descriptions and quotes from this event come from two articles: "The Cause of Liberty in Jefferson County," *Albany Patriot*, July 16, 1845, and one in *Liberty Press*, June 28, 1845.

11. Estate of Bailey Ormsby, JCSC.

12. Haddock, *Growth of a Century*, 474.

13. Ibid., 473. According to L. H. Everts, *Jefferson County History*, eight of Silas Spicer's nine daughters were teachers. Clarissa, born in 1830, would marry Melzer Fowler; their daughter, Nettie, attended the Troy Female Seminary and later married Cyrus McCormick. See <http://www.usgennet.org/usa/ny/town/brownville/Spicer.html>.

14. Haddock, *Growth of a Century*, 473; *Liberty Press*, June 28, 1845, 34, in Smith Papers; *Black River Journal*, July 28, 1843, party nominations; *Northern State Journal*, November 11, 1846. Hugh Smith also ran on the Liberty Party ticket for prison inspector in 1851. See *Frederick Douglass' Paper*, October 9, 1851.

15. Haddock, *Growth of a Century*, 474, 473. Henry Spicer served as a member of the legislature and a presidential elector; Hugh's brother, Levi Smith, had been a postmaster in Watertown; and Hugh Smith himself became a member of the New York Assembly in 1873. Open support for escaping fugitives grew over time and perhaps was inevitable due to Jefferson County's proximity to Canada. See, for example, *Frederick Douglass' Paper*, June 3, 1852.

16. "Proceedings of a Public Meeting held in Clayton, New York," NARA. I am grateful to Judith Wellman for alerting me to this and other petitions from Jefferson County and to Katherine Mollan of the Center for Legislative Archives at the National Archives for providing a copy of them.

17. *Liberty Press*, November 1, 1845, Smith Papers. The *Albany Patriot*, October 22, 1845, listed the candidates. Quote is from *Liberty Press*.

18. Three petitions against slavery from March 1850 include these names. All are in NARA.

19. Subscribers to Liberty Party paper (year illegible, 1849?), Smith Papers. These commitments continued into the 1850s. *Frederick Douglass' Paper* published subscription lists on October 9, 1851; June 10, 1853; February 23, 1855; and August 10, 1855 that listed $2.00 from Hugh Smith. On January 1, 1852, and June 1, 1855, the paper reported that Joseph Osborn contributed $2.00 and $3.00, respectively. Finally, on October 15, 1852, *Frederick Douglass' Paper* listed Osborn as one of three delegates from Jefferson County to the Liberty Party national convention in Syracuse two weeks earlier.

20. Hough, *History of Jefferson County*, 71 and, e.g., 85.

21. Ellsworth, "Settlement of the North Country," 198; Fox, *Decline of Aristocracy*, 102.

22. Hough, *History of Jefferson County*, 176; Ellsworth, "Settlement of the North Country," quote on 199. Massey letter also in Hough, *History of Jefferson County*, 459.

23. Hough, *History of Jefferson County*, 459. William Cooper "made the best of a bad situation by shipping produce and goods north from Otsego to DeKalb for smuggling across the border to Canada" even as his son James "was posted on a naval brig in nearby Lake Ontario with orders to seek and seize smugglers' boats and cargoes" (Alan Taylor, *William Cooper's Town*, 325).

24. Landon, *North Country*, 1:157; also in Ellsworth, "Settlement of the North Country," 202.

25. Their ties to Jefferson's party were in some cases deeply personal. During the Revolution, Pierre Penet had introduced Benjamin Franklin to a French supporter of American independence, Jacques Le Ray de Chaumont, at whose estate, Passy, Franklin stayed for several years. While there, Franklin taught English to his host's son, James Donatien Le Ray de Chaumont. Enthralled with Franklin's stories, James came to the United States in 1785, married Grace Coxe of New Jersey, renounced his French citizenship, and began purchasing land in the North. See Moore, "Some French Influences," 122–26; Hough, *History of Jefferson County*, 442, 445.

26. Powell, *Penet's Square*, 183.

27. Hough, *History of Jefferson County*, 344. See, for example, "Report of the Committee on Canals, for the Extension of the Black River Canal" and "An Act to Provide for the Location of the Northern Termination of the Black River Canal," *Jeffersonian*, April 12, 1841; "Black River Canal," *Jeffersonian*, May 3, 1841.

28. *Jeffersonian*, July 5, 1841.

29. Ibid., February 17, 1841. Several meetings about the incomplete Black River canal followed.

30. *Northern New-York Journal*, November 20, 1851. A Watertown and Rome railroad had been incorporated as early as 1832, but it took, in Hough's understated words, "years of patient and persevering effort" before the work began in 1848; see Hough, *History of Jefferson County*, 324, 330.

31. On the 1821 convention, see, for example, Fox, *Decline of Aristocracy*, chap. 8; Peterson, *Democracy, Liberty, and Property*; Meyers, *Jacksonian Persuasion*, 237–53; Scalia, *America's Jeffersonian Experiment*. Interestingly, "a majority of the members of the constitutional convention of 1821 . . . were of New England stock" (Ellis et al., *Short History of New York State*, 192).

32. Keyssar, *Right to Vote*, 17–18.

33. Jean H. Baker, *Affairs of Party*, 268.

34. Fox, *Decline of Aristocracy*, 254–55.

35. Benson, *Concept of Jacksonian Democracy*, 10; Fox, *Decline of Aristocracy*, 239.

36. Benson, *Concept of Jacksonian Democracy*, 7–8; Jean H. Baker, *Affairs of Party*, 145.

37. Ellis et. al., *Short History of New York State*, 123.

38. McCurdy, *Anti-Rent Era*, 246.

39. See ibid., 121–30, quotes on 122.

40. *Jefferson County Democrat*, February 19, 1846.

41. For an excellent discussion of Free Soil Democrats, see Earle, *Jacksonian Antislavery*.

42. Editorial, *New York Evening Post*, July 8, 1834, in White, *Democratick Editorials*, 191; "Reward for Arthur Tappan," *New York Evening Post*, August 26, 1835, in ibid., 200–201.

43. "Abolitionists," *New York Evening Post*, September 7, 1835, in ibid., 206–7; "Slavery No Evil," *New York Evening Post*, September 9, 1835, in ibid., 209.

44. *New York Evening Post*, January 14, 1837, in ibid., 212–17.

45. *Plaindealer*, July 29, 1837, in ibid., 229.

46. Earle, *Jacksonian Antislavery*, 7.

47. *North Star*, July 21, 1848; *National Era*, March 22, 1849, 47; *Northern State Journal*, June 14, 1848. The *Albany Atlas*, a Barnburner newspaper, is a good source for information on meetings of the various Democratic factions throughout 1848 and 1849.

48. Susan, "Small Comforts," *New Genesee Farmer and Gardener*, April 1840, 63.

49. Jean H. Baker, *Affairs of Party*, 27–29.

50. *Jeffersonian*, July 5, 1841.

51. *Frederick Douglass' Paper*, July 27, August 10, 1855. Increasingly, "Friends of Freedom and Free Men" met to nominate candidates for office; on Wednesday, October 13, 1852, the meeting was to be held in Depauville; see *Frederick Douglass' Paper*, October 8, 1852. Remoteness also, of course, meant a continuing familiarity with Canada and its mores. Frederick Douglass believed this 1855 meeting was "the first time in the history of First of August celebrations" that a white militia, the Northern Rangers, marched in support of "British magnanimity"; in addition, "God Save the Queen" was played by the Watertown Brass Band. See *Frederick Douglass' Paper*, August 10, 1855.

52. H. C. Wright to W. L. Garrison, May 6, 1840, Antislavery Collection. For an excellent account of one Garrisonian's complicated interaction with New York's Liberty Party, see Sterling, *Ahead of Her Time*, chap. 10.

53. Nationally, the party's electoral impact was small, with only 62,300 votes (or 2.3 percent) cast for James Birney's presidential campaign in 1844. Greeley's *New York Tribune* claimed that approximately 90 percent of its votes came from Whig ranks. See Benson, *Concept of Jacksonian Democracy*, 208.

54. Stanton quoted in Hallowell, *James and Lucretia Mott*, 185–86; Stanton to Elizabeth Pease, February 12, 1842, Antislavery Collection. See also Ginzberg, *Women and the Work of Benevolence*, 82–93.

55. *Friend of Man*, February 22, 1837.

56. In northern New York, voters gave Orville Hungerford considerably more votes than the victorious "indominatable, whole-souled Whig" Joseph Mullin for Congress in 1846; see *Northern State Journal*, November 18, 1846. Jefferson voters

even chose William Marcy, the Democratic candidate for governor in 1838, when Whig William Seward won the state; see Hough, *History of Jefferson County*, 371.

57. Landon, *North Country*, 1:396.

58. *National Anti-Slavery Standard*, November 2, 1843, 86; Wellman, *Grass Roots Reform in the Burned-Over District*, 154. On the 1844 vote, see Benson, *Concept of Jacksonian Democracy*, 139 n. 23.

59. *Jefferson County Democrat*, May 7, 1846. The April 28 election must have resonated within the Liberty Party community on a personal level. Liberty Party candidate Aaron Porter, a thirty-nine-year-old South Rutland doctor, died on April 30. The Jefferson County Anti-Slavery Convention, held five months after Porter's death, offered the unusually lengthy resolution that "in the death of our lamented brother, Dr. Porter, the benevolent and moral enterprises of the age have lost a valued, faithful and steadfast friend. Honored be his memory! But while we mourn his loss, we are admonished of the uncertainty of human life, and of the importance of being found in the way of duty, in all the relations of life." Prayer for his family followed. See *Albany Patriot*, October 28, 1846. Porter's wife, Isabel (or Isabella) Twitchell Porter, still lived in the area in 1850, but I have been unable to find further connections with the petitioning families or with Greene.

60. *Northern State Journal*, November 18, 1846. See also Field, *Politics of Race in New York*.

61. McKivigan, *War against Proslavery Religion*, 162; Earle, *Jacksonian Antislavery*, 13, 55.

62. *Albany Patriot*, November 12, 1845; McCurdy, *Anti-Rent Era*, 145.

63. Landon, *North Country*, 1:421.

64. *Liberty Press*, June 28, 1845, 34. Hough, *History of Jefferson County*, 439, says Judge Keyes died in 1834. Perhaps it is coincidence that Jay Ormsby, Hiram and Amy's son, an antislavery petition signer and Lydia Osborn's heir, named his own son Perley in 1877, but it was surely not a common name.

65. Pierson, *Free Hearts and Free Homes*, 44.

66. Appleton Howe to A. A. Phelps, June 25, 1839, Antislavery Collection.

67. *Michigan Liberty Press*, June 20, 1848.

68. *Frederick Douglass' Paper*, October 9, 1851, and March 4, 1853.

69. *Albany Patriot*, November 12, 1845.

70. Ibid., April 29, 1846.

CHAPTER SIX

1. *Albany Patriot*, August 12, 1846. "Cute" meant devious or underhanded in the parlance of the day.

2. Ibid., September 9, 1846.

3. "New-York Constitutional Convention," *New-York Daily Tribune*, August 17, 1846.

4. The convention reporters list his age as fifty, but he was about nine years older.

Hough claims that he was sixty-four when he died in 1851. The federal census for Utica (Whitestown), New York, in 1850, which lists inmates in the New York State Lunatic Asylum, reports his age as sixty-five. For information on Greene, see Hough, *History of Jefferson County*, 430–31; Alpheus S. Greene obituary, *Northern New-York Journal*, February 5, 1851; listing for (nephew) W. W. Greene in Haddock, *Growth of a Century*, 288.

5. JCD, K/120; JCD, C2/385.

6. Hough, *History of Jefferson County*, 399.

7. "Our National Anniversary," *Jeffersonian*, June 7, 1841; see also *Jeffersonian*, June 21, 1841.

8. *Northern State Journal*, March 3, 1847. His antislavery neighbors in Jefferson County resolved in October 1846 to support "the present 'No License' law of the State" ("Jefferson Co. Anti-Slavery Convention," *Albany Patriot*, October 28, 1846).

9. *Northern New-York Journal*, February 5, 1851. He served as well on the board of the Watertown Academy when it was founded in 1835. See Hough, *History of Jefferson County*, 379.

10. Mintz, *Moralists and Modernizers*, 71; Fitch, *Watertown Directory*, 22.

11. "Our National Anniversary," *Jeffersonian*, June 7, 1841.

12. Hastings, *Essay on Constitutional Reform*, 12–13.

13. See Peterson, *Democracy, Liberty, and Property*; Scalia, *America's Jeffersonian Experiment*; Jacob Katz Cogan, "Look Within."

14. Federal Writers' Project, *Proceedings of the New Jersey State Constitutional Convention of 1844*, lxv.

15. See Berthoff, "Conventional Mentality," on how these conventions defined business corporations, but not white women or African Americans, as equal persons.

16. On Pennsylvania, see *Journal of the Convention of the State of Pennsylvania*, and Keyssar, *Right to Vote*, 16. On Ohio, see J. V. Smith, *Report of the Debates and Proceedings . . . of the State of Ohio*, 56, 75–76, 458, and Quillin, *Color Line in Ohio*, 61. For a late-nineteenth-century summary of suffrage restrictions, see Naar, *Law of Suffrage and Elections*. For an excellent overview of these issues, see Keyssar, *Right to Vote*.

17. "The Right of Suffrage," *Albany Patriot*, December 4, 1844.

18. *Journal of the Constitutional Convention, of the Territory of Minnesota*, 60. Wisconsin's constitution had similar wording. See Keyssar, *Right to Vote*, 55.

19. McCurdy, *Anti-Rent Era*, 121–30, 192.

20. On the constitutional convention of 1846, see Galie, *Ordered Liberty*, 95–116; Gunn, *Decline of Authority*, 170–97; Lincoln, *Constitutional History of New York*, 2:9–217; Dougherty, *Constitutional History of the State of New York*, 162–81.

21. Meyers, *Jacksonian Persuasion*, 85.

22. "The Times! The Times!," *Cultivator*, June 1837, 61.

23. Earle, *Jacksonian Antislavery*, 57; Meyers, *Jacksonian Persuasion*, 83–84; Galie, *Ordered Liberty*, 97–98.

24. McCurdy, *Anti-Rent Era*, xiii. See also Huston, *Land and Freedom*.

25. Quoted in McCurdy, *Anti-Rent Era*, 260.

26. Field, *Politics of Race in New York*, 34–37. Field notes the black population incorrectly on 37, correctly on 36.

27. Hough, *History of Jefferson County*, 359. In 1830 there were 139 African Americans in Jefferson County; in 1840 there were 141.

28. Field, *Politics of Race in New York*, 37. On how African American New Yorkers fared compared with those of other states, see Keyssar, *Right to Vote*, 54–59.

29. McCurdy, *Anti-Rent Era*, 5.

30. "Albany Convention of Colored Citizens," in Foner and Walker, *Proceedings of the Black State Conventions*, 11. Some Whigs waffled on black political rights, but William Seward argued in 1845 that the "large mass of citizens disfranchised on the ground of color . . . must be invested with the right of suffrage" (*Address of the Southern and Western Liberty Convention*, 19).

31. *Albany Patriot*, June 4, 1845.

32. On married women's property rights in New York, see esp. Basch, *In the Eyes of the Law*; Rabkin, *Fathers to Daughters*; Stanley, *From Bondage to Contract*. On Herttell, see Basch, *In the Eyes of the Law*, 115–19; Herttell, *Argument in the House of Assembly*.

33. Hurlbut, *Essays on Human Rights*, 9–10, 147.

34. The vote was 213,257 to 33,860 according to "The New-York Constitutional Convention," *United States Democratic Review* 19 (November 1846): 406–7; 6,397 of the votes for a convention were from Jefferson County. See also Gunn, *Decline of Authority*, 181–82.

35. *Jefferson County Democrat*, March 12, April 2, 1846.

36. McCurdy, *Anti-Rent Era*, 192–93; Galie, *Ordered Liberty*, 9.

37. *New York Morning News*, March 21, 1846, and *New York Tribune*, April 21, 1846, quoted in Benson, *Concept of Jacksonian Democracy*, 318–19.

38. Hastings, *Essay on Constitutional Reform*, 32–33.

39. *Albany Patriot*, January 28, 1845. In the face of several African American activists' support for the Whig Party, Gerrit Smith expressed outrage at associating with men "who cling to proslavery parties, [and] cannot be trusted on any question affecting that of slavery." See *North Star*, September 15, 1848; Gerrit Smith, *Reply to Colored Citizens of Albany*, Library Company of Philadelphia; "Address to the Voters in the State of New York, by the People of Color," *Albany Patriot*, February 11, 1845.

40. This listing of town votes for delegates is in *Jefferson County Democrat*, May 7, 1846. Total votes in the county numbered some 8,000. In Clayton the three Whig candidates got 196, 195, and 196 votes, respectively. But among the three Democratic candidates, Danforth and McNeil each got 231 votes and Greene got 234. In Brownville, interestingly, Hugh Smith got 3 more votes (37) than the other two Liberty Party candidates.

41. *New York Herald*, June 1, 1846.

42. Ellis et al., *Short History of New York State*, 222. See also Galie, *Ordered Liberty*, 99–100.

43. *Documents of the Convention of the State of New-York*, doc. no. 136, 2:8.

44. See listing of delegates in Bishop and Attree, *Report of the Debates and Proceedings*. The breakdown of occupations varies in different reports.

45. The list of where delegates boarded is in *Documents of the Convention of the State of New-York*, doc. no. 9, vol. 1.

46. See, for example, Charles O'Conor's remarks in Bishop and Attree, *Report of the Debates and Proceedings*, 268.

47. Bishop and Attree, *Report of the Debates and Proceedings*, all quotes on 65–67. Women in Washington, D.C., frequently attended hearings at the Capitol, filling its galleries almost as soon as it was completed in 1825. See Allgor, *Parlor Politics*.

48. Basch, *In the Eyes of the Law*, 47.

49. Quoted in Lincoln, *Constitutional History of New York*, 2:116–7.

50. Bishop and Attree, *Report of the Debates and Proceedings*, 1053.

51. Ibid., 111–12.

52. *Albany Patriot*, June 3, 1846; Bishop and Attree, *Report of the Debates and Proceedings*, 537, 539.

53. Bishop and Attree, *Report of the Debates and Proceedings*, 1014, 1016–17.

54. Ibid., 1018.

55. Wisconsin delegate, quoted in Keyssar, *Right to Vote*, 57.

56. J. V. Smith, *Report of the Debates and Proceedings . . . of the State of Ohio*, e.g., 458; Quillin, *Color Line in Ohio*, 61–62, 9. The notion of suffrage as an inducement to immigration was an old one. In the 1788 constitutional debate in North Carolina, one delegate feared that abolishing religious tests for office "was an invitation for Jews and pagans of every kind to come among us. . . . All those who have any religion are against the emigration of those people from the eastern hemisphere" (Neil H. Cogan, *Complete Bill of Rights*, 68). In contrast, western states sought to expand suffrage for immigrants as a means to *encourage* settlers; see Keyssar, *Right to Vote*, 38.

57. Bishop and Attree, *Report of the Debates and Proceedings*, 1019, 1030.

58. Ibid., 1027.

59. Ibid., 1027–29.

60. Ibid., 1029–1030.

61. Ibid., 1034, 1033. In fact, 20 percent of Swackhamer's constituents in Kings County would vote that fall for equal suffrage for African Americans. See Field, *Politics of Race in New York*, app. B, 236.

62. Bishop and Attree, *Report of the Debates and Proceedings*, 1043, 540.

63. Ibid., 1017.

64. Ibid., 80, 196.

65. Basch, *In the Eyes of the Law*, 39.

66. Bishop and Attree, *Report of the Debates and Proceedings*, 1042, 1058–59, 1039.

67. Meyers, *Jacksonian Persuasion*, 201–2. For a comparable analysis, see Carey, *Appeal to the Wealthy of the Land*.

68. See Rabkin, *Fathers to Daughters*, 93–94; Basch, *In the Eyes of the Law*, 152–53.

69. Bishop and Attree, *Report of the Debates and Proceedings*, 1039–41.

70. Ibid., 1060.
71. Rabkin, *Fathers to Daughters*, 96–97; Bishop and Attree, *Report of the Debates and Proceedings*, 1060.
72. Bishop and Attree, *Report of the Debates and Proceedings*, 1042.
73. Ibid., 1038.
74. See "Charles O'Conor" in *American National Biography*, 16:610–1. Quotes are in Bishop and Attree, *Report of the Debates and Proceedings*, 269, 1038, 1057; Rabkin, *Fathers to Daughters*, 93.
75. Quoted in Rabkin, *Fathers to Daughters*, 80.
76. Bishop and Attree, *Report of the Debates and Proceedings*, 1058, 1057.
77. Ibid., 1042.
78. Ibid., 1035. Danforth and McNeil joined him in this vote.
79. Lincoln, *Constitutional History of New York*, 2:126.
80. Basch, *In the Eyes of the Law*, 138; "The New-York Constitutional Convention," *United States Democratic Review* 19 (November 1846): 347.
81. Greene's sisters directly benefited from married women's property acts. One of them, Nancy Moore, died in 1858 and left to her husband land, furniture, and "capital stock in the Jefferson county Bank at Watertown New York, and any balance or residue of my brother's estate, Alpheus S. Green [*sic*], deceased, due me and which shall not have been received at the time of my death" (Paper of Individuals, Estate of Alpheus S. Greene, JCSC). On W. W. Greene's wife, Ingham by birth, see Haddock, *Growth of a Century*, 289.
82. Bishop and Attree, *Report of the Debates and Proceedings*, 1042.
83. Quoted in Basch, *In the Eyes of the Law*, 153.
84. Bishop and Attree, *Report of the Debates and Proceedings*, 1056–57.
85. Ibid., 1059–60.
86. Basch, *In the Eyes of the Law*, 135.
87. Quoted in Keyssar, *Right to Vote*, xvii.
88. Hurlbut, *Essays on Human Rights*, 158.
89. Bishop and Attree, *Report of the Debates and Proceedings*, 1039; Basch, *In the Eyes of the Law*, 56–57.
90. Basch, *In the Eyes of the Law*, 120, 143, 138; Rabkin, *Fathers to Daughters*, 97.
91. Caleb Cushing, "The Legal Condition of Woman," *North American Review* 26 (April 1828): 318.
92. Bishop and Attree, *Report of the Debates and Proceedings*, 540.
93. Ibid., 1027.
94. *Albany Patriot*, June 3, 1846; Bishop and Attree, *Report of the Debates and Proceedings*, 1031.
95. Bishop and Attree, *Report of the Debates and Proceedings*, 1031, 1046–47, 272.
96. Ibid., 250, 269.
97. Basch, *In the Eyes of the Law*, 162.
98. See Wellman, "Women's Rights, Republicanism, and Revolutionary Rhetoric in Antebellum New York State," 381.
99. Croswell and Sutton note only that Greene moved to have a petition "in favor of

'woman's rights'" read and referred to committee; see Croswell and Sutton, *Debates and Proceedings*, 480.

100. Bishop and Attree, *Report of the Debates and Proceedings*, 96, 1031, 220. John Hunt, a delegate from New York City, also presented a petition to enfranchise the clergy and women; see Croswell and Sutton, *Debates and Proceedings*, 701.

101. Meyers, *Jacksonian Persuasion*, 256.

102. Gerrit Smith, *To the Voters of the State of New York*, Library Company of Philadelphia.

103. *Memorial to the Honorable Senate and House of Representatives*, 2. See also Eric Ledell Smith, "End of Black Voting Rights in Pennsylvania."

104. Vote counts differ slightly. Field, *Politics of Race in New York*, 61, says it was 224,336 to 85,406. Galie, *Ordered Liberty*, 108, says 223,834 to 85,306, close to the vote to ratify the constitution itself, which was 221,528 to 92,436, according to Gunn, *Decline of Authority*, 181, and Lincoln, *Constitutional History of New York*, 2:213.

105. Field, *Politics of Race in New York*, app. B. The vote in Jefferson County against equal suffrage was 4,536 to 2,791; see Hough, *History of Jefferson County*, 370.

106. Keyssar, *Right to Vote*, 29.

107. *North Star*, November 2, 1849, and September 1, 1848.

108. Basch, *In the Eyes of the Law*, 156.

109. Rothman, *Discovery of the Asylum*, 149.

110. Obituary in *Northern New-York Journal*, February 5, 1851; "Affidavit by John G. Webb" and "Inventory," Estate of Alpheus S. Greene, JCSC. Hough, *History of Jefferson County*, 431, says he died on February 28, 1851, after the obituary date. The list of deaths from 1843 to 1852 is in the *Tenth Annual Report* (1853), 17. The *Annual Reports of the Managers of the State Lunatic Asylum* are useful for understanding nineteenth-century notions of insanity, as is the *American Journal of Insanity*. A report titled "Fair at the State Lunatic Asylum" appears in the *Liberty Press*, February 22, 1845.

CONCLUDING THOUGHTS

1. This is a vast literature. See, for example, Stoler, "Tense and Tender Ties" and commentaries that follow; Sinha, "Gender and Nation"; "Negotiating Nations"; Bender, *Rethinking American History in a Global Age*. Other works that have been particularly useful are Badran, *Feminists, Islam, and Nation*; Margot Badran, "Competing Agenda: Feminists, Islam, and the State in Nineteenth- and Twentieth-Century Egypt," in Kandiyoti, *Women, Islam, and the State*; Moghadam, *Gender and National Identity*; Narayan, *Dislocating Cultures*.

2. Herttell, *Argument in the House of Assembly*, 23.

3. Stanton, *Eighty Years and More*, 83, 81; [Bradburn], *Memorial of George Bradburn*, 245–46.

4. J. V. Smith, *Report of the Debates and Proceedings . . . of the State of Ohio*, 76, 107.

5. Personal e-mail correspondence in 2002 and 2003 with Debbie Quick, director

of the Historical Association of South Jefferson, and the great-great-great-great-granddaughter of Anna Bishop; Thelma Moye, Eleanor Vincent's third great-granddaughter; Stephen R. Ormsby, Amy Ormsby's fourth great-grandson; Richard Osborn, Lydia Osborn's great-great-nephew.

6. See "Announcements by Susan B. Anthony," in Ann D. Gordon, *Selected Papers of Stanton and Anthony*, 291, 301.

7. Personal e-mail correspondence with Richard Osborn.

8. *Albany Patriot*, October 28, 1846.

9. Ibid., November 12, 1845.

10. "Last Will and Testament of Joseph Osborn," Estate of Joseph Osborn, JCSC, bk. 12, pp. 209–11.

11. *Proceedings and Debates of the Virginia State Convention of 1829–30*, 340.

12. *Debates of the Convention to Amend the Constitution of Pennsylvania*, 540.

13. Wyman, *Selections from the Autobiography of Elizabeth Oakes Smith*, 61.

14. Interestingly, while American supporters of woman suffrage embraced the rhetoric of Christian respectability, French women's suffrage was delayed until after World War II in part because radical politicians feared the political effects of their religious loyalties. See Karen Offen, "Women, Citizenship, and Suffrage with a French Twist, 1789–1993," in Daley and Nolan, *Suffrage and Beyond*, 161.

15. Fulton, *True Woman*, 3, 35.

16. Brekus, *Strangers and Pilgrims*, 334.

17. Susan E. Marshall, *Splintered Sisterhood*, 11, 37, 49.

18. See, for example, Kaplan, *Crazy for Democracy*; Cott, *Grounding of Modern Feminism*.

19. Docekal, "In Defense of Same Sex Marriage."

20. Massachusetts State House News Service, Constitutional Convention Proceedings.

21. Henderson, "Queer Theory, New Millennium," 376.

22. Ibid.

23. Sinha, "Gender and Nation," 268.

Bibliography

MANUSCRIPT AND GOVERNMENT SOURCES

Antislavery Collection. Courtesy of the Boston Public Library/Rare Books Department. Boston, Mass.

Estate and Administrative Probate Papers. Jefferson County Surrogate's Court. Watertown, N.Y.

Estate of Alpheus S. Greene, 1800G-272

Estate of Timothy O'Connor, 1800O-83, and Minute Books, B-499 and B-559

Estate of Bailey Ormsby, 1800O-275

Estate of Susan Ormsby, 1800O-115, and Minute Books, V-229, S-453, Q-701, Q-702

Estate of Joseph Osborn, 1800O-106, and Minute Books, bk. 12, pp. 209–11

Estate of Lydia Osborn, 1800O-91, and Minute Books, K-315

Estate of Nahum D. Williams, 1800W-110, and Minute Books, F-201, F-580

Genealogy Department. Flower Memorial Library. Watertown, N.Y.

Bishop Family File

Osborn Family File

Jefferson and St. Lawrence Counties. New York State. *1810 and 1820 Federal Population Census Schedules. Transcript and Index.* Edited by Ralph V. Wood Jr. 1963.

Jefferson County Deeds. Office of the County Clerk, Jefferson County. Watertown, N.Y.

Jefferson County Historical Society. Watertown, N.Y.

Orleans File

Marshall, A. G. "Historical Sketch of Orleans Township." Typescript.

Orleans Tax Assessment, 1824

Pamphlets

Clayton on the St. Lawrence, 1872–1972. 1972.

The Patriot War. Radio Broadcast Series, "Memories of Northern New York." 1947.

Library Company of Philadelphia. Philadelphia, Pa.

Smith, Gerrit. *Reply to Colored Citizens of Albany.* March 13, 1846. Broadside.

——. *To the Voters of the State of New York.* October 19, 1846. Broadside.

Petitions to Congress. National Archives and Records Administration. Washington, D.C.

Petition of the Women of Harrisville, Ohio, for Abolition of Slavery in the District of Columbia and Immediate Enfranchisement, June 13, 1834. HR23A-HRG4.3, Record Group 233.

Petitions from Smithville, Jefferson County, 1839. HR25A-H1.8, Record Group 233. February 4, 1839, folder 33, tray 12.

"Proceedings of a Public Meeting held in Clayton, New York, against the annexation of Texas." Records of the U.S. House of Representatives. HR28A-G7.5, Record Group 233. NA box 39 of LC box 137.

Three petitions against slavery from Jefferson County. HR31A-G4.1 (March 13–21, 1850); HR31A-G9.5 (March 14–21, 1850); HR31A-G23.1 (March 15–22, 1850), Record Group 233.

Gerrit Smith Papers. Microfilm Collection. Special Collections Research Center. Syracuse University Library, Syracuse, N.Y.

State of New-York. *Census.* 1825, 1835, 1855.

U.S. Bureau of the Census. *Seventh Census of the United States, 1850, Population.*

———. *Eighth Census of the United States, 1860, Population.*

———. *Ninth Census of the United States, 1870, Population.*

CONSTITUTIONAL CONVENTION PROCEEDINGS

Bishop, William G., and William H. Attree, reporters. *Report of the Debates and Proceedings of the Convention for the Revision of the Constitution of the State of New-York, 1846.* Albany: Evening Atlas, 1846.

Clarke, L. H. *Report of the Debates and Proceedings of the Convention of the State of New-York.* New York: J. Seymour, 1821.

Croswell, S., and R. Sutton, reporters. *Debates and Proceedings in the New-York State Convention for the Revision of the Constitution, 1846.* Albany: Albany Argus, 1846.

Debates of the Convention to Amend the Constitution of Pennsylvania. Harrisburg: Benjamin Singerly, 1873.

Documents of the Convention of the State of New-York, 1846. 2 vols. Albany: Carroll and Cook, 1846.

Federal Writers' Project of the Works Progress Administration for the State of New Jersey. *Proceedings of the New Jersey State Constitutional Convention of 1844.* Trenton, 1942.

Journal and Debates of the Constitutional Convention of the State of Wyoming. Cheyenne: Daily Sun Printing, 1893.

Journal of the Constitutional Convention, of the Territory of Minnesota. St. Paul: Earle S. Goodrich, 1857.

Journal of the Convention of the State of Pennsylvania, to Propose Amendments to the Constitution. 2 vols. Harrisburg: Thompson and Clark, 1837–38.

Massachusetts State House News Service. Constitutional Convention Proceedings. 2004. <http://www.statehousenews.com/public/cc2-11-4.htm>.

Perley, Jeremiah. *The Debates, Resolutions, and Other Proceedings, of the Convention of Delegates, Assembled . . . for the Purpose of Forming a Constitution for the State of Maine*. Portland: A. Shirley, 1820.

Proceedings and Debates of the Virginia State Convention of 1829–30. Richmond: Samuel Shepherd and Co., 1830.

Quaife, Milo M., ed. *The Convention of 1846*. Madison: Publications of the State Historical Society of Wisconsin, 1919.

———. *The Struggle over Ratification, 1846–1847*. Madison: Publications of the State Historical Society of Wisconsin, 1920.

Smith, J. V. *Report of the Debates and Proceedings . . . for the Revision of the Constitution of the State of Ohio, 1850–51*. 2 vols. Columbus: S. Medary, 1851.

NEWSPAPERS

Albany Evening Journal

Albany Patriot

American Agriculturist

American Journal of Insanity (Utica)

American Jurist and Law Magazine

American Missionary Register

The Beacon

Black River Gazette

Black River Journal

Brother Jonathan

Colored American (Accessible Archives at <http://www.accessible.com>)

Cultivator

Daily Albany Argus

Frederick Douglass' Paper (Accessible Archives at <http://www.accessible.com>)

Free Enquirer

Friend of Man (Utica)

Genesee Farmer (Rochester)

Home Missionary

Jefferson County Democrat

Jefferson County Journal

Jeffersonian (Watertown)

Journal of the New-York State Agricultural Society

Ladies' Repository

Liberty Press

Mechanic's Free Press

Michigan Liberty Press (Battle Creek) (microfilm of originals in the Michigan Historical Collections)

Monthly Genesee Farmer

National Anti-Slavery Standard

National Era (Accessible Archives at <http://www.accessible.com>

New Genesee Farmer and Gardener
New-Harmony Gazette
New York Herald
New-York Daily Tribune
North American Review (<http://cdl.library.cornell.edu/moa/>)
Northern New-York Journal (Watertown)
Northern State Journal
North Star (Accessible Archives at <http://www.accessible.com>)
The Revivalist, a Quarterly (Adams, Jefferson County)
The Telescope
United States Democratic Review (<http://memory.loc.gov/cgi-bin/query/>)
Watertown Daily Times Collection of New York State Newspapers on Micro-
   film
   Black River Gazette. 1826–1846, scattered issues.
   Black River Journal. 1843–1846. Subsequently became *Northern State Journal.*
   Jefferson County Democrat (Adams). July 18, 1844–June 18, 1846. Reel 1.
   The Jeffersonian (Watertown). January 4, 1841–September 21, 1854, scattered.
      Reels 23, 29.
   Northern State Journal (Watertown). August 26, 1846–December 28, 1853. Reel
      25.
Watertown Eagle
Working Farmer
Yankee and Boston Literary Gazette

BOOKS, ARTICLES, DISSERTATIONS, AND ESSAYS

*Address of the Southern and Western Liberty Convention, To the People of the United
   States; The Proceedings and Resolutions of the Convention; The Letters of Elihu
   Burrit, Wm. H. Seward, William Jay ... and Others.* Cincinnati, 1845.
Ahlstrom, Sydney E. *A Religious History of the American People.* 2 vols. Garden
   City, N.Y.: Image Books, 1975.
Ahmed, Leila. *Women and Gender in Islam.* New Haven: Yale University Press, 1992.
Allgor, Catherine. *Parlor Politics: In Which the Ladies of Washington Help Build a
   City and a Government.* Charlottesville: University Press of Virginia, 2000.
American Baptist Home Missionary Society. *Annual Reports of the Executive Com-
   mittee.* New York: John Gray, 1835–43.
American National Biography. Edited by John A. Garraty and Mark C. Carnes. New
   York: Oxford University Press, 1999.
Anderson, Bonnie S. *Joyous Greetings: The First International Women's Movement,
   1830–1860.* New York: Oxford University Press, 2000.
Badran, Margot. *Feminists, Islam, and Nation: Gender and the Making of Modern
   Egypt.* Princeton: Princeton University Press, 1995.
Baker, Jean H. *Affairs of Party: The Political Culture of Northern Democrats in the
   Mid-Nineteenth Century.* Ithaca: Cornell University Press, 1983.

Baker, Paula. "The Domestication of Politics: Women and American Political Society, 1780–1920." *American Historical Review* 89 (June 1984): 620–47.

Barron, Hal S. *Those Who Stayed Behind: Rural Society in Nineteenth-Century New England.* Cambridge: Cambridge University Press, 1984.

Barry, Kathleen. *Susan B. Anthony: A Biography of a Singular Feminist.* New York: New York University Press, 1988.

Basch, Norma. *In the Eyes of the Law: Women, Marriage, and Property in Nineteenth-Century New York.* Ithaca: Cornell University Press, 1982.

Bender, Thomas, ed. *Rethinking American History in a Global Age.* Berkeley: University of California Press, 2002.

Benson, Lee. *The Concept of Jacksonian Democracy: New York as a Test Case.* Princeton: Princeton University Press, 1961.

Berthoff, Rowland. "Conventional Mentality: Free Blacks, Women, and Business Corporations as Unequal Persons, 1820–1870." *Journal of American History* 76 (December 1989): 753–85.

Borden, Morton. *Jews, Turks, and Infidels.* Chapel Hill: University of North Carolina Press, 1984.

Boydston, Jeanne. *Home and Work: Housework, Wages, and the Ideology of Labor in the Early Republic.* New York: Oxford University Press, 1990.

——. "Making Gender in the Early Republic: Judith Sargent Murray and the Revolution of 1800." In *The Revolution of 1800: Democracy, Race, and the New Republic,* edited by James Horn, Jan Ellen Lewis, and Peter S. Onuf, 240–66. Charlottesville: University of Virginia Press, 2002.

——. "The Woman Who Wasn't There: Women's Market Labor and the Transition to Capitalism in the United States." *Journal of the Early Republic* 16 (Summer 1996): 183–206.

Boydston, Jeanne, Mary Kelley, and Anne Margolis. *The Limits of Sisterhood: The Beecher Sisters on Women's Rights and Woman's Sphere.* Chapel Hill: University of North Carolina Press, 1988.

Boylan, Anne M. *The Origins of Women's Activism: New York City and Boston, 1797–1840.* Chapel Hill: University of North Carolina Press, 2002.

Brackenridge, H. M., W. G. D. Worthington, and John S. Tyson. *Speeches on the Jew Bill, in the House of Delegates of Maryland.* Philadelphia, 1829.

[Bradburn, Frances H.] *A Memorial of George Bradburn.* By His Wife. Boston: Cupples, Upham and Co., 1883.

Brekus, Catherine A. *Strangers and Pilgrims: Female Preaching in America, 1740–1845.* Chapel Hill: University of North Carolina Press, 1998.

Brown, Elsa Barkley. "Negotiating and Transforming the Public Sphere: African American Political Life in the Transition from Slavery to Freedom." *Public Culture* 7 (1994): 107–46.

Carey, Matthew. *Appeal to the Wealthy of the Land.* 2nd ed. Philadelphia: L. Johnson, 1833.

Clarke, T. Wood. *Émigrés in the Wilderness.* New York: Macmillan, 1941. Reprint, Port Washington, N.Y.: Ira J. Friedman, 1967.

Cogan, Jacob Katz. "The Look Within: Property, Capacity, and Suffrage in Nineteenth-Century America." *Yale Law Journal* 107 (November 1997): 473–98.

Cogan, Jacob Katz, and Lori D. Ginzberg. "Archives: 1846 Petition for Woman's Suffrage, New York State Constitutional Convention." *Signs* 22 (Winter 1997): 427–39.

Cogan, Neil H., ed. *The Complete Bill of Rights: The Drafts, Debates, Sources, and Origins.* New York: Oxford University Press, 1997.

Conklin, Henry. *Through "Poverty's Vale": A Hardscrabble Boyhood in Upstate New York, 1832–1862.* Edited by Wendell Tripp. Syracuse: Syracuse University Press, 1974.

Cott, Nancy F. *The Grounding of Modern Feminism.* Cambridge, Mass.: Harvard University Press, 1987.

———. *Public Vows: A History of Marriage and the Nation.* Cambridge, Mass.: Harvard University Press, 2000.

Cott, Nancy F., Jeanne Boydston, Ann Braude, Lori D. Ginzberg, and Molly Ladd-Taylor. *Root of Bitterness.* 2nd ed. Boston: Northeastern University Press, 1996.

Coughlin, Jere, comp. *Jefferson County Centennial, 1905.* Watertown, N.Y.: Hungerford-Holbrook, 1905.

Daley, Caroline, and Melanie Nolan. *Suffrage and Beyond: International Feminist Perspectives.* New York: New York University Press, 1994.

Darby, William. *A Tour from the City of New York, to Detroit.* 1819. Chicago: Quadrangle Books, 1961.

Demaree, Albert Lowther. *The American Agricultural Press, 1819–1860.* New York: Columbia University Press, 1941. Reprint, Philadelphia: Porcupine Press, 1974.

Docekal, Su. "In Defense of Same Sex Marriage." Speech at Seattle rally, February 14, 2004. <www.radicalwomen.org>.

Dougherty, J. Hampden. *Constitutional History of the State of New York.* 2nd ed. New York: Neale Publishing, 1915.

Douglass, Frederick. *Oration, Delivered in Corinthian Hall, Rochester, July 5th, 1852.* Rochester, N.Y., 1852.

Dublin, Thomas. *Women at Work: The Transformation of Work and Community in Lowell, Massachusetts, 1826–1860.* New York: Columbia University Press, 1979.

DuBois, Ellen Carol. *Elizabeth Cady Stanton, Susan B. Anthony: Correspondence, Writings, Speeches.* New York: Schocken Books, 1981.

———. *Feminism and Suffrage: The Emergence of an Independent Women's Movement in America, 1848–1869.* Ithaca: Cornell University Press, 1978.

———. "Making Women's History: Activist Historians of Women's Rights, 1880–1940." *Radical History Review* 49 (Winter 1991): 61–84.

Earle, Jonathan H. *Jacksonian Antislavery and the Politics of Free Soil, 1824–1854.* Chapel Hill: University of North Carolina Press, 2004.

Eitches, Edward. "Maryland's 'Jew Bill.'" *American Jewish Historical Quarterly* 60 (March 1971): 258–79.

Ellis, David M., James A. Frost, Harold C. Syrett, Harry J. Carman. *A Short History of New York State.* Ithaca: New York State Historical Society and Cornell University Press, 1957.

Ellsworth, Richard C. "The Settlement of the North Country." Chapter 6 of *Conquering the Wilderness*, vol. 5 of *History of the State of New York, in Ten Volumes*, edited by Alexander C. Flick. New York: Columbia University Press, 1934.

Emma Willard and Her Pupils, or Fifty Years of the Troy Female Seminary, 1822–1872. New York: Mrs. Russell Sage, 1898.

Emmons, Ebenezer. *Agriculture in New-York*. 5 vols. Albany: C. Van Benthuysen and Co., 1846–54.

Everett, L. S. *An Exposure of the Principles of the "Free Inquirers."* Boston, 1831.

Fairfield, Roy P., ed. *The Federalist Papers*. 2nd ed. Baltimore: Johns Hopkins University Press, 1981.

Faragher, John Mack. *Sugar Creek: Life on the Illinois Prairie*. New Haven: Yale University Press, 1986.

Feldman, Stephen M. *Please Don't Wish Me a Merry Christmas: A Critical History of the Separation of Church and State*. New York: New York University Press, 1998.

Field, Phyllis F. *The Politics of Race in New York: The Struggle for Black Suffrage in the Civil War Era*. Ithaca: Cornell University Press, 1982.

Finley, Ruth. *The Lady of Godey's, Sarah Josepha Hale*. Philadelphia: J. B. Lippincott, 1931.

Fitch, J. P. *The Watertown Directory, for 1840*. Watertown, N.Y.: Knowlton and Rice, 1840.

Flexner, Eleanor. *Century of Struggle: The Woman's Rights Movement in the United States*. New York: Atheneum, 1974.

Flick, Alexander C., ed. *History of the State of New York, in Ten Volumes*. New York: Columbia University Press, 1934.

Foner, Philip, and George E. Walker, eds. *Proceedings of the Black State Conventions, 1840–1865*. Vol. 1. Philadelphia: Temple University Press, 1979.

Foucault, Michel. *The History of Sexuality*. Vol. 1. New York: Pantheon, 1978.

Fox, Dixon Ryan. *The Decline of Aristocracy in the Politics of New York, 1801–1840*. Edited by Robert Remini. New York: Harper Torchbook, 1965.

———. *Yorkers and Yankees*. New York: New York University Press, 1940.

French, J. H. *Gazetteer of the State of New York*. Syracuse: R. P. Smith, 1861.

Friedman, Lawrence J. *Gregarious Saints: Self and Community in American Abolitionism, 1830–1870*. Cambridge: Cambridge University Press, 1982.

Fulton, Rev. J. D. *The True Woman. To Which is Added Woman vs. Ballot*. Boston: Lee and Shepard, 1869.

Galie, Peter J. *Ordered Liberty: A Constitutional History of New York*. New York: Fordham University Press, 1996.

Garand, Rev. P. S. *Historical Sketch of the Village of Clayton, N.Y., and a Complete History of St. Mary's Parish*. Clayton, N.Y.: G. H. Bates, 1902.

Gates, Paul Wallace. *The Farmer's Age: Agriculture, 1815–1860*. New York: Holt, Rinehart and Winston, 1960.

Gaustad, Edwin Scott. *Historical Atlas of Religion in America*. Rev. ed. New York: Harper and Row, 1976.

Gillette, William. *History of Depauville*. 1905. Reprint, 1993. Supplement to *The Thousand Islands Sun Vacationer*, August 27, September 3, 10, 1997.

Ginzberg, Lori D. " 'The Hearts of Your Readers Will Shudder': Fanny Wright, Infidelity, and American Freethought." *American Quarterly* 46 (June 1994): 195–226.

———. "The Nation's Mission: Social Movements and Nation-Building in the United States." *Histoire Sociale / Social History* 33 (November 2000): 325–41.

———. " 'Pernicious Heresies': Women's Political Identities and Sexual Respectability in the Nineteenth Century." In *Women and the Unstable State in Nineteenth-Century America*, edited by Alison Parker and Stephanie Cole, 139–61. Lubbock: Texas A&M University Press, 2000.

———. *Women and the Work of Benevolence: Morality, Politics, and Class in the Nineteenth-Century United States*. New Haven: Yale University Press, 1990.

Golden, John. "Feminism Roots Found in the North." *Watertown Daily Times*, September 3, 1995.

Goodell, William. *Address Read at the New-York State Liberty Convention, Held at Port Byron, on Wednesday and Thursday, July 25 and 26, 1845*. 1845.

Gordon, Ann D., ed. *The Selected Papers of Elizabeth Cady Stanton and Susan B. Anthony*. Vol. 1, *In the School of Anti-Slavery, 1840–1866*. New Brunswick, N.J.: Rutgers University Press, 1997.

Gordon, Sarah Barringer. "Blasphemy and the Law of Religious Liberty in Nineteenth-Century America." *American Quarterly* 52 (December 2000): 682–719.

Gordon, Thomas F. *Gazetteer of the State of New York*. Philadelphia: T. K. and P. G. Collins, 1836.

Greer, Allan. *The Patriots and the People: The Rebellion of 1837 in Rural Lower Canada*. Toronto: University of Toronto Press, 1993.

Grossberg, Michael. *Governing the Hearth: Law and the Family in Nineteenth-Century America*. Chapel Hill: University of North Carolina Press, 1985.

———. *A Judgment for Solomon: The D'Hauteville Case and Legal Experience in Antebellum America*. New York: Cambridge University Press, 1996.

Guillet, Edwin C. *The Lives and Times of the Patriots: An Account of the Rebellion in Upper Canada, 1837–1838, and of the Patriot Agitation in the United States, 1837–1842*. Edinburgh: Thomas Nelson and Sons, 1938. Reprint, Toronto: University of Toronto Press, 1968.

Gunn, L. Ray. *The Decline of Authority: Public Economic Policy and Political Development in New York, 1800–1860*. Ithaca: Cornell University Press, 1988.

Haddock, John A. *The Growth of a Century as Illustrated in the History of Jefferson County, New York, from 1793 to 1894*. Philadelphia: Sherman and Co., 1894.

Hahn, Steven, and Jonathan Prude, eds. *The Countryside in the Age of Capitalist Transformation: Essays in the Social History of Rural America*. Chapel Hill: University of North Carolina Press, 1985.

Hallowell, Anna Davis, ed. *James and Lucretia Mott: Life and Letters*. Boston: Houghton, Mifflin, 1884.

Halsey, Francis Whiting. *The Old New York Frontier: Its Wars with Indians and Tories, Its Missionary Schools, Pioneers and Land Titles, 1614–1800*. New York: Charles Scribner's Sons, 1901.

Hansen, Debra Gold. *Strained Sisterhood: Gender and Class in the Boston Female Anti-Slavery Society*. Amherst: University of Massachusetts Press, 1993.

Hardin, George A., ed. *History of Herkimer County, New York*. Syracuse: D. Mason and Co., 1893.

Hartog, Hendrik. "Abigail Bailey's Coverture: Law in a Married Woman's Consciousness." In *Law in Everyday Life*, edited by Austin Sarat and Thomas R. Kearns, 63–108. Ann Arbor: University of Michigan Press, 1993.

——. *Man and Wife in America: A History*. Cambridge, Mass.: Harvard University Press, 2000.

Hastings, Hiram P. *An Essay on Constitutional Reform*. New York: Globe Job Office, 1846.

Hatch, Nathan O. *The Democratization of American Christianity*. New Haven: Yale University Press, 1989.

Haydon, Roger, ed. *Upstate Travels: British Views of Nineteenth-Century New York*. Syracuse: Syracuse University Press, 1982.

Hedrick, Ulysses Prentiss. *A History of Agriculture in the State of New York*. Albany: New York State Agricultural Society, 1933.

Henderson, Lisa. "Queer Theory, New Millennium." *Journal of Homosexuality* 45, no. 2/3/4 (2003): 375–79.

Herttell, Thomas. *Argument in the House of Assembly of the State of New York, in the Session of 1837, in Support of the Bill to Restore to Married Women "The Right of Property" as Guaranteed by the Constitution of this State*. New York: Henry Durell, 1839.

Hesse, Carla. *The Other Enlightenment: How French Women Became Modern*. Princeton: Princeton University Press, 2001.

Hewitt, Nancy A. *Women's Activism and Social Change: Rochester, New York, 1822–1872*. Ithaca: Cornell University Press, 1984.

Higgins, Ruth L. *Expansion in New York*. New York: Columbia University Press, 1931. Reprint, Philadelphia: Porcupine Press, 1976.

Hoff, Joan. *Law, Gender, and Injustice: A Legal History of U.S. Women*. New York: New York University Press, 1991.

Hoffert, Sylvia D. *When Hens Crow: The Woman's Rights Movement in Antebellum America*. Bloomington: Indiana University Press, 1995.

Horn, James, Jan Ellen Lewis, and Peter S. Onuf, eds. *The Revolution of 1800: Democracy, Race, and the New Republic*. Charlottesville: University of Virginia Press, 2002.

Horowitz, Daniel. *Betty Friedan and the Making of the Feminine Mystique: The American Left, the Cold War, and Modern Feminism*. Amherst: University of Massachusetts Press, 1998.

Hough, Franklin B. *A History of Jefferson County in the State of New York*. Albany: Joel Munsell, 1854.

Hurlbut, Elisha P. *Essays on Human Rights, and their Political Guaranties*. New York: Fowler and Wells, 1848.

Huston, Reeve. *Land and Freedom: Rural Society, Popular Protest, and Party Politics in Antebellum New York*. New York: Oxford University Press, 2000.

Irwin, Inez Haynes. *Angels and Amazons: A Hundred Years of American Women*. Garden City, N.Y.: Doubleday, Doran, 1934.

Isenberg, Nancy. *Sex and Citizenship in Antebellum America*. Chapel Hill: University of North Carolina Press, 1998.

Jensen, Joan M. *Loosening the Bonds: Mid-Atlantic Farm Women, 1750–1850*. New Haven: Yale University Press, 1986.

Jones, Samuel. *A Treatise on the Right of Suffrage*. Boston: Otis, Broaders and Co., 1842.

Journal of the Rev. John Taylor, on a Mission through the Mohawk and Black River Country, in the year 1802. In *The Documentary History of the State of New-York*, edited by E. B. O'Callaghan, 3:673–96. Albany: Weed, Parsons and Co., 1850.

Kandiyoti, Deniz, ed. *Women, Islam, and the State*. Philadelphia: Temple University Press, 1991.

Kann, Mark E. *A Republic of Men: The American Founders, Gendered Language, and Patriarchal Politics*. New York: New York University Press, 1998.

Kaplan, Temma. *Crazy for Democracy: Women in Grassroots Movements*. New York: Routledge, 1996.

Kelley, Robin D. G. *Hammer and Hoe: Alabama Communists during the Great Depression*. Chapel Hill: University of North Carolina Press, 1990.

Kelly, Catherine E. *In the New England Fashion: Reshaping Women's Lives in the Nineteenth Century*. Ithaca: Cornell University Press, 1999.

Kerber, Linda K. *No Constitutional Right to Be Ladies: Women and the Obligations of Citizenship*. New York: Hill and Wang, 1998.

Keyssar, Alexander. *The Right to Vote: The Contested History of Democracy in the United States*. New York: Basic Books, 2000.

Kirby, Edmund. *Address Delivered Before the Jefferson County Agricultural Society*. Watertown, N.Y.: Woodward and Calhoun, 1831.

Klinghoffer, Judith Apter, and Lois Elkis. " 'The Petticoat Electors': Women's Suffrage in New Jersey, 1776–1807." *Journal of the Early Republic* 12 (Summer 1992): 159–93.

Kolmerton, Carol A. *The American Life of Ernestine L. Rose*. Syracuse: Syracuse University Press, 1999.

Kraditor, Aileen. *Means and Ends in American Abolitionism: Garrison and His Critics on Strategy and Tactics, 1834–1850*. New York: Random House, 1967.

Landes, Joan. *Women and the Public Sphere in the Age of the French Revolution*. Ithaca: Cornell University Press, 1988.

Landon, Harry F. *The North Country*. 3 vols. Indianapolis: Historical Publishing Co., 1932.

Le Ray de Chaumont, James. *An Address Delivered Before the Jefferson County Agricultural Society*. 1829.

Le Ray de Chaumont, Vincent. *Address Delivered Before the Jefferson County Agricultural Society.* 1830.

Lincoln, Charles Z. *The Constitutional History of New York.* 5 vols. Rochester: Lawyers Co-operative Publishing Co., 1906.

Linklater, Andro. *Measuring America: How the United States Was Shaped by the Greatest Land Sale in History.* New York: Penguin, 2002.

Macauley, James. *The Natural, Statistical, and Civil History of the State of New-York.* 3 vols. New York: Gould and Banks, 1829.

Managers of the State Lunatic Asylum. *Annual Reports.* Albany, 1843–90.

Mansfield, Edward D. *The Legal Rights, Liabilities and Duties of Woman.* Cincinnati: John P. Jewett and Co., 1845.

Marshall, Susan E. *Splintered Sisterhood: Gender and Class in the Campaign against Woman Suffrage.* Madison: University of Wisconsin Press, 1997.

Marty, Martin E. *Pilgrims in Their Own Land: 500 Years of Religion in America.* Boston: Little, Brown, 1984.

Massey, Solon. *Links in the Chain.* Edited by Julia Fitch Stanton. Watertown, N.Y.: n.p., 1981.

Matthews, Jean V. *Toward a New Society: American Thought and Culture, 1800–1830.* Boston: Twayne, 1991.

Mayer, Henry. *All On Fire: William Lloyd Garrison and the Abolition of Slavery.* New York: St. Martin's Press, 1998.

McCurdy, Charles. *The Anti-Rent Era in New York Law and Politics, 1839–1865.* Chapel Hill: University of North Carolina Press, 2001.

McKivigan, John R. *The War against Proslavery Religion: Abolitionism and the Northern Churches, 1830–1865.* Ithaca: Cornell University Press, 1984.

McMurry, Sally. *Transforming Rural Life: Dairying Families and Agricultural Change, 1820–1885.* Baltimore: Johns Hopkins University Press, 1995.

Meinig, D.W. "Geography of Expansion, 1785–1855." Chapter 8 of *Geography of New York State*, edited by John H. Thompson, 140–71. Syracuse: Syracuse University Press, 1966.

Memorial to the Honorable Senate and House of Representatives of the Commonwealth of Pennsylvania by the Colored Citizens of Philadelphia. 1853. Philadelphia: Historical Publications No. 226, 1969.

Meyers, Marvin. *The Jacksonian Persuasion: Politics and Belief.* Stanford, Calif.: Stanford University Press, 1957.

Mintz, Steven. *Moralists and Modernizers: America's Pre–Civil War Reformers.* Baltimore: Johns Hopkins University Press, 1995.

Moghadam, Valentine M. *Gender and National Identity: Women and Politics in Muslim Societies.* London: Zed Books, 1994.

Moore, William A. "Some French Influences in the Early Settlement of the Black River Valley." *Proceedings of the New York State Historical Association* 14 (1915): 123–31.

Mott, Frank Luther. *American Journalism: A History, 1690–1960.* New York: Macmillan, 1962.

Naar, M. D. *The Law of Suffrage and Elections.* Trenton: Naar, Day and Naar, 1880.

Narayan, Uma. *Dislocating Cultures: Identities, Traditions, and Third World Feminism.* New York: Routledge, 1997.

"Negotiating Nations: Exclusions, Networks, Inclusions." Special Issue of *Histoire Sociale/Social History* 33 (November 2000).

Newman, Louise Michele. *White Women's Rights: The Racial Origins of Feminism in the United States.* New York: Oxford University Press, 1999.

"The Old State Road. An Address by George L. Johnson of Ilion, Delivered to the Herkimer County Historical Society." November 2, 1904. <http://www.rootsweb. com/~nyherkim/history/oldstateroad.html>.

Osterud, Nancy Grey. *Bonds of Community: The Lives of Farm Women in Nineteenth-Century New York.* Ithaca: Cornell University Press, 1991.

Parker, Alison, and Stephanie Cole, eds. *Women and the Unstable State in Nineteenth-Century America.* Lubbock: Texas A&M University Press, 2000.

Pateman, Carole. *The Disorder of Woman: Democracy, Feminism, and Political Theory.* Stanford, Calif.: Stanford University Press, 1989.

———. *The Sexual Contract.* Stanford, Calif.: Stanford University Press, 1988.

Peterson, Merrill D., ed. *Democracy, Liberty, and Property: The State Constitutional Conventions of the 1820's.* Indianapolis: Bobbs-Merrill, 1966.

Phillips, Anne. *Engendering Democracy.* University Park: Pennsylvania State University Press, 1991.

Pierson, Michael D. *Free Hearts and Free Homes: Gender and American Antislavery Politics.* Chapel Hill: University of North Carolina Press, 2003.

Powell, Thomas F. *Penet's Square: An Episode in the Early History of Northern New York.* Lakemont, N.Y.: North Country Books, 1976.

Quillin, Frank U. *The Color Line in Ohio: A History of Race Prejudice in a Typical Northern State.* Ann Arbor: George Wahr, 1913.

Rabkin, Peggy A. *Fathers to Daughters: The Legal Foundations of Female Emancipation.* Westport, Conn.: Greenwood Press, 1980.

Randall, Oran E. *History of Chesterfield, Chester County, N.H.* Brattleboro, Vt.: D. Leonard, 1882.

Rose, Anne C. *Transcendentalism as a Social Movement, 1830–1850.* New Haven: Yale University Press, 1981.

Rothman, David J. *The Discovery of the Asylum: Social Order and Disorder in the New Republic.* Boston: Little, Brown, 1971.

Rupp, Leila J. *Worlds of Women: The Making of an International Women's Movement.* Princeton: Princeton University Press, 1997.

Ryan, Mary P. *Cradle of the Middle Class: The Family in Oneida County, New York, 1790–1865.* New York: Cambridge University Press, 1981.

———. *Women in Public: Between Banners and Ballots, 1825–1880.* Baltimore: Johns Hopkins University Press, 1990.

Scalia, Laura J. *America's Jeffersonian Experiment: Remaking State Constitutions, 1820–1850.* DeKalb: Northern Illinois University Press, 1999.

Scharer, Laura Lynne. "African-Americans in Jefferson County, New York: 1810–1910." *Afro-Americans in New York Life and History* 19 (January 1995): 7–16.

Schlesinger, Arthur M., Jr. *The Age of Jackson.* Boston: Little, Brown, 1945.

Scott, Joan Wallach. *Only Paradoxes to Offer: French Feminists and the Rights of Man.* Cambridge, Mass.: Harvard University Press, 1996.

Silas Wright. New York: Columbia University Press, 1949. Reprint, New York: AMS Press, 1970.

Sinha, Mrinalini. "Gender and Nation." In *Women's History in Global Perspective,* edited by Bonnie Smith. Urbana: University of Illinois Press, 2004.

Smith, Eric Ledell. "The End of Black Voting Rights in Pennsylvania: African Americans and the Pennsylvania Constitutional Convention of 1837–38." *Pennsylvania History* 65 (Summer 1998): 279–99.

Smith, Rogers M. *Civic Ideals: Conflicting Visions of Citizenship in U.S. History.* New Haven: Yale University Press, 1997.

Stanley, Amy Dru. *From Bondage to Contract: Wage Labor, Marriage, and the Market in the Age of Slave Emancipation.* New York: Cambridge University Press, 1998.

Stanton, Elizabeth Cady. *Eighty Years and More: Reminiscences, 1815–1897.* 1898. Reprint, New York: Schocken Books, 1971.

Stanton, Elizabeth Cady, Susan B. Anthony, and Matilda Joslyn Gage. *The History of Woman Suffrage.* Vol. 1. New York: Fowler and Wells, 1881.

Sterling, Dorothy. *Ahead of Her Time: Abby Kelley and the Politics of Antislavery.* New York: W. W. Norton, 1991.

Stilwell, Louis D. *Migration from Vermont.* Montpelier: Vermont Historical Society, 1948.

Stoler, Ann Laura. "Tense and Tender Ties: The Politics of Comparison in North American History and (Post) Colonial Studies." *Journal of American History* 88 (December 2001): 829–65.

Suhl, Yuri. *Ernestine L. Rose: Women's Rights Pioneer.* 1959. Reprint, New York: Biblio Press, 1990.

Sweet, William Warren. *Religion on the American Frontier: The Baptists, 1783–1830.* New York: Henry Holt, 1931.

Taylor, Alan. *William Cooper's Town: Power and Persuasion on the Frontier of the Early American Republic.* New York: Vintage, 1995.

Taylor, Barbara. *Mary Wollstonecraft and the Feminist Imagination.* New York: Cambridge University Press, 2003.

Terborg-Penn, Rosalyn. *African American Women in the Struggle for the Vote, 1850–1920.* Bloomington: Indiana University Press, 1998.

Tetrault, Lisa. "The Memory of a Movement: Woman Suffrage, Political Economy, and Reconstruction America, 1865–1895." Ph.D. diss., University of Wisconsin, 2004.

Thompson, John H., ed. *Geography of New York State.* Syracuse: Syracuse University Press, 1966.

Tocqueville, Alexis de. *Democracy in America*. 2 vols. New York: Alfred A. Knopf, 1980.

Trouillot, Michel-Rolph. *Silencing the Past: Power and the Production of History*. Boston: Beacon Press, 1995.

Tryon, Rolla Milton. *Household Manufactures in the United States, 1640–1860*. Chicago: University of Chicago Press, 1917.

Tyrrell, Ian. *Woman's World/Woman's Empire: The Woman's Christian Temperance Union in International Perspective, 1880–1930*. Chapel Hill: University of North Carolina Press, 1991.

Ulrich, Laurel Thatcher. *A Midwife's Tale: The Life of Martha Ballard, Based on her Diary, 1785–1812*. New York: Random House, 1990.

VanBurkleo, Sandra F. *"Belonging to the World": Women's Rights and American Constitutional Culture*. New York: Oxford University Press, 2001.

Varon, Elizabeth R. *We Mean to Be Counted: White Women and Politics in Antebellum Virginia*. Chapel Hill: University of North Carolina Press, 1998.

Wagner, Sally Roesch. *Sisters in Spirit: Haudenosaunee (Iroquois) Influence on Early American Feminists*. Summertown, Tenn.: Native Voices, 2001.

Waldstreicher, David. *In the Midst of Perpetual Fetes: The Making of American Nationalism, 1776–1820*. Chapel Hill: University of North Carolina Press, 1997.

[Warner, Henry Whiting]. *An Inquiry into the Moral and Religious Character of the American Government*. New York: Wiley and Putnam, 1838.

Weed, Harriet A., ed. *Life of Thurlow Weed*. Vol. 1, *Autobiography of Thurlow Weed*. New York: DaCapo Press, 1970.

Weed, Zeruvia Porter. *Faith and Works, or the Life of Edward Weed*. New York: C. W. Benedict, 1853.

Wellman, Judith. *Grass Roots Reform in the Burned-Over District of Upstate New York: Religion, Abolitionism, and Democracy*. New York: Garland, 2000.

———. "Women's Rights, Republicanism, and Revolutionary Rhetoric in Antebellum New York State." *New York History* 69 (July 1988): 353–84.

White, Lawrence H., ed. *Democratick Editorials: Essays in Jacksonian Political Economy by William Leggett*. Indianapolis: Liberty Press, 1984.

Winch, Julie. *A Gentleman of Color: The Life of James Forten*. New York: Oxford University Press, 2002.

Wyman, Mary Alice, ed. *Selections from the Autobiography of Elizabeth Oakes Smith*. Lewiston, Maine: Lewiston Journal Co., 1924.

Zaeske, Susan. *Signatures of Citizenship: Petitioning, Antislavery, and Women's Political Identity*. Chapel Hill: University of North Carolina Press, 2003.

Zagarri, Rosemarie. "The Rights of Man and Woman in Post-Revolutionary America." *William and Mary Quarterly*, 3rd ser., 55 (April 1998): 203–30.

Index

Abolition. *See* Antislavery

Adams, Abigail, 30

Adams, John, 30, 149, 178 (n. 29)

Adams, John Quincy, 153

Adirondack Mountains, 49, 53

African Americans: and 1846 convention, 122–23, 126–27, 134–35, 136–37, 140–44, 151–52; disfranchisement of, 132, 141, 154–55; and equal suffrage referendum, 122–23, 144, 154–55; in Jefferson County, 56, 134; petitions by, 134, 154, 160; rhetorical ties to woman suffrage, 151–52; rights of, 15, 28, 66, 107, 126, 134–35, 136–37, 140–44, 148; votes to exclude from states, 141. *See also* Antislavery; Citizenship; Slaves

Age of Reason, 86

Agricultural press, 94, 181 (n. 78); and "book farming," 94–95, 186 (n. 57); and civic concerns, 94–95; correspondents to, 72, 93–97; and girls' education, 93–94; and migration west, 79; and woman's rights, 96, 186 (n. 59); women readers of, 95–97

Agricultural societies, 94–95

AIDS, 168

Albany Atlas, 79

Albany Evening Journal, 99

Albany memorial (1846), 16–17, 153

Albany Patriot, 16, 91, 112, 129, 137, 141; letter from Joseph Osborn, 125; "One of the Disfranchised" letter, 104–5; and woman's rights, 125–26. *See also* Liberty Party

Alexander, Edward, 109

Allen, Stephen, 138

American Anti-Slavery Society, 104

American Baptist Home Missionary Society, 87

American Farmer, 95

American Revolution: impact on rights talk, 27–32, 36; influence on Patriot War, 101–2

Andrews, William, 85

Angel, William, 60, 105, 179 (n. 43)

Annexation of Texas: 112, 117

Anthony, Susan B., 9, 14–15

Anti-rent war, 139–40

Antislavery: and First of August celebrations, 108, 121, 191 (n. 51); in Jefferson County, 110–13, 122–23, 137, 166; petitions for, 15, 112; schism within, 104, 107; women's involvement in, 107–8; and woman's rights, 103, 108–9. *See also* Liberty Party

Astor, John Jacob, 55

Attree, William, 8, 143

Atwood v. Walton, 39

Banks, 133

Baptists, 88, 89, 130

Barnburner-Hunker split. *See* Democratic Party; Free soil

Barnburners. *See* Democratic Party; Free soil

Bascom, Ansel, 139, 140, 145, 150, 153

Bascomb, Rev. Mr., 87

Bateham, Josephine A. P. [Cushman], 186 (n. 59)

Bateham, Louisa Jane [Lovell], 186 (n. 59)

DATE DUE

HIST 1730	

UPI   PRINTED IN U.S.A.